HELLENIC STUDIES SERIES 86

WHO AM I?

T0339179

Recent Titles in the Hellenic Studies Series

WHO AM I?

(MIS)IDENTITY AND THE POLIS
IN *OEDIPUS TYRANNUS*

Efimia D. Karakantza

Center for Hellenic Studies
Trustees for Harvard University
Washington, D.C.
Distributed by Harvard University Press
Cambridge, Massachusetts, and London, England
2020

Who Am I? (Mis)Identity and the Polis in Oedipus Tyrannus
Efimia D. Karakantza

Copyright © 2020 Center for Hellenic Studies, Trustees for Harvard University
All Rights Reserved.

Published by Center for Hellenic Studies, Trustees for Harvard University,
    Washington, D.C.
Distributed by Harvard University Press, Cambridge, Massachusetts,
    and London, England
Production: Jen Jackowitz
Cover design: Joni Godlove
Cover image: Photo illustration, collection of old, used passports (ID 7411195),
    and passport of Greece (ID 8295240). 123RF.com, editorial license.

EDITORIAL TEAM

Senior Advisers: W. Robert Connor, Gloria Ferrari Pinney, Albert Henrichs,[†]
    James O'Donnell, Bernd Seidensticker
Editorial Board: Gregory Nagy (Editor-in-Chief), Casey Dué (Executive Editor),
    Mary Ebbott (Executive Editor), Scott Johnson, Olga Levaniouk, Leonard
    Muellner
Production Manager for Publications: Jill Curry Robbins
Web Producer: Noel Spencer
Multimedia Producer: Mark Tomasko

Library of Congress Cataloging-in-Publication Data

Names: Karakantza, E. D. (Euphēmia D.), author.
Title: Who am I? : (mis)identity and the polis in Oedipus tyrannus / Efimia
    Karakantza.
Other titles: Hellenic studies ; 86.
Description: Washington : Center for Hellenic Studies, Trustees for Harvard
    University, 2020. | Series: Hellenic studies ; 86 | Includes
    bibliographical references and index.
Identifiers: LCCN 2019021518 | ISBN 9780674237940
Subjects: LCSH: Oedipus (Greek mythological figure) | Sophocles. Oedipus
    Rex. | Identity (Philosophical concept) in literature.
Classification: LCC PA4413.O7 K37 2019 | DDC 882/.01--dc23
LC record available at https://lccn.loc.gov/2019021518

To my beloved children
Aspasia, Dimitris, and Athina
Who had to learn how to fall
Before learning how to fly

They all fly now, with elegance and kindness ...

Contents

Contents

Acknowledgements

In the long years devoted to the research and writing of this book on Oedipus, I came to realize that I cannot really distinguish between the people who supported me emotionally and those with whom I was engaged in an intellectual dialogue. In most cases the two categories happily overlapped. Now is the time to say thank you to them all.

I begin by expressing my deep gratitude to Gregory Nagy, who cherished me with his intellectual support and precious friendship. Over the years he stood by me whenever I needed guidance and encouragement, and it was always with great kindness that he offered them to me. The Center for Hellenic Studies in Washington, DC, this hospitable place for the Hellenists of the entire world, became my home for the Fall semester of the academic year 2010–11, when I held a residential fellowship; and again, in the winter of 2016, during my brief stay as a visiting scholar. At the Center, I was fortunate to be able to discuss intellectual matters with the fellows of the year 2010–11, and the three 'wise men'—Gregory Nagy, Leonard Muellner and Douglas Frame. Friendly faces made my life easier, too, and facilitated my research greatly: I thank with all my heart Zoie Lafis, Noel Spencer, Lanah Koelle, and the wonderful librarian, Temple Wright, who were always kind and supportive. For this beautiful book I also owe much to Jill Curry Robbins and the CHS publications team (of course, I alone am to blame for all its faults).

My very special thanks go to Gonda Van Steen, who was actually *the* first reader of my finished manuscript, and gave me her sincere approbation even before the book was accepted for publication. Her enthusiasm and encomiastic comments gave me an unprecedented stimulus to continue.

Back at my home institution, the University of Patras, I feel the need to thank wholeheartedly my colleagues at the Department of Philology, who approved my sabbatical leave, which enabled me fully to engage with this book. I owe a special debt of gratitude to Spyridon Rangos, who read part of the book at an earlier stage and generously gave me his learned advice; he was also among the first to read the book in its final version and render his approbation. Angeliki Syrkou, an esteemed colleague and a dear friend, patiently listened and cleverly responded to my ideas about Oedipus. As expected, the innumerable discussions

Acknowledgements

I have had with my students of the University of Patras (especially my classes on Sophocles, Greek Myth, the Reception of Ancient Greek Drama in Literary Criticism and Art, and, lately, on Feminist Thought and Classics) have been an abiding source of inspiration. With my students I have talked—inside or outside the classroom—about all the thorny issues in the interpretation of Oedipus, in antiquity as well as in modern criticism and reception. I thank them all.

From among my former students I single out a few, who are now valuable friends, and to whom I address from here my deepest gratitude for their love and support. Marietta Kotsafti has always been there for me; she supported me greatly when I was in dire straits, and she has been my unfailing and perceptive interlocutor over the years—I simply owe her much more than I can tell in a few lines. Gesthimani Seferiadi and Alexandros Velaoras are still working with me; their intelligence and kindness make me feel that my role as a teacher is duly justified. My 'junior' former students Andreas Filippopoulos and Alexandros Frantzis are promising examples of the new generation educated in Classics.

In the long years of the making of the book, I relied on my editor, the recently deceased Jonathan Smith, when struggling with the language and the sometimes-convoluted ideas about Oedipus. His intelligence, erudition, and linguistic sensibility gave my text elegance and clarity. I consider myself fortunate to have had a friend like him in times of great distress.

My love for the tales of the ancient Greeks began with the greatest storyteller I have known, my father, whose bedtime stories always involved Heracles, the wise centaur Chiron, and the angry Achilles. I can trace the very remote beginnings of this book back to those stories of his. Even in his very old age, he sought to refresh his clouded memory of those tales. "What did Hector reply to Andromache?" he asked me a few weeks before he died, only to hear his favorite answer: "I have to go back to the fray, my beloved Andromache, for I have learned to be one of the best, always fighting in Troy's first ranks for all the Trojans." With his life and mind, my father always served unfailingly the common good.

This book is dedicated to my beloved children: Aspasia, Dimitris and Athina. Raising them has been the joy of my life. They are now beautiful young adults pursuing their own paths of life; but most of all, they are kind, generous, and compassionate toward other human beings. I am simply very proud of being their mother.

Lastly, there is Takis Zambetis, whom I cannot but thank for loving me the way he does. He makes my life beautiful. Σ' ευχαριστώ Τάκη μου.

Athens/Piraeus 2019

Note on Translations and Editions
of *Oedipus Tyrannus*

I quote Lloyd-Jones' translation of *Oedipus Tyrannus* used throughout, unless otherwise indicated. The edition of the original text is by Lloyd-Jones & Wilson (1990), for I had nearly completed my book when the edition/commentary by Finglass (2018) appeared. However, I adopt the newer edition in places where I disagree with Lloyd-Jones & Wilson, changing the translation accordingly.

Part 1

Prologue
How It All Began

1

Sophocles' *Hypsipolis–Apolis* Antithesis, and Castoriadis's Imaginary Institution of Classical Athens

Εἶναι παιδιά πολλῶν ἀνθρώπων τά λόγια μας.
Σπέρνουνται γεννιοῦνται σάν τά βρέφη
ριζώνουν θρέφουνται μέ τό αἷμα.
Ὅπως τά πεῦκα
κρατοῦνε τή μορφή τοῦ ἀγέρα
ἐνῶ ὁ ἀέρας ἔφυγε, δέν εἶναι ἐκεῖ
τό ἴδιο τά λόγια
φυλάγουν τή μορφή τοῦ ἀνθρώπου
κι ὁ ἄνθρωπος ἔφυγε, δέν εἶναι ἐκεῖ.

Our words are children of many men. / Begotten and born like
infants / they are rooted, nourished in blood. / As the pines, / keep
the shape of the wind / when the wind has gone, is no longer there, /
words in the same way / frame the image of man / and the man has
gone, is no longer there.

Γιώργος Σεφέρης *Τρία Κρυφά Ποιήματα* / Giorgos Seferis
Three Secret Poems. Translated by R. Beaton.

FOR MORE THAN FIFTEEN YEARS, I have been studying the works of
Sophocles. In class, in print, as well as in diverse academic settings, I have
reflected on various aspects of his work. The more deeply I have immersed
myself in his poetry, the more profoundly I appreciate his dramatic artistry. To
me, one of the most beautiful lines of poetry ever written is one of exquisite
simplicity and poignancy from *Ajax* (394) σκότος, ἐμὸν φάος—"ah darkness, that
you are my light"—three everyday words imbued with all the emotion of a man
on the point of suicide. At the same time, my sense that Sophocles' work is also

extremely political has grown. I am aware that this is no novel conviction; at least since the time of the invaluable Paris School, Hellenists can no longer see Attic drama in a cultural and ideological vacuum. Instead, we contextualize it within the confines of the polis that incubates it. Of course, interpretations vary in orientation and intensity. My own particular political approach, focusing on the autonomous individual in a self-instituting society, will be elaborated in the course of this book. Here, however, I admit to two starting points that have informed my reading of the Sophoclean corpus since I first encountered them.

In the famous first *stasimon* of *Antigone*, for no apparent reason, the playwright exalts the many achievements of man in creating human culture. Among the many practical skills essential to mere survival (building, sea-faring, agriculture, the crafts of hunting and fishing, medicine), he also proudly lists more sophisticated forms of human invention engendering arts and sciences: letters, numbers, religion, oracles, and, above all of these, laws safeguarding the survival of human societies. Laws are, of course, the major issue in Sophocles' *Antigone*. Without debating the reasons for the enforced disjunction between human and divine laws, I shall dwell briefly on the antithesis in line 370 between the *hypsipolis* and *apolis* citizen. Man inclines, says Sophocles, sometimes towards evil and sometimes towards good (367); consequently, life in the polis bears the marks of these twofold tendencies. The ideal citizen (*hypsipolis* = thought of highly in his polis) applies the laws of men (νόμους χθονός, 368) *and* the justice of gods ensured by the gravity of oaths (θεῶν τ' ἔνορκον δίκαν, 369). The chorus establishes this conjunction, which will be seriously undermined in the course of the play. Conversely, the individual who defies the conjoined laws, an individual consorting with evil, should be expelled from the city. He becomes *apolis*, a social and political outcast (μήτ[ε] παρέστιος ... /... μήτ' ἴσον φρονῶν, 373–374). I argue that this crucial dichotomy runs throughout the extant works of Sophocles, and marks his reflection on contemporary reality. The major preoccupation of his plays is to explore the dilemmas of characters from the perspective of their suitability as citizens in the discourse of the Athenian polis.

This readjustment of civic ideology can *only* be done effectively in a society that is *autonomous* rather than *heteronomous*; that is, in a self-legislating society, where "nothing is enforced as inviolable law by a higher authority, a god, an emperor, or a religious or political elite."[1] In an autonomous society, such as radically democratic Athens, the *dêmos* (the citizenry), who are also *autodikos* (self-judging), and *autotelês* (self-governing), is the same body that watches en masse the dramatic performances in the Theater of Dionysus. To engage there, as audience, in debates over all the issues concerning life in the polis becomes

---

[1] As I argue at length in the following chapter, p. 13.

possible through the dynamic medium of dramatic art. Issues including identity, kinship, political loyalty, religious sanctions, and ethics are fiercely debated among the dramatis personae faced with extreme situations and dilemmas within a society of peers. The same body politic will later debate issues in "real" political life in the Assembly of the citizens; issues crucial to sustaining a democratic polis.

How is this apparently "standard" procedure of political praxis transferable from the realm of the imaginary to the "real" world? Comprehending this process is facilitated by an understanding of the sophisticated procedures involved in the twofold structure of human institutions, as argued by the contemporary Greek political philosopher, Cornelius Castoriadis.[2] An institution, says the philosopher, is a "socially sanctioned, symbolic network in which a *functional* and an *imaginary* component are combined in variable proportions and relations."[3] In order to be able to establish or reform an institution (the term "institution" is understood here in its broadest meaning: everything institutionalized by human political activity), the body politic needs the ability to create and re-create its social significations on the imaginary level—it needs to *imagine* first what it would be like to have such and such a law/reform/ institution in society. This is inextricably linked with the people having a certain *concept* of themselves—what it is to be a citizen of Athens, what can be tolerated, and what cannot.[4] Castoriadis argues eloquently about how philosophical questions were tackled and formulated in poetry, "long before philosophy existed as an explicit reflection"; and he continues, "... [man] is a poetic animal that gave in imaginary the answers to those questions."[5] The social imaginary significations (responsible for the radical activity of the social creation and thus the radical direct democratic system of Athens) is what holds a society together and empowers the body politic to reform the political reality in which they live.

Now, we can understand better the *hypsipolis*/*apolis* antithesis that Sophocles embedded in his tragic vision. Sophocles, a great artist as well as an important intellectual, "tries out" the thoughts and actions of his characters that make them *apolides*: undeserving of being part of their polis. This is not necessarily

---

[2] A short biography of the radical left political philosopher Cornelius Castoriadis can be found in Appendix 1. From his long career as philosopher and political activist, I mention here two major involvements. The famous journal and eponymous political group *Socialisme ou Barbarie* (*Socialism or Barbarism*), which he co-founded with Claude Lefort, lasted from 1948–1966. The second is the publication in 1975 of his seminal book *L'Institution Imaginaire de la Société* (*The Imaginary Institution of Society*), where he presents his theory of the self-instituting society, social imaginary significations, and social change as a radical creation developed over years.

[3] Castoriadis 1997a:132.

[4] These ideas are presented at great length in the next chapter.

[5] 1997a:147; see p. 27.

done with disdain. Antigone can be considered *apolis*, as can Oedipus. However, what is it to be *apolis*, despite one's fortitude and courage? How does one disrupt the civic order, despite the sincere wish to be part of it? How is this order reconstituted, while the protagonists are expelled or die? And finally, what constitutes an ideal citizen and what does not?

Through this lens, civic identity in this radical and direct democracy becomes one of the focal points of tragic discourse. Thus the recalibration of the consideration of *Oedipus Tyrannus* as a play about identity positions it at the inception of existence in the polis. The *"Who Am I?"* of my title does not refer to any modern existential or philosophical category of being. Rather, Oedipus' deficit in knowledge about his identity incapacitates him as an esteemed member of his polis. In the Introduction to my close reading (*"Who Am I? A Tragedy of Identity"*), I explain that there is a very simple idea triggering the refocusing of my interpretation: "Oedipus' major handicap in life is 'not knowing who he is'; the parricide and incest come about as the result of this ignorance."[6] Of course, any examination of civic identity inevitably embraces the concomitant notions of political, religious, and societal systems and their codes of behavior and thinking. Thus, viewed through the lens of civic identity, a wealth of other issues concerning the well-being of Athenian society are revealed. However, because of the long history of the reception of *Oedipus Tyrannus* in philosophy, ethics, social sciences, and psychoanalysis, we have been distracted from considering the simple fact that the playwright constructs the conceptual plot of his play around the discovery of the identity of Oedipus, as will be argued in the course of this book. Sophocles has transformed a popular legend, common to many cultures, into a profound reflection on identity, in the absence of which one's position in the polis is jeopardized.

I have acknowledged thus far the two major starting points informing my reading of Greek antiquity, Attic drama, and *Oedipus Tyrannus* in particular: the Sophoclean *apolis* and the Castoriadian imaginary institution of society. However, this is far from being the end of the story. I am also much indebted to many other intellectuals and scholars for, as Nobel laureate Giorgos Seferis reminds us, εἶναι παιδιά πολλῶν ἀνθρώπων τά λόγια μας, "our words are children of many men": Claude Lévi-Strauss for understanding the laws of kinship; Charles Taylor and Alasdair MacIntyre for the construction of civic identity; Michel Foucault for mapping power relations and their ensuing ideologies in human societies, as informed by historical circumstances; Luce Irigaray, Judith Butler, and contemporary feminist critics for reconfiguring gender identity and the laws of kinship establishing patriarchy; Josiah Ober for understanding the

---

[6] See p. 41.

functioning and success of the radical and direct Athenian democracy. Lastly, although prior to all the above, are Jean-Pierre Vernant, Pierre Vidal-Naquet, Nicole Loraux, and their peers from the Paris School, who so strongly established the *polis* on the map of Hellenic scholarship. Had they not paved the way, we would still be wandering, bereft of our intellectual *poleis*, as was Oedipus.

Part 2

Theoretical Considerations

2

Defining the Polis

IN DEFINING WHAT A POLIS IS, we can begin with its basic meaning in the archaic and classical periods: a polis is a settlement and a community. As a settlement a polis is "primarily a large nucleated settlement," that is to say, a city. As a community it is "an institutionalized political community," that is to say, a state.[1] Of course a polis is also "inextricably linked to its hinterland,"[2] which is demarcated by a series of extra-urban sanctuaries that symbolically, through ritual practices, consolidate the appropriation of, and the sovereignty over, the land and the territory around the city.[3] Communal action defines the possession of this territory, since it has to be defended militarily. Protecting the most remote parts of the city territory becomes part of the initiation rites of the Athenian *ephebes*, as beautifully shown in the classic "The Black Hunter and the Origin of the Athenian *Ephebia*" of Pierre Vidal-Naquet.[4] But also, and very importantly, extra-urban sanctuaries constitute a symbolic bulwark beyond which lies the domain of the "undifferentiated, disordered, and ephemeral, all that is dominated by abnormal relations and placed under the sign of cunning and noninstitutionalized violence: relations without mediation between men and gods ... , between human beings themselves ... , and between man and animals";[5] in short, all things abhorrent to the culture of the polis.

Even when defining the urban and the extra-urban dimensions of the polis, the settlement and its hinterland, we have already entered into the realm of the symbolic demarcation of what *is* and what *is not* the domain of the polis, what *belongs* and what *does not belong* to it. These distinctions become even more important to delineate when we move to the notion of the "institutionalized

---

[1] Hansen 2006:56. Also, "every *polis*-city was the centre of a *polis*-state, and every *polis*-state had a *polis*-city as its political centre" (59).

[2] Hansen 2006:57, 101–105.

[3] de Polignac 1995:21–24, 32–88.

[4] Original publication in 1968 as "Le chasseur noir et l'origine de l'ephébie athénienne," *Annales* 23:947–964.

[5] de Polignac 1995:35–36.

political community" and its activity. The polis is the community of the citizens in a political context and the system of the institutions that define and enforce a legal order over the population.[6] A "polis" comprises the two aspects described above, the settlement and the community. But, quite early on in Greek thought, a polis becomes not "just a walled city but rather a community of men ready to defend their society."[7] In the Greek democratic mentality, the polis *is* the people/citizenry of a city-state. "You would be a fine ruler over a deserted city!" Haemon exclaims sarcastically (*Antigone* 739) when his father, the king Creon, asks, "Is not the city thought to belong to its ruler?" (*Antigone* 738)[8]—a notion extraordinary to the average Athenian ear.

To this mentality we shall now turn. The people and the institutions,[9] policy and the making of it,[10] along with the modes of thought and the imaginary social significations that create a world, in reference to which the society exists[11]—all these elements *are* the Greek polis, and the Athenian democratic polis, in particular, in which tragedy is a constituent part.

In order to better understand this notion of the polis, we need to contextualize it within the broader confines of fifth-century democratic Athens. Josiah Ober has argued convincingly that contrary to the common assumption that democracy is the rule of the majority[12] (an interpretation that may itself have pejorative resonances originating largely from democracy's Greek critics), the original meaning of the word democracy (*dêmos* + *kratos* = the power of the people)[13] points to the notion of "power" as the capacity of the citizens to do things together in the public realm, "to make things happen."[14] *Dêmos* is a term referring to a collective body, which is *not* the equivalent of the "tyrannical" or "monopolistic domination of government apparatus by the many who were

---

[6] Hansen 2006:64.

[7] Hansen 2006:98.

[8] ΚΡ. Οὐ τοῦ κρατοῦντος ἡ πόλις νομίζεται;

AI. Καλῶς ἐρήμης γ᾽ ἂν σὺ γῆς ἄρχοις μόνος.

[9] Hansen 2006.

[10] Ober 2008a:1.

[11] Castoriadis 1997a:359.

[12] Even a critic as sensitive and well informed as Hansen, who directed the Copenhagen Polis Center from 1993–2005, refers to Athenian democracy as the majority rule of the "little people" or the "less wealthy." Note the following statement: "under a rule of the people (*demokratia* or *politeia*) it is the 'little people' (*dêmos*), the majority in fact, of the less wealthy citizens who exercise power through a People's Assembly in which all citizens have the right to speak and vote irrespective of their property status" (2006:111).

[13] The "how many people may occupy official positions of authority" is denoted by the -*arche* suffix: monarchy, oligarchy, anarchy (the last term denoting that magisterial offices of the government are vacant); the equivalent of the "majority rule" would be "*polloi-archia*," which does not exist in classical Greek (Ober 2008b:6).

[14] Ober 2008b:7.

poor," but it refers to the "whole of citizenry."[15] *Dêmos* with the *-kratos* suffix becomes an empowered collective body and, consequently, democracy is "the regime in which the *dêmos* gains a collective capacity to effect change in the public realm."[16] Additionally, this capacity does not imply a simple matter of control, but a "collective *strength* and *ability* to act within that realm, and indeed to *reconstitute the public realm through action*."[17]

This last sentence leads us to reflect on the mechanisms that enable the body politic to reconstitute the public realm through its political *praxis*. Reforms, of course, are the result of tangible political action: new laws are introduced, the distribution of power among the members of the body politic is redesigned, the political system is reorganized—to name just a few possibilities. Some of the reforms might seem to be the result of a long evolutionary process. There are moments, however, in the history of the Athenian democratic system that are thoroughly radical, such as Cleisthenes' redesign of the political system by introducing the ten political tribes. Without going into the philosophy of historical change in general, one should reflect in particular on the conditions that made these reforms possible. My approach is formulated in the light of the uprising of the *dêmos* preceding the reforms, what Ober calls the "Athenian Revolution," without which "the Cleisthenic reforms would have remained empty words."[18] It is also informed by Castoriadis's insight into the nature of human institutions and the social imaginary significations that symbolize political *praxis*. Such a radical moment, moreover, is a moment when history is seen as creation.

Reforming the political reality presupposes the action of *re-imagining* it. This process of *re-imagining* becomes possible because classical Athens is the self-instituting society par excellence, for what defines the instituting activity of the citizens is their *autonomy*, not *heteronomy*. The *dêmos* is *autonomos* (self-legislating), *autodikos* (self-judging), and *autotelês* (self-governing).[19] This overstressed autonomy (nothing in this society is enforced as inviolable law by a higher authority, a god, an emperor, or a religious or political elite) creates the preconditions for the *creation* of "a new *eidos*, a new essence, a new form in the full and strong sense: new determinations, new norms, new laws."[20] Such a new *eidos* is the Cleisthenic radical reform consisting in ten blatantly artificial Athenian tribes; these new *forms* had to be conceptualized, that is to say to be *imagined* first.

---

[15] Ober 2008b:8.
[16] Ober 2008b:7.
[17] Ibid., the last emphasis is mine.
[18] Ober 1996:41.
[19] Castoriadis 1997b:275 (the original essay, "Greek Polis and the Creation of Democracy," appeared in 1983, *Graduate Faculty Philosophy Journal* 9:79–115); the terms are found in Thucydides.
[20] Castoriadis 1997b:269.

In order to understand this action of being *imagined* (which is the functioning of the radical social imagination), we need to reflect on the nature of a human institution, taking the meaning of an 'institution' in its broadest sense. In his seminal book *The Imaginary Institution of Society*, Castoriadis defines an institution as "a socially sanctioned, symbolic network in which a functional component and an imaginary component are combined in variable proportions and relations."[21] The imaginary component is responsible for the radical activity of the social creation: of the new institutions, the new ways of living and thinking, and the new significations on the social plane, what are defined as "the social imaginary significations."[22] The latter is what holds a society together. In Castoriadis's words:

> Society exists in positing the requirement of signification as universal and as total, and in positing its world of significations as what can satisfy this requirement. And it is only in correlation with this world of significations as it is instituted in each case that we reflect on the question raised above: what is the 'unity' and the 'identity', that is to say the *ecceity* of a society, and what is it that holds a society together? What holds a society together is the holding-together of its world of significations. What permits us to think of it in its *ecceity*, as *this particular* society and not another, is the particularity or specificity of its world of significations as the institution of *this* magma of social imaginary significations, organized in a particular way and not otherwise.[23]

The shared social significations make you what it is to be an Athenian. How do you *imagine* yourself to be? *What is your perception of yourself?* In the case of the Athenians, at that important moment of their history after the abolition of Tyranny (510 BCE) and just before the Cleisthenic reforms (508 BCE), a salient question might have been articulated thus: does it make sense for us, the Athenians, to belong to a clientele adherent to a local aristocrat serving

---

[21] Castoriadis 1997a:132.

[22] Charles Taylor in his *Modern Social Imaginaries* (2004:24) defines the social imaginary as follows: "Our social imaginary at any given time is complex. It incorporates a sense of the *normal expectations* we have of each other, the kind of *common understanding* that enables us to carry out the collective practices that make up our social life. This incorporates some sense of how we all fit together in carrying out the common practice. Such understanding is both *factual* and *normative*; that is, we have a sense of how things usually go, but this is interwoven with the idea of how they ought to go, of what missteps would invalidate the practice" (my emphasis). And further down: "Humans operated with a social imaginary well before they ever got into the business of theorizing about themselves (26)." In a similar manner, Castoriadis (1997a:147) refers to the action of the humans to deliberate in the realm of the imaginary (and the symbolic) as prior to any systematic philosophical thinking; see also Chapter 3 below, p. 27.

[23] Castoriadis 1997a:359.

individual centers of power, rival to each other (as must have been the case in late-seventh- and most of sixth-century Attica)?[24] Or, do we consider ourselves as members of a body politic belonging to the collectivity of our polis, serving common goals and aiming at reconstituting political reality so as to lay the ground for the well-being of the entirety of the citizenry to which we belong? And (depending on the answer to the above questions), how do we organize our political *praxis*? Do we try to work together and avoid conflict with each other, as civic strife (*stasis*) needs to be prevented at all costs?

The Athenian Revolution of the years 508/7 BCE, as interpreted by Josiah Ober,[25] and the subsequent Cleisthenic reforms are fine examples of the working of the social imaginary significations and of the collective capacity to effect change in the public realm. They exemplify a political *praxis* that bears all the characteristics of a collectivity being *imagined* first, then empowered to implement major reforms (the ten new artificial tribes) that made this social imagination reality.

This is how things happened. In 508 BCE Athens experienced a three-day riot of the *dêmos*, fueled by the aggressive political decision of the Spartan King Cleomenes I, who was in control of Attica, to dissolve the *Boulê* of the Athenians. His intention was clearly to turn Athens into a client-state, with a status similar to the other Peloponnesian allies. He was backed up by the archon Isagoras and the pro-Spartan elite, who had exiled Cleisthenes and some 700 families. The *Boulê* resisted and, in reaction, Cleomenes and Isagoras occupied the Acropolis (Herodotus *Histories* 5.72.1–20). There, they were besieged by the Athenians for two days and on the third, after a truce, the Spartans fled Attica (5.72.1–2). Some of their Athenian supporters were summarily executed.[26] From the scarce evidence of our sources, Ober infers[27] a spontaneous and sudden riot of the

---

[24] Ober 1989:57–59, 66–69.

[25] The two extensive accounts, and interpretation, of the events are found in "The Athenian Revolution" (1996), and in "I Besieged that Man. Democracy's Revolutionary Start" (2007:83–104). The idea of the Athenian Revolution as a spontaneous leaderless uprising of the *dêmos* permeates all Ober's writings.

[26] The two sources that record the events are Herodotus *Histories* 5.66, 69–78, and Aristotle *Athênaiôn Politeia* 20–22.1.

[27] What is offered here is an "inferential but plausible sequence" of the events (1996:43), which Ober also reiterates later in his work (2007:92–93). Of course, historians do not agree as to various aspects of the events and the consequent reforms of Cleisthenes: do we detect here the "real" origins of Athenian democracy? Was it truly a leaderless revolution? What were the motives of Cleisthenes in introducing his reforms: his self-interest or the interest of the people? Ehrenberg (1973) and Lewis (1963) detect individualistic motives, while de Ste. Croix (2004:136) argues: "we cannot know what Cleisthenes' motives were in 508." Ehrenberg reads the events as a person-to-person communication between Cleisthenes and Isagoras. Ostwald (1986:16–17) remarks: "... Cleisthenes was ... no ideological democrat but a practical politician concerned with eliminating the roots of internal conflict from the society in which he lived. ... Cleisthenes acting as a

dêmos that spread quickly without being led by any figure of the elite, for the sources name none. The sudden uprising took Cleomenes off his guard; he then occupied the Acropolis, probably without securing enough supplies, and he was thus forced to surrender within three days.

What made the Athenian Revolution possible? Was it the new abstract notions of "Athens" and "Athenians"? The perception of oneself as an Athenian involved the imaginary signification of a citizen attached to his polis, and *not* of a client attached to his aristocrat lord, *nor* of a subject of Sparta. The emerging awareness of citizenship can be traced back to the reforms of Solon that "undercut the traditional authority associated with birth."[28] But just as emphatically, the sense of connection to the polis as a prime locus of the Athenian identity can be traced back to the policy of Peisistratus, who seriously undermined the ties between the landholder aristocrats and their clientele. Public festivals, celebrations, and extensive building programs to reconstruct and embellish the face of the urban polis all aimed at "fostering closer ideological identification of the citizenry as a whole with the Athenian state."[29] Of course, this was initiated by Peisistratus in order to "legitimize his own position"[30] but an indirect and inevitable result of the reforms was that "a greater meaning was attached to Athenian citizenship,"[31] which then became not simply "protection from ultimate status degradation, but something much more positive and potentially more politically meaningful."[32]

This "potentiality" became social and political reality in the new reorganization of the body politic into the ten artificial tribes. Experts before me have analyzed the reforms extensively.[33] What I would like to stress here, in the context of my argument, is that these reforms are a paradigm of a pure and radical political *creation*, resulting in what, in Castoriadian terms, we would call a new *eidos*. This unprecedented "form," consisting of new determinations, norms, and laws, reestablished and redefined the political time, space, and identity of the Athenians. The new institutions forming the legislative, judicial, and executive bodies of the new political organization were the functional component

---

private citizen in opposition to the ruling *archôn*, used the *dêmos*—presumably meaning Council and Assembly—as the forum for passing his reforms. That this was a revolutionary step to take is evident, but it does not follow that the political aims to be achieved by this procedure were equally radical." My own thesis, evident throughout these pages, supports clearly the radicalism of the Athenian Revolution and the reforms of Cleisthenes.

28 Ober 1996:38.
29 Ober 1989:66.
30 Ibid.
31 Ibid.
32 Ober 1989:67.
33 For major publications on Cleisthenes' reforms, as well as a short history of how ancient historians shifted their interest from Solon and Pericles to Cleisthenes, see Appendix 2.

part of this creation. In order for the creation to acquire *this* form, it needed to be *imagined* first at the collective imaginary level. The Athenians needed to have a differentiated perception of themselves, as we saw manifested in the Athenian Revolution a few months prior to the reforms. The collective social significations had changed (in a long process starting from the time of Solon), laying the preconditions for Cleisthenes to initiate a radical new concept of the organization and institutionalization of the polis and its citizens. Cleisthenes evaluated the mass action and designed institutions "capable of framing and stabilizing a new ideology."[34]

The new concept and its political application aimed at undermining the strong local ties between aristocrats and their clients or other locality-based bonds with possible political implications. The body politic was reorganized on a cross-class and cross-regional basis. The radical character of the reforms is masterfully exemplified in the combination of the three equal thirds (*trittyes*) from the coastal, urban, and inland regions of Attica in order for each new tribe to be created. In their year of service, the fifty Councilmen of each new tribe, people who had never met before, had to work closely together as members of the same tribe. During the thirty-five or thirty-six-day period that the tribe had the presidency of the Council (*Boulê*), one third of the Councilmen of the same tribe had to sleep, eat, and spend each day together in the public building of *Tholos*, where they were constantly on duty, ready to respond to any political emergency. The random mixing of the populace in the formation of the tribes and the imperative for close collaboration was not confined to the political *praxeis* of the Council; other important venues were the People's Courts, the groups created ad hoc to deal with various administration issues, and, of course, the military service, with the majority of the Athenians serving as heavy infantry, *hoplites*, or oarsmen in the war ships. A powerful symbol of the new social order was tribal participation in civic celebrations. For example, dithyrambic choruses composed of one hundred members (fifty men and fifty adolescent boys) of each tribe opened the celebrations of the Great Dionysia—one of the prime venues where Athenian civic identity was consolidated. The result was that the Athenians made polities, deliberated, fought and died, or danced together as citizens of the same tribe, albeit coming from distant localities (*demes*), different backgrounds, and various social classes.[35]

---

[34] Ober 1996:33.

[35] See the same idea, albeit differently formulated, by Ober (2008a:142): "The experience of marching, fighting, sacrificing, eating, and dancing, together in this newly 'intermixed' grouping, would, according to Cleisthenes' plan, lead to a strengthened collective identity at the level of the polis."

One of the effective tools for reshaping the new social-imaginary signification attached to the abstractions "Athenians" and "Athens" was a novel networking system, starting from the local level of the *demes* and embracing the whole of Attica, fostering a "master" network.[36] This master network, the result of a complex and extremely sophisticated concept, created new ties among the diverse and dispersed members of the ten new tribes, consolidating a new civic identity extending across the whole of Attica. This was perhaps the first time that such a conscious and consistent effort had been made to create the ground for a political system that would promote equality, collaboration, and solidarity among otherwise disparate citizens. The master network formed a platform where people coming from isolated, small, or unimportant *demes* had to work together with the wealthy or the better educated people from the city, the port, or other important *demes*. They worked as equals on a cooperative basis sharing the "collective responsibility for decisions that could not be enforced by external authority";[37] their political *praxis* was the result of their self-instituting activity. The transfer of individuals' knowledge[38] from the administration of their local networks to the master network favored an unprecedented aggregation of knowledge of political affairs, thus producing the successful paradigm of the participatory and deliberative political system of Athens. In terms of assessing its performance compared to contemporary rival cities, Athens outpaced its rivals by a substantial margin. In all domains where success is normally measured—growth, wealth, intellectual life, artistic

---

[36] Ober in his *Democracy and Knowledge* (2008a) studies extensively how, starting with small-scale local networks, information/knowledge was transferred across the extended network of the entire polis by building bridges between the local administration of *demes* (and the accumulation of social, technological, and political knowledge there) and the numerous political bodies created by the new system of the ten artificial Cleisthenic tribes; the latter form the "master" plan of the administration of the city, where an extensive aggregation of knowledge ensured the success of the "epistemic democracy" of classical Athens (see also n38 below). "Athens knows what the Athenians know," remarks Ober (150).

[37] Ober 1989:73.

[38] What Ober calls "social epistemology" (2008a:34). The Athenian democracy as a political system, based on aggregated knowledge transferable from individuals to the collective bodies of citizens materializing political *praxis*, is termed by the author "epistemic democracy," to which he dedicates his contribution in J. Elster and H. Landemre (eds.) titled: "Epistemic Democracy in Classical Athens; Sophistication, Diversity, and Innovation" (2012:118–147). At the very beginning of the Introduction, we read: "A democracy may be said to be 'epistemic' to the degree to which it employs collective wisdom to make good policy. Scott Page (this volume) offers a formal model of collective wisdom, in the sense of accurately predicting or characterizing an outcome that is produced by two factors: the individual sophistication of participants and the diversity of their perspectives. The city-state of Athens, from the late sixth century through the late fourth century B.C.E, is a case study of a participatory epistemic democracy: an intensively-studied historical example of a community whose remarkable success can, at least in part, be explained by ... sophistication and diversity" (118).

creations—"Athens was an outstandingly successful state."[39] During the exceptional performance of the 180 years of democracy (508–338 BCE), the Athenians managed to sustain a large hegemony, accumulate public and private wealth, establish institutions that prioritized the common well-being, erect public buildings of unique beauty, and produce unparalleled intellectual life. In Ober's words:

> Participatory and deliberative government, dedicated to and constrained by moral values, can be grounded in choices made by interdependent and rational individuals—people who are concerned (although not uniquely) with their own welfare and aware that it depends (although not entirely) on others' behavior. Bringing normative political theory together with the philosophy of joint action and the political science of rational choice creates space for conceptual advances in democratic theory and social epistemology: it leads to defining democracy as *the capacity of a public to do things* (rather than simply as majority rule), to focusing on *the relationship between innovating and learning* (not just bargaining and voting), and to designing institutions *to aggregate useful knowledge* (not merely preferences or interests).[40]

In the last sentence of the quotation, my emphases point to the essential characteristics of Athenian democracy. One final point emerges that, although stated as a feature of the political system, complements the overall picture of the identity of an Athenian of the classical period: the perception of being highly experimental, innovative, and daring,[41] powerful witness to which is found in the funeral oration of Pericles, as reconstructed by Thucydides (*History of the Peloponnesian War* 2.40.3.1–4.1):

> διαφερόντως γὰρ δὴ καὶ τόδε ἔχομεν ὥστε <u>τολμᾶν</u> τε οἱ αὐτοὶ μάλιστα καὶ περὶ ὧν ἐπιχειρήσομεν ἐκλογίζεσθαι· ὃ τοῖς ἄλλοις ἀμαθία μὲν θράσος, λογισμὸς δὲ ὄκνον φέρει. κράτιστοι δ' ἂν τὴν ψυχὴν δικαίως κριθεῖεν οἱ τά τε δεινὰ καὶ ἡδέα σαφέστατα γιγνώσκοντες καὶ διὰ ταῦτα μὴ ἀποτρεπόμενοι ἐκ τῶν κινδύνων.

And this is another point where we differ from other people. We are capable at the same time of taking risks and of estimating them

---

[39] Ober 2008a:78.
[40] Ober 2008a:5, my emphasis.
[41] Ober 2008a:275.

beforehand. Others are brave out of ignorance; and, when they stop to think, they begin to fear. But the man who can most truly be accounted brave is he who best knows the meaning of what is sweet in life and what is terrible, and then goes out undeterred to meet what is to come.[42]

The Athenian ideology of civic identity, pervasive in the funeral oration (and in other Thucydidean passages) "valued innovation as a good in itself."[43] The powerful drives of innovation and experimentation manifest in all aspects of Athenian life—in war, as well as in peace—can be said to be employed at a symbolic level to "test" the sustainability or viability of their institutions. This last characteristic brings us full circle back to the Castoriadian concept of the self-institution of the society and the human activity of constantly creating and re-creating one's own institutions. Experimenting and innovating *are* the qualities that secure the *re-imagining*[44] and re-design of an institution if changing circumstances demand.

2.1 Tragedy as a Self-Restraining Mechanism of Athenian Democracy

This is where tragedy comes into play. Castoriadis argues that tragedy, a purely Athenian intellectual product, is one of the controlling, corrective, and self-restraining mechanisms of democracy. The philosopher maintains this on the grounds that tragedy reflects on and warns against cases of overweening arrogance[45] manifested in words, thoughts, and behavior, what is commonly understood as *hybris*. It is worth noting that the word τολμᾶν found in the above passage of Thucydides is cognate with τόλμας in the *hypsipolis/apolis* passage with which I began my overall argument (ἄπολις ὅτῳ τὸ μὴ καλὸν / ξύνεστι τόλμας χάριν, *Antigone* 370–371), where Sophocles juxtaposes the positive and negative potentialities of civic identity.[46] The fine line between them is embodied in the word τόλμα (Attic τόλμη).[47] Audacity and its intrinsic tendency

---

[42] Translated by Warner.

[43] Ober 2008a: 275.

[44] We should note, that "whatever has been *imagined* strongly enough to shape behaviour, speech, or objects can, in principle, be *re-imagined* (re-represented) by somebody else" in the long process of the self-creation of this society, Castoriadis 1997b:270.

[45] Castoriadis 2008:337.

[46] See chapter 1 above.

[47] In the twenty-eight passages of τόλμας - τολμᾶν and their cognates found in Sophocles, all have negative connotations, denoting an unrestrained, malign action or thought; one passage only is contextualized positively (εὖ τολμᾷ τελεῖν, *Ajax* 528).

towards innovation and experiment, although highly esteemed and praised in Pericles' funeral oration as social and cultural capital, can so easily transform into one of the major pitfalls of Athenian democracy, and reveal the "dark" side of citizenship.

To my mind, however, the major contribution of tragedy as a controlling, correcting, and self-restraining mechanism of the political system lies in its ability to mediate deliberation about the viability of the current institutions. As an example, I will consider here the abandonment of the corpse of a traitor to the city unburied to be eaten by animals, as the ultimate dishonoring sanction of the polis, as in *Ajax* and *Antigone*. In both tragedies, the playwright favors burial, contrary to the widespread practice in Athens of forbidding such burials in its land and its hegemony.[48] Honoring and dishonoring the dead is part of the discourse of civic identity. I am *not* suggesting that the solution that Sophocles advocates is a straightforward suggestion to the body politic to change or modify the practice. *I am* suggesting that the playwright calls for deliberation on an institutionalized political action that touches upon issues that often follow civil strife and political upheaval, issues capable of profoundly traumatizing the Athenians. In his treatment, the playwright introduces to the story complex matters interwoven with family ethics and divine justice, together with notions of personal honor and pride, thus throwing the subtle complexities of these issues into stark relief. In characteristic Sophoclean manner, the denouements of both plays refrain from offering any unequivocal solution (a feature that perplexed scholars often call the "open-endings" of his plays). Of course, the social order (seen in tragedy as integral to the wider cosmic order) must be re-established, but the intense tragic feeling of the endings eats into the very essence of this order; the restoration always comes at a high price.

The final point that I would like to raise in reference to the contribution of tragedy in the *re-imagining* and consequent redefining of existing institutions is that the particular issues of each play invoke a higher notion of justice to be debated. In the deliberative system of Athenian democracy the concept of

---

[48] I think one of the most apt formulations regarding the polis' right to deny burial to Polyneices, who is a traitor and not just an enemy to Thebes, has been made by Christiane Sourvinou-Inwood: "The funeral was a family affair, but this does not affect the fact that *it was the polis that sanctioned funerary discourse and practice*. In Athens the war-dead were given public burial by the polis ... . The mirror image of the public funerals of the war heroes, *the disposal of the traitor's body, also belonged to the public sphere*. It was normal Athenian practice for traitors, sacrilegers and certain other categories of transgressors to be denied burial" (1989:137, with n20, my emphasis). This is corroborated by the following quotation from [Plutarch] *Vita X Oratorum* regarding Archeptolemus and Antiphon who were charged, and condemned, for treason (προδοσία) in relation to the regime of the Four Hundred: καὶ μὴ ἐξεῖναι θάψαι Ἀρχεπτόλεμον καὶ / Ἀντιφῶντα Ἀθήνησι, μηδ᾽ ὅσης Ἀθηναῖοι κρατοῦσι· (834 Β.1–2). For relevant recent discussion on the matter, see Karakantza 2011a:40, 40n41; Patterson 2006; Hame 2008.

justice is paramount and runs through all aspects of life, a prerequisite for the constant activity of decision-making. We are aware of at least one major change of decision in the case of the dissent of Mytilene (428 BCE) as a result of fierce deliberation, which Thucydides recorded.

In a stormy meeting of the Assembly, the Athenians decided to change the brutal decision taken in the previous meeting to punish the rebels by killing the entire adult male population and selling the rest into slavery.[49] According to the historian,[50] while the trireme was still on route to convey and implement the decision, the anger of the Athenians was supplanted by remorse, leading to the second Assembly that voted for the moderate decision to spare the *dêmos* and punish only the oligarchic leaders of the revolt. The notion of justice in various forms had been brought into the debate, even if the deliberation was in part about "whether justice [had] anything to do with the decision."[51] Whether it *was* about justice, or about *the utility* for the Athenians of preserving the Mytilenean *dêmos*, as the argument of Diodotus went, is not at question here. The fact was that everything concerning the life of the polis had to be debated publicly, and measured against common assumptions of "what is right, and what is not," even if this argument was not openly expressed. In the Mytilenean debate, a multitude of other issues of vital importance at the time were implicitly touched upon, among them "the relationship between the deployment of power, domestic politics, and social diversity," "the relationship between an individual speaker's personal interests and the public interest," "the discontinuity between public and private interests," and the reconciliation between "prudent ... policy and decisive action."[52]

In many other debates in the Assembly as reconstructed by Thucydides, similar issues were raised, as is the case with particular issues debated by the dramatis personae of tragedy. Every aspect of civic life was discussed in the Assembly, as well as in tragedy, where a higher notion of justice is constructed as a measure and a goal. And if in the Mytilenean debate Cleon and Diodotus claimed that their argument *was not* about justice, in the famous Melian deliberation, as every student of the *Histories* knows, everything *was* about justice.

In the argument for tragedy as a controlling and correcting mechanism of democracy, it is evident by now that it is not merely through the *hybris* of the

---

49 Thucydides *History of the Peloponnesian War* 3.36.2.1–3: ὑπὸ ὀργῆς ἔδοξεν αὐτοῖς οὐ τοὺς παρόντας μόνον ἀποκτεῖναι, ἀλλὰ καὶ τοὺς ἅπαντας Μυτιληναίους ὅσοι ἡβῶσι, παῖδας δὲ καὶ γυναῖκας / ἀνδραποδίσαι.

50 Thucydides *History of the Peloponnesian War* 3.36.4.2–5.1: καὶ τῇ ὑστεραίᾳ μετάνοιά τις εὐθὺς ἦν αὐτοῖς καὶ ἀναλογισμὸς ὠμὸν τὸ βούλευμα καὶ μέγα ἐγνῶσθαι, πόλιν ὅλην διαφθεῖραι μᾶλλον ἢ οὐ τοὺς αἰτίους.

51 Ober 1998:101.

52 Ober 1998:102.

individual that this is accomplished; it is also through a complex deliberation on issues that are pivotally significant to the survival of the polis and its citizens. In a sense, Attic tragedy depicts a polis in civil strife (*stasis*) when members of the same body politic find themselves driven by divisive pathos in the context of the disintegration of the ethical and ideological system of the polis.[53] Every time that a tragic play is staged, disintegration and the countervailing healing processes are enacted in the realm of the imaginary; possible solutions of the crisis are tried out—they are *imagined* during the performance and the ensuing discourse that a successful play is bound to inspire. How true this is for the two most successful plays of Sophocles, *Oedipus Tyrannus* and *Antigone*: through their long history of reception and criticism, they have produced a robust discourse well into the twenty-first century.

2.2 Summing Up

My effort to define the notion of the polis started with the strict definition of the polis as a technical term. It took us from the walled city and its hinterland to the political community and its institutions. In both cases we could read the symbolic that resides in the imaginary. The importance of the construction of new social imaginary significations regarding the identity of the "Athenians" and "Athens" (what Ober calls the "new abstractions" of the terms) is manifested in (and is a prerequisite of) the Athenian Revolution, just before the radical reforms of Cleisthenes in 508 BCE. Those reforms are explained as an act of radical creation in the Castoriadian sense, that is, a moment in history when a society creates itself. This self-creation presupposes a period when important social significations had been modified (in the case of Athens this happened throughout the sixth century BCE) and projected onto the imaginary, that is, they were *re-imagined*. As the Athenian polis is a *societas instituans*[54] (and not a *societas instituta*), nothing, no law or institution, is enforced by an external or higher authority. Everything is the result of the self-instituting activity of its citizens. Therefore, the activity of imagining and re-imagining its social significations is constant and paramount, and it is interwoven with the autonomy of the political *praxis*. In this context, controlling and self-restraining mechanisms of the political system have been devised,[55] for the body politic is responsible for deliberating on and modifying the institutions.

---

[53] Karakantza 2011a:27.
[54] "The instituting society is the social imaginary in the radical sense," Castoriadis 1997b:269.
[55] Castoriadis 1995:202–203.

Tragedy, a product of the imaginary, is one of the prime mechanisms of imagining, re-imagining, and redefining the ideology that underlies the creation and modification of institutions. One of its avenues is the notion of *hybris* that warns the Athenians against any excess in behavior and thought; another is the deliberation over the sustainability and viability of the existing institutions. Finally, and of great importance, is the discourse constructed around a higher notion of justice that permeates all political *praxeis* of the body politic.

One last word of clarification: although the notion of the polis comprises all the partial characteristics stated at the outset of this chapter, each of them being a necessary, but not sufficient, condition for the entirety, the most important of all is the notion of the community of citizens mutually bound by strong bonds. "Athens" is primarily "the Athenians" and not the urban settlement. When Themistocles was hard pressed by the Peloponnesians to engage in naval battle, not in Salamis but in the Isthmus, the main argument of the Corinthian general Adeimantus was that the Athenians did not have a country and a polis anymore to protect, for the Persians had just conquered the city of Athens and burnt it to ashes. "Since Athens does not exist anymore," the argument went, "the sensible action is to protect the remaining of the Greek cities in Peloponnese."[56] To this, the Athenian general replied that the Athenians *had* a country and a polis, greater than any other Greek city, as long as they had their ships and could conquer any city they wanted. But most importantly, Themistocles said that as long as there were Athenians, the city could be founded somewhere else. The general threatened to embark all the Athenians on the ships, sail to Italy, and settle there, thus re-founding Athens.[57] Athens existed as long as the Athenians existed.

---

[56] I condense here the argument of Adeimantus in the fierce debate between himself, Eurybiades, and Themistocles in relation to the location of the naval battle. The Greek text (Herodotus *Histories* 8.61.1-6) runs as follows: Ταῦτα λέγοντος Θεμιστοκλέος αὖτις ὁ Κορίνθιος Ἀδείμαντος ἐπεφέρετο, σιγᾶν τε κελεύων τῷ μὴ ἔστι πατρὶς καὶ Εὐρυβιάδην οὐκ ἐῶν ἐπιψηφίζειν ἀπόλι ἀνδρί· πόλιν γὰρ τὸν Θεμιστοκλέα παρεχόμενον οὕτω ἐκέλευε γνώμας συμβάλλεσθαι. Ταῦτα δέ οἱ προέφερε, ὅτι ἡλώκεσάν τε καὶ κατείχοντο αἱ Ἀθῆναι ("During his speech Themistocles was again attacked by the Corinthian Adeimantus, who told him to hold his tongue because he was a man without a country, and tried to prevent Eurybiades from putting any question to the vote at the instance of a mere refugee. Let Themistocles, he cried, provide himself with a country before he offered his advice. The point of the jibe was, of course, the fact that Athens had fallen and was in Persian hands"; trans. de Sélincourt/Burn).

[57] Herodotus *Histories* 8.61–62.

3

The Self in the Polis

THE PRIOR CHAPTER'S DEFINITIONS—of what constitutes a polis, of political creation, and of social imaginary significations that add meaning to the perceptions of "Athens" and the "Athenians" at the turn of the fifth century BCE—have already touched upon the notion of identity in the polis. What it is to be an "Athenian" is the collective notion applied to, and experienced by, the citizenry in Athens. Vigorous debate and participation, creation of policies, extensive networks of collaboration between the citizens, public festivities, rituals, commonality of action—in peace, as well as war—all these constitute the public, collective notion of being a political and social subject; they define what it is to be a citizen.

But what about the individual? For a contemporary reader the notion of the individual resonates strongly with that of privacy; an individual private person, living their own life, relatively unaffected by the social or political practices of their society if they so choose. Moreover, identity in the Kantian vein can be a universalized version of an ethical self, transcending historically determined circumstances.[1] Taken thus, the issue of identity is not inextricably bound to the polis, leaving aside the banal observation that any human society consists of individuals. However, if—as I argue—*Oedipus Tyrannus* is a tragedy about identity, how is this relevant to the "polis" of my book's title? How does personal identity become so located at the heart of the polis? The goal of this book is to answer these questions, especially through the close reading of Sophocles' drama. Before this, however, we should reflect on specific issues concerning the self in the Greek classical polis, pursuing the vein of analysis proposed in the preceding chapter. These issues expose the special characteristics that inform ideas of the self and of the identity of the individual[2] in classical Athens; without

---

[1] Sorabji 2006:7–8. See also Gill 1996:406 for the post-Cartesian framework of thought in defining the self.

[2] "Personal identity cannot be detached from the notion of the self, of which it is a constituent and indispensable part" (Sorabji 2006:2).

clarifying those we are bound to adopt ahistorical assumptions that distort our understanding of the different concepts of classical times.

3.0.1 Public Self

The paramount postulate that we need to bear in mind is that the self in ancient Greece is essentially public.[3] This is not to say that any individualistic characteristics are excluded from the ambient notion of the self in ancient Athens. But, what is a "self"? At this point we should consider the definition provided by Richard Sorabji:

> What I am postulating is not an undetectable soul or immaterial ego, but an embodied individual whose existence is plain to see. This individual is something that has or owns psychological states as well as having or owning a body and bodily states. ... In asking about the self I am not asking what it is to be a human being, or a higher animal in general, but about what it is to be an individual one.[4]

Similarly, my preoccupation is not with the "undetectable soul or immaterial ego," but with the embodied individual who lives in a classical city-state and within the specific social and political environment of the polis, possessing its own ideological structures regarding the perception of a self. This is my working definition of the self. A modern-day Athenian is not an individual in the same sense as an Athenian of classical Athens, for the notion of the self, as a multitude of other cultural constructs, is historically determined, which raises the following question: "how did the ancients understand what it is that I am, fundamentally, as an acting and affected subject, interpreting the world around me, being distinct from others like and unlike me?"[5]

A further issue complicates my argument. We understand what it is to be Pericles, Alcibiades, or Socrates, but what about Oedipus, Achilles, or Odysseus? Is there any chance to reconstruct the notion of the self in classical Athens by means of fictional characters? In the previous chapter I dealt with the new perception of "what it is to be an Athenian" in the aftermath of the Athenian Revolution of 508 BCE. The Athenians thought of themselves as autonomous individuals in an autonomous city-state and thus repudiated any possibility of becoming a dependent client state to Sparta. In the Castoriadian vein of interpreting political *praxis*, this was possible because the Athenians first imagined

---

[3]   Taylor 1989:16–17, 25–52; MacIntyre 2007:141–69.
[4]   Sorabji 2006:4, 20.
[5]   Remes and Sihvola 2008:1.

themselves differently and then effected change in the public realm. The action of imagining must happen as a prior prerequisite to change. In the social imaginary, human beings pose and answer questions that in time become seminal questions of philosophy. Castoriadis says:

> Man is an unconsciously philosophical animal posing the questions of philosophy concerning things long before philosophy existed as an explicit reflection; and he is a poetic animal that gave in imaginary the answers to those questions.[6]

Thus poetry becomes both the setting and the agency for building up individual characters that think, act, deliberate, and take decisions within the framework of their polis. Alongside the viability of the current institutions, the playwright presents us with individuals who face personal dilemmas and who are also accountable to their community for their thoughts and actions. Moreover, individual characters in poetry present individual traits. What it is to be Oedipus or Orestes or Achilles can be understood by considering the particular assemblage of traits that constitute the unique psychological and mental make-up of these persons;[7] and in some cases (such as Oedipus or Odysseus) comprise their bodily traits as well (the marks on the ankles and thigh, respectively). Viewed from this perspective, my question can be formulated as follows: how do we balance the individual and the public dimensions of defining the self in classical Greece?

3.0.2 Particularity and Accountability

I will begin by quoting Alasdair MacIntyre's definition of the heroic self, for I firmly believe that understanding Attic tragedy requires a thorough appreciation of the heroic self of the Homeric epics, a concept with which the later genre is in constant dialogue:[8]

> Identity in heroic society involves particularity and accountability. I am answerable for doing or failing to do what anyone who occupies my role owes to others and this accountability terminates only with death. I have until my death to do what I have to do. Moreover this

---

[6] Castoriadis 1997a:147.

[7] Three meanings of personality attached to "personality" and "self" are also most relevant here: 1. individual distinctiveness or uniqueness; 2. psychological structure, either common to us as human beings, or distinctive to us as individuals; and 3. our essence as persons (in a normative sense); see Gill 1996:1.

[8] A much longer exposition of my views on the heroic self, as well as a radical reformulation of the well-known dichotomy between the cooperative and competitive values in the Homeric epics advocated by Adkins, can be found in Appendix 2.

accountability is particular. It is to, for and with specific individuals, members of the same local community, that I am accountable. The heroic self does not itself aspire to universality even although in retrospect we may recognize universal worth in the achievements of that self.[9]

It is interesting to note that the two traits defining the heroic self are "particularity" and "accountability." Both Achilles and Hector have their own particular characteristics, their "individual distinctiveness or uniqueness," which is one of the prerequisites of the notion of "self" and "selfhood." However, what is important to understand as especially applicable to ancient Greece is what MacIntyre calls "accountability." As a person in a heroic society I am accountable to my community for doing or failing to do what I owe to others, depending on my position in this particular community—as are Hector (doing) and Achilles (failing to do). Public esteem, the respect of others, and the reputation of heroic deeds pass from father to son (the *kleos* of the family). The public character is so emphasized that honor in Homeric society assumes a tangible material dimension plain for all to see. The famous speech of Sarpedon to Glaukos, when he urges him to take their stand in the frontline of battle, lays out the twofold character of *timê*: they are highly esteemed among the Lycians, as if they were gods; and fighting in the frontline brings them fine estates, beautiful orchards, riverside fields, and prime portions at symposia (*Iliad* 12.310–321):

> Γλαῦκε τί ἢ δὴ νῶϊ <u>τετιμήμεσθα</u> μάλιστα
> ἕδρῃ τε κρέασίν τε ἰδὲ πλείοις δεπάεσσιν
> ἐν Λυκίῃ, πάντες δὲ θεοὺς ὣς εἰσορόωσι,
> καὶ τέμενος νεμόμεσθα μέγα Ξάνθοιο παρ' ὄχθας
> καλὸν φυταλιῆς καὶ ἀρούρης πυροφόροιο;
> τὼ νῦν χρὴ Λυκίοισι μέτα πρώτοισιν ἐόντας
> ἑστάμεν ἠδὲ μάχης καυστείρης ἀντιβολῆσαι,
> ὄφρά τις ὧδ' εἴπῃ Λυκίων πύκα θωρηκτάων·
> 'οὐ μὰν ἀκλεέες Λυκίην κάτα κοιρανέουσιν
> ἡμέτεροι βασιλῆες, ἔδουσί τε πίονα μῆλα
> οἶνόν τ' ἔξαιτον μελιηδέα· ἀλλ' ἄρα καὶ ἲς
> ἐσθλή, ἐπεὶ Λυκίοισι μέτα πρώτοισι μάχονται.'

Glaucus, why is it that we two are most held in honor, with a seat of honor and meats and full cups, in Lycia and all men gaze on us as

---

[9]   2007:147.

gods? And we possess a great estate by the banks of Xanthus, a fair tract of orchard and a wheat-bearing plough-land. Therefore now we must take our stand among the foremost Lycians and confront blazing battle so that many a one of the mail-clad Lycians may say: "Surely no inglorious men are these who rule in Lycia, our kings, and they eat fat sheep and drink choice wine, honey-sweet: but their might too is noble, since they fight among the foremost Lycians."[10]

But tragedy deals with the heroic self in a refracted way. When the "virtues move to Athens," to paraphrase the title of MacIntyre's chapter that deals with the self in classical Athens,[11] there is a significant change inextricably bound up with the creation of the polis. As discussed in the previous chapter, new perceptions of the notions of "Athens" and "Athenians," a new political creation privileging the collective and the system of "working together," new social imaginary significations that reject clientelism to aristocrats or to a foreign political authority are created. Thus autonomy, rather than heteronomy, is promoted as the quintessence of the new collective identity of the Athenians. So, where now stands the individual?

Moving from heroic society to classical Athens, we should note that the paramount constituent of identity remains accountability to others, but this time in the context of the city-state. A good man is, overall, a good citizen in terms of the collectivity of his polis. Moreover, the much-celebrated autonomy on the collective level defers now to the law representing a higher authority to which an individual is subject.[12] The laws and the civic system that enforces and supports them assume a much greater authority in the polis—the citizen owes obedience only to them. Interestingly, we should bear in mind that, since the laws are also the product of the legislative activity of the citizens (the highest legislative body being the Assembly), an individual is subject to no one other than his own (collective) authority.

In the context of the polis, and within the grid formed by the notion of justice, an individual faces dilemmas regarding all aspects of life: with family, friends, gods, political power, fellow-warriors—dilemmas that require citizens to take an ethical stance to retain their personal sense of honor within their community. "In Homer," MacIntyre claims, "the question of honor is what is due to a king; in Sophocles the question of honor has become the question of

---

[10] All translations from Homer are by Murray (revised by Wyatt), unless otherwise stated.

[11] Chapter 11 "The Virtues at Athens" in 2007:153–69.

[12] See also chapter 5.3 below, where I discuss at length Vernant's idea of the emergence of the self in the face of the law in the widespread judicial practices of the democratic law courts.

what is due to a man."[13] In this last sentence, I would substitute "citizen" for "man" since "the common Athenian assumption is that the virtues have their place within the social context of the city-state. To be a good man will on every Greek view be at least closely allied to being a good citizen";[14] and, thus, "to be successful is to be successful in a particular city."[15]

Needless to say, being successful in one's city does not correlate with merely efficiently managing its administration. Success requires nurturing the ethical self, constructing the system of values of society. Each individual needs to define what comprises an honorable and meaningful life; in this endeavor, citizens attempt to determine what is good, intrinsically valuable, just, and appropriate: what should be endorsed and what repudiated.[16] A successful citizen in ancient Greece needs to be *dikaios*, *sôphrôn*, and *sophos* (to name just the capital virtues). In this society "the most valued existence"[17] embraces such notions as *agathon*, *eudaimonia*, *eu prattein*, *agathos bios*, and their like.[18] MacIntyre considers at least four groups of texts (the sophists, Plato, Aristotle, and the tragedians, especially Sophocles) in order to draw a picture of the moral vocabulary of the Greek texts. The wide variance in terminology amongst the texts points to a number of Athenian views, but the author continues:

> Yet before I consider these four let me underline at least one thing that they all do share. All do take it for granted that the milieu in which the virtues are to be exercised and in terms of which they are to be defined is the polis.[19]

Thus the most important and common ground on which the self is constituted in classical Athens is the polis; the particular characteristics of the individual remain salient,[20] but it is "accountability" to others in the political and social

---

[13]   2007:155.

[14]   2007:158.

[15]   2007:162.

[16]   Taylor 2004:50. See also Herman (2006:264): "Norms and values remain constant through time only so long as social structures and conditions are constant; as soon as these change, norms and values change too."

[17]   Adkins 1960:249. As for the "triple standard of behavior," Adkins quotes Plato *Crito* 48b, where Socrates is the speaker: "Are we still agreed that to live *eu*, to live *kalôs*, and to live *dikaiôs*, are one and the same thing"? For the construction of systems of values in ancient Greek society, the following books are indispensable: Adkins 1972; Dover 1974; Ferguson 1989; Christ 2006; Herman 2006.

[18]   Karakantza 2011a:25.

[19]   2007:157-158.

[20]   "Athenian democracy pragmatically acknowledged the legitimacy of personal self-interest, which was intimately connected with individual freedom, and incorporated this into its ideology of citizenship," Christ 2006:9.

context that takes precedence over the traits of selfhood. This is very much the case, I argue, in tragedy, as well, despite the overwhelming presence of themes that, in the long reception of the genre, were considered as timeless and universal. The "reality" in the tragedy of classical Athens is that "the moral protagonist stands in relation to his/her community and his/her social role."[21]

3.1 The "Lonely" Sophoclean Hero as Not-So-Lonely After All

For thinking about Sophocles, MacIntyre articulates a central interpretative principle: "the Sophoclean protagonist would be nothing without his or her place in the social order, the city, the army at Troy."[22] This formulation challenges the widespread assumption created by Bernard M. W. Knox's *The Heroic Temper* (1964). Knox's elegantly expressed (and debated) views of over fifty years ago still exert a strong hold on mainstream interpretations of the Sophoclean hero, who is found to be intransigent, stubborn, unyielding to friends' and family's pleas for moderation, and, above all, enmeshed in the heroic temper; the Sophoclean hero is a lonely and isolated figure.[23] Such a characterization conflicts, it is argued here, with perceptions of the identity of a person (real or imaginary) held by Athenians contemporary with Sophocles. The tragic hero's supposed isolation, his "shutting off" from the world with decisions that divide his psychic life and that cast him out of the community, is an evidently romanticized construction stemming from *our* perception of a tragic hero. Knox's description of the Sophoclean hero resonates with later assumptions of a turbulent romantic psyche:

> To those who face him, friends and enemies alike, the hero seems unreasonable almost to the point of madness, suicidally bold, impervious to argument, intransigent, angry; an impossible person whom only time can cure. But to the hero himself the opinion of others is irrelevant. His loyalty to his conception of himself, and the necessity to perform the action that conception imposes, prevail over all other considerations.[24] [...] The disrespect and mockery of the world lock them even more securely in the prison of their passionate hearts, fill

---

[21] MacIntyre 2007:158.
[22] Ibid.
[23] Knox 1964:32.
[24] 1964:28.

them with fierce resentment against those they regard as responsible for their sufferings.[25]

For Sophocles' contemporaries, a hero like this would not make any sense. Although it is the hero's own decisions that result in his becoming an outcast from the community, it is precisely his ardent desire to remain within the community that makes him act, think, and argue as he does; the hero's honor within the community cannot be impugned. Knox's claim that "to the hero himself the opinion of others is irrelevant" cannot be correct. An obvious "suspect" is Ajax, who is "deaf" to his sailors' words of persuasion, as well as to the desperate pleading of Tecmessa. He insists—to the point of committing suicide—that his damaged heroic honor (that is, the high esteem he enjoys among his peers) is irreparable, and so he decides to die, because to live without the respect and esteem of the Achaeans is to endure a life not worth living. This is put eloquently in the following celebrated lines of *Ajax* (479–480):

> ἀλλ' ἢ καλῶς ζῆν ἢ καλῶς τεθνηκέναι
> τὸν εὐγενῆ χρή. Πάντ' ἀκήκοας λόγον

> The noble man must live with honor or be honorably dead; you have heard all I have to say.[26]

Because his public self has been destroyed, his life becomes unbearable. The only time he tries to persuade himself to change is in response to his wife's pleas, *because* he has been sensitive to her pleas and *listened* to her arguments. In the "deception speech" he makes a sincere attempt to convince himself, measuring himself against the recurrent cosmic circle of change. Everything seems to be going well until Ajax begins to reflect on the issue of *philia* within the army of the Achaeans. *Philia*, as we very well know, is not only an individual feeling of affection (and the manifestation of it) toward our friends—as it can be today— but a tangible network of socially sanctioned loyalties.[27] Political and social alliances, alongside family ties, form strong social bonds that mark one's position in society.[28] When Ajax begins to reflect (in the "harbor of friendship" passage) on the instability and untrustworthiness of these alliances, he despairs of being a part of such a duplicitous system and returns to his determination to die. *Philia* fails twice in the story of Ajax: first in the Judgment of Arms and second in the

---

[25] 1964:31.

[26] All translations of *Ajax* and *Electra* are by Lloyd-Jones unless stated otherwise.

[27] Karakantza 2011c:42–43, and nn1–3.

[28] *Philia* and *philos* imply "a network of stable human loyalties that are bound by reciprocal favor and affection," Karakantza 2011c:41.

raid of Ajax against his fellow-warriors; the shift of loyalties undermines the social standing in the army at Troy. This is not just a casual mutation of the reciprocal bonds implied in *philia*; rather it entails extreme danger, as is shown in the fearful appeal of the Salaminian sailors to Ajax to recover his senses and stand by them, for without his protection the Atreidae threaten to execute them publicly (*Ajax* 251–256):

> τοίας ἐρέσσουσιν ἀπειλὰς δικρατεῖς Ἀτρεῖδαι
> καθ' ἡμῶν· πεφόβημαι λιθόλευστον Ἄρη
> ξυναλγεῖν μετὰ τοῦδε τυπείς,
> τὸν αἶσ' ἄπλατος ἴσχει.

> Such angry threats are hurled against us by the brother-kings, the sons of Atreus; I fear to share a bitter death by stoning, smitten at this man's side, who is swayed by a fate to which none may draw nigh.[29]

Fear has been in the air ever since the *parodos* of the play: "I quake exceedingly and am sore afraid, like a winged dove with troubled eyes" (μέγαν ὄκνον ἔχω καὶ πεφόβημαι / πτηνῆς ὡς ὄμμα πελείας, *Ajax* 139–140), says the chorus. The rumor of Ajax' sally upon the cattle the previous night haunts the Salaminians in the *parodos*, destroying Ajax' *kleos* and their own: "loud murmurs beset us for our shame" (μεγάλοι θόρυβοι κατέχουσ' ἡμᾶς / ἐπὶ δυσκλείᾳ, *Ajax* 142–143). Publicly acclaimed honor leads to the threat of publicly administered revenge. Moreover, public humiliation of the enemy, whose image is thus sullied and stature destroyed, is what the goddess Athena suggests: "and to mock at foes—is not that the sweetest mockery?" (οὔκουν γέλως ἥδιστος εἰς ἐχθροὺς γελᾶν; *Ajax* 79); it is also what Ajax most dreads: "Alas, the mockery! How have I been shamed?" (οἴμοι γέλωτος, οἶον ὑβρίσθην ἄρα, *Ajax* 367). There are, in fact, fourteen references in the play to malicious laughter against Ajax and his pitiful failure to take proper revenge on his enemies, as an Iliadic warrior would (γέλως / γελᾶν 79, γέλων 303, γέλωτος 367, γέλωθ' ὑφ' ἡδονῆς 382, γελᾷ 383, ἐπεγγελῶσιν 454, γελᾷ 957, γέλωτα 958, γελώντων 961, ἐπεγγελῷεν 969, ἐπεγγελᾶν 989, γελᾶν 1011, γελῶν 1043).

Thus a betrayed notion of *philia*, which leads to injustice and to public ridicule that vitiates honor—the connecting thread running through the entire play—fatally compromises the standing of Ajax amongst the Achaeans. Ajax

---

[29] Translations of *Ajax* on this page are by Jebb.

cannot survive, because "he would be nothing without his place in the social order of the army at Troy."[30]

My second counter-example to the claims of Knox is Sophocles' *Electra*, whose protagonist is commonly considered to be "locked" in the "prison of [her] passionate heart," with a "fierce resentment against those [she] regard[s] as responsible for [her] sufferings." Such claims seem to be unequivocally applicable to the behavior of Electra because of her protracted lamentation and her fierce resentment against her mother and her mother's lover. She is "deaf" to calls from the chorus for moderation and, although conscious of her transgression, admits that she cannot but keep lamenting her dead father for this abnormally long period of time. (Of course, dramatic time does not equal real time, but the period of mourning of Electra parallels dramatically the period of the coming-of-age of Orestes.) She laments "over much and over long" with such an intensity that on the modern stage she can be interpreted in purely Freudian terms, as in Peter Stein's production with the National Theater of Greece in 2007, which portrayed her as a "psychopath," a "hysterical person," and a "wild neurotic."[31] Thus, Knox's reading of Electra, "locked in her passionate heart" and "fierce [in her] resentment," has entered the performance tradition, and with ever stronger Freudian overtones.

But, again, nothing could be further from the truth. In order to endorse such readings, one would need to confine all the sentiments, thoughts, and actions of Electra to a familial conflict, with the daughter harboring strong emotions towards both mother and father. But the *oikos* in classical Greek thought is an indispensable part of the polis. Electra and her actions should be seen against the background of her degraded social and political status and her diminished position in the rituals of the family and the polis. I will begin with the notorious abasement of her social status when she is forced to serve as a lowborn slave, with meager food and clothing, in the palace of her own father (*Electra* 189–192):

ἀλλ' ἀπερεί τις ἔποικος ἀναξία
οἰκονομῶ θαλάμους πατρός, ὧδε μὲν
ἀεικεῖ σὺν στολᾷ,
κεναῖς δ' ἀμφίσταμαι τραπέζαις.

---

[30] See MacIntyre 2007:167

[31] Peter Stein's controversial production of *Electra* in 2007 with the National Theatre of Greece prompted my response in "Throwing out the *Menos* with the Bath Water: The Sophoclean Text vs Peter Stein's *Electra* (2007)." There I discuss how limited his reading is, as it reduces everything to a single focus, that of Electra's *psychopatheia* and vindictiveness. Stein said in an interview that the original play was "ugly" and "uneventful," Karakantza 2013:61–62.

... like a lowborn slave serve in the chambers of my father, in such
mean attire as this, and stand at empty tables!

Pursuing the same vein of persecution and humiliation, Electra is forced
to remain unwed (ἀνύμφευτος, 165), with neither a husband (οὔτις ἀνὴρ
ὑπερίσταται, 188) nor a male of her house to protect her.[32] Denied the chance
to produce offspring (ἄτεκνος, 164) that would empower her in her husband's
oikos, Electra is virtually suspended between the *oikos* of her father, which is
being destroyed, and the *oikos* of a husband she is denied. It is important at this
point to note that Clytemnestra has had other children by Aegisthus (πατέρα
τὸν ἀμὸν πρόσθεν ἐξαπώλεσας, / καὶ παιδοποιεῖς, "in time past you killed
my father, and getting children by him" [Aegisthus], 588–589), thus usurping
the old line of Agamemnon's *oikos* with a new one. Moreover, since she and
Aegisthus also attempted to kill Orestes in infancy, it is clear that they intend to
exterminate the bloodline of the former ruler, with obvious social and political
consequences.[33]

We should now consider the observance of rituals of the family and the polis,
where the transgression of Electra is egregiously marked. She laments "over
much and over long,"[34] to such an extent that even in modernity "Mourning
Becomes Electra."[35] Mourning, together with funeral rites, is a family matter,
but it is also regulated by the polis, in degree and extent, to avoid excess in
either. Lamenting for such a protracted period of time marks a transgression
and exacerbates the marginality of the mourner and her exclusion from normal
life. On at least three occasions, Electra herself admits her excess. A celebrated
line addressed to the chorus, ἔξοιδ', οὐ λάθει μ' ὀργὰ ("I know, my passion does
not escape me," 222), is corroborated by Electra admitting the shame that the
excess of lamentation brings upon her and the members of the chorus (*Electra*
254–255):

αἰσχύνομαι μέν, ὦ γυναῖκες, εἰ δοκῶ
πολλοῖσι θρήνοις δυσφορεῖν ὑμῖν ἄγαν

I am ashamed, women, if you think I grieve too much with my
numerous laments.

---

[32] Karakantza 2013:66–67; Giosi 1996:174–175.

[33] Karakantza 2013:67.

[34] Karakantza 2013:69–73.

[35] I am referring of course to the emblematic title of the play cycle *Mourning Becomes Electra* written
by the American playwright Eugene O'Neill, which premiered in 1931. The cycle parallels the
Aeschylean trilogy *The Oresteia* with three plays *The Homecoming*, *The Hunted*, and *The Haunted*.

Even to her mother, Electra admits that she is aware that her actions are inappropriate for her age and go against her nature (ἔξωρα πράσσω κοὐκ ἐμοὶ προσεικότα, *Electra* 618).

However, there are tangible benefits from her excessive lamentation, which extend to public and political as well as private realms, that need consideration before passing hasty judgment on her "passionate love for her father." First, Electra keeps the memory of her father alive, preventing it from being extinguished. This is very important when there is a *nostos* to be accomplished, because—as in the case of Orestes—the returning son needs to be informed that there is an ally at home waiting to help take revenge for the murder of the father. Without that memory being kept alive at home (as in the archetypical *nostos* of Odysseus and the constant quasi-lament of Penelope), the *nostos* cannot be accomplished (or might be seriously endangered). Second, lamentation sets the loss of a person within the social, cultural, and religious framework of his society. In the case of Agamemnon, it serves as a catalyst for an as yet unfulfilled vengeance, for it brings a private familial matter into the public realm. Third, Electra responds with her own abnormal rituals to Clytemnestra's perverted ritual of commemoration for the murder of Agamemnon in the performance of dances and sacrifices every month on the day of the slaughter of her husband: "Mother and daughter thus take up diametrically opposite positions, each transgressing against the proper rites in her own way."[36]

Electra's excessive and protracted lamentation does not spring forth from the obscure depths of her passionate heart; rather, it responds to still unresolved issues that are directly connected with her position, and her dead father's position, within their society. Electra will stop when the tottering house of Agamemnon is re-founded by Orestes; until then, she needs to remind everybody (especially Clytemnestra and Aegisthus) publicly of the unredeemed murder, the usurpation of the bloodline, and the perverted rituals: "A lamenting Electra is a dangerous Electra, since by drawing attention to the still unpaid penalty for her father's murder she becomes a threat on a social level."[37]

---

[36] Karakantza 2013:72. See also Seaford's similar statement formulated nearly thirty years earlier than mine: "[Electra] must respond to the perverted and protracted rites of her mother with anomalously protracted lamentation of her own" (1985:317).

[37] Karakantza 2013:69; see also Alexiou 1974:21. When dealing with Sophocles' *Electra*, Goff (2004:310-311) stresses the idea that "Elektra uses her mourning as a political tool against those now in power" and that "[her] mourning is so effective that, … Aigisthos and Klytaimestra are determined to hide it and to shut Elektra in a dungeon." According to Foley (1993:143): "a mourning woman is not simply a producer of pity, but dangerous"; see also Bakogianni 2011:1.41-42.

It has become clear by now that in Sophocles it is "the individual in his or her role, representing his or her community, who is ... the dramatic character."[38] The self in Attic tragedy is a self in the polis.

3.1.1 Narrating One's Life

One last remark is indispensable to complete our notion of identity within the framework we have delineated so far and to build a bridge to the dramatic genre as the retelling of a story. A person should be able to "tell a narrative [of his/ her] life, because without that one will not have an identity."[39] The narrative should be coherent, lest it result in a refracted notion of identity, which makes the position of the individual in the polis ambiguous. But more importantly, the narrative of a life, with all its moral decisions, leaves its imprint in the public domain, where it participates in a discourse of debate around these decisions—posing the causes and effects of actions, articulating lines of thought and arguments that support those actions. The narrative of a life is part of its identity. MacIntyre argues along these lines in reference to the Sophoclean protagonist:

> The life of the Sophoclean protagonist has its own specific narrative form just as that of the epic hero had. ... If a human life is understood as progress through harms and dangers, moral and physical, which someone may encounter and overcome in better and worse ways and with greater or lesser measure of success, the virtues will find their place as those qualities the possession and exercise of which generally tend to success in this enterprise and the vices likewise as qualities which likewise tend to failure. Each human life will then embody a story whose shape and form will depend upon what is counted as a harm and danger and upon how success and failure, progress and its opposite, are understood and evaluated.[40]

We are, as Taylor claims, linguistic animals; as we express our motivations and evaluations in words and images, we give a "shape" to what initially might be confused or partially formulated thoughts and emotions.[41] And as we try to make sense of our lives and, for that matter, to possess an identity, "we need an orientation to the good"; the latter is woven into our understanding of our lives

---

[38] MacIntyre 2007:168.
[39] Sorabji 2006:8.
[40] MacIntyre 2007:167–168.
[41] Taylor 1985:36, 103.

"as an unfolding story," which in plain words means that "our lives exist also in this space of questions, which only a coherent narrative can answer."[42]

With these last remarks, we lay the groundwork for considering the narrative of the life of Oedipus and how the incoherence of his narrative hinders any attempt to make sense of his life, as the story told by Sophocles shows. This incoherence confuses not just "what I am" but also "what I have become" and "how I have come here."[43] The narrative relates to the public space that is also the place where our moral decisions are taken. It is also apposite to break down the facets of one's identity into the basic constituents of the question "who am I": "where do I stand in life," "how do I relate to my family tree," "how do I relate to my social function and status?" Parallel to these fundamental questions are other important aspects of a life's narrative: "from where do I speak and to whom," and "how do I relate to these webs of interlocution, since I am a self among other selves?" These questions will be pursued at the beginning of a close reading of *Oedipus Tyrannus*, where I raise the issue "Who Am I?" as the central focal point of my reading of the drama.

[42]   Taylor 1989:47.
[43]   Ibid.

Part 3

Close Reading of *Oedipus Tyrannus*

4

Who Am I?

A Tragedy of Identity

Simon had been right.
You saw things differently
when you changed your perspective and location.
All blind spots could be compensated for.

Jo Nesbo, *The Son*

OEDIPUS' MAJOR HANDICAP in his life is not knowing who he is; the parricide and incest come about as the result of this ignorance. This extremely
simple and stark statement sounds self-evident but, save for a very few
exceptions,[1] has never been the main focus of interpretation of the play. In the
nineteenth century Oedipus is the Philosopher, at the turn of the twentieth
century Freud detects the Oedipus complex in the play—an interpretation that
has become the overwhelmingly popular assumption in contemporary versions
of Oedipus' story. Under the influence of German Idealism, scholarship has seen
the protagonist's endeavors as indicative of the relentless human struggle to
attain knowledge. The play explores, in this interpretive view, how precarious
human knowledge and happiness are. Although not a subscriber to this view, I
do often quote the following exquisite formulation by E. R. Dodds, from his 1966
paper "On Misunderstanding the *Oedipus Rex*," as the epitome of the "humanistic" approach to classics (which was very much in fashion even into the late
70's):

> To me personally, Oedipus is a kind of symbol of the human intelli-
> gence, which cannot rest until it has solved all the riddles—even the

---

[1] Cameron 1968; Dugdale 2015; Euben 1990:96–129.

last riddle, to which the answer is that human happiness is built on an illusion.[2]

Psychoanalysis, philosophy, and German Idealism (with the subsequent humanistic trend that held sway well into the twentieth century) do not exhaust formulations of the play's cardinal "meaning." In the political vein, Oedipus is seen as a tyrant in the polis, or as Pericles, or as the wounded body of the Athenian democracy itself (the date of the play is circa 425 BCE). Of course, the artistic merits of the play have been praised ever since the *Poetics* of Aristotle and have contributed immensely to the unquestionable popularity the play has enjoyed since its rediscovery in the Renaissance. Furthermore, under the "weight" of the widespread Christian morality of our times a long debate has been waged as to the existence and extent of Oedipus' guilt for his transgressions. And if guilty, what is he to blame for: intellectual pride, or political arrogance imbued with a disposition for tyranny?

Finally, and significantly, substantial efforts have been made to investigate the degree of divine intervention in the drama. Even in the most casual of discussions, students of Greek antiquity wonder whether there is any possibility of speaking about freely willed action on the part of Oedipus, since the existence of the oracle(s) predetermines the course of his actions and decisions. Contemporary scholarship has approached this thorny issue with a slew of suggestions, ranging from Oedipus as a "puppet" in the hands of the gods, to the hero as a human being who transcends his limitations to carve out his own courses of action. In this endeavor, the insistence on divine intervention is like exploring "Apollo's ways" in a quasi-biblical vein of thought. I will discuss these issues below.[3] However, I will mention briefly here that, despite the crucial functional importance of the oracles received by Laius and Oedipus in shaping the history of the family, the playwright constructs the conceptual plot of his play around the discovery of Oedipus' identity, *not* around the god's ways. The latter form the general framework given by the tradition and are freely used by Sophocles to build up *his* version of the story.

Three major cycles of questions run through the play: "Who is the murderer of Laius," "Am I the murderer of Laius," and finally, "Who am I?"[4] It has been said that *Oedipus Tyrannus* is written like a detective story, with the difference that the audience knows the truth all along. However, *Oedipus Tyrannus* is *not* a detective story, for what constitutes the objective here is not to solve the murder of Laius, but to construct—piece by piece—the identity of Oedipus. The whole life

---

[2] Dodds 1966:48.
[3] See below, chapter 5, sections 2 and 3, pp. 125–147
[4] Cameron 1968:32–33.

of Oedipus has been narrated; the "who am I?" is answered in relation to "how I have come here" and "what I have become." What Taylor calls "a narrative understanding of [one's] life"[5] is something that makes sense only if the narrative acquires coherence, which is the objective of the investigation initiated by Oedipus. *Oedipus Tyrannus* is a quest for Oedipus' identity.[6]

We need to reorient our perspective on the *Oedipus Tyrannus*, in contrast to much of the scholarship on the play, so as to see things differently.[7] No matter how important all the other issues are, it is the omnipresent question of identity that dominates the entire Sophoclean tragedy, and with this question on his mind (and on his lips) Oedipus comes to visit the oracle at Delphi. He asks the god "who he is and who his father is"—this is how the questions should be formulated when we render the indirect question(s) to the oracle (ζητῶν ἑαυτὸν καὶ γένους φυτοσπόρον), found in the ancient hypothesis by Aristophanes the Grammarian (line 6), into direct speech. In reality, what obsesses Oedipus is, above all, the question "who am I?" in relation to his genealogy. This is, of course, the first and cardinal question that springs to one's mind when talking about identity: your name and genealogy.[8] This destabilizing uncertainty intrudes abruptly into Oedipus' life when a fellow-drinker at a banquet in Corinth accuses him of being the bastard son of the king. Up to that moment, Oedipus had been living under the comforting delusion that he knew who he was and where he stood in life, all founded on the figment of his false identity. How and why I attach such a primal importance to Oedipus' false and true identities will be clarified in a close reading of the play, after first posing some fundamental directive lines so as to follow the steps of Oedipus, as they are delineated by Sophocles.

Charles Taylor, in his seminal book, *The Sources of the Self: The Making of the Modern Identity* (1989), breaks down the primal question "who am I?" into "where do I speak from and to whom?" and "where do I stand in life?" In an expanded formulation this reads as follows:

> ... *where I speak from*, in the family tree, in social space, in the geography of social statuses and functions, in my intimate relations to the ones I love, and also crucially *in the space of moral and spiritual orientation* within which my most important defining relations are lived out.[9]

---

5 Taylor 1989:48; see also chapter 3 above, pp. 36–37.
6 MacIntyre 2007:203–204.
7 See also the examination of the play by Finglass (2018:40–82) under a number of (overlapping) headings, responding to the initial question of the Introduction to chapter 4: "What Kind of Play is This?": 1. Suppliant drama 2. Recognition tragedy 3. Nostos-play 4. Foundling narrative 5. A work of theodicy and 6. Tragicomedy.
8 Taylor 1989:27.
9 Taylor 1989:35, my emphases.

Thus, the "who am I?" relates to three major components of the construction and understanding of a person's identity. First, genealogy and position in the family tree; second, the public (moral) space that determines our orientation to the good; and lastly, the definition of our interlocutors in life, for what we are depended on "to whom we speak and from where"; this constitutes our webs of interlocution, for we become ourselves when we are introduced into language,[10] and as human beings we are "potential interlocutor[s] in a society of interlocutors."[11]

Starting from the second point, the "where I stand" obviously places a person in a space, a locality that is primarily spatial (for example, "I was born in Corinth, but now I live in and reign over Thebes"). This spatial dimension is not innocently (or indifferently) demarcated, for it fuses with the public space, the theater of our activities as social beings. This is where we react to, or take decisions in respect to, ethical issues: the notion of justice, respect for other people's lives, their wellbeing and dignity, as well as our own dignity and pride—this is where we realize a meaningful life.[12] The public space is "potentially one of respect or contempt, of pride or shame,"[13] and how we move in a public space can command respect and can empower our sense of dominating it (or failing to do so).[14] The public space becomes a moral space, a place where our moral choices are formulated: "what is good or bad, what is worth doing and what is not, what has meaning and importance for you and what is trivial and secondary";[15] it is where our morality is tried and tested. It is clear that physical space becomes a metaphor for moral space;[16] an identity crisis is very often seen as an acute sense of disorientation,[17] and the story of Oedipus is a prime case in point. The "disoriented" Oedipus leaves Corinth plunged into doubt about his identity, reaches Delphi where he becomes stricken with terror, and sets out on his road once more in desperation, without knowing where to go. As he leaves Delphi, he is utterly confused (in Taylor's terminology he is 'disoriented'),

---

[10] Reminiscent of (but not congruent with) the Lacanian introduction to language through the Name of the Father. For the latter, see also section 4.2, p. 53.

[11] Taylor 1989:29; see also section 4.2, pp. 52–53.

[12] Taylor 1989:14–15; consider also a similar formulation: every orientation in life is necessarily an orientation to the good, as we take a stance "on questions of what is good, or worthwhile, or admirable, or of value" (Taylor 1989:27).

[13] "The very way we walk, move, gesture, speak is shaped from the earliest moments by our awareness that we appear before others, that we stand in *public space*, and that this space is potentially one of respect or contempt, of pride or shame" (Taylor 1989:15).

[14] Taylor 1989:5.

[15] Taylor 1989:28.

[16] Ibid.

[17] Taylor 1989:27.

driven only by his fear of ever returning home—distancing himself as far as he can, with the help of the stars, from Corinth (794–797):

κἀγὼ 'πακούσας ταῦτα τὴν Κορινθίαν
ἄστροις τὸ λοιπὸν τεκμαρούμενος χθόνα
ἔφευγον, ἔνθα μήποτ' ὀψοίμην κακῶν
χρησμῶν ὀνείδη τῶν ἐμῶν τελούμενα.

When I heard this I left the land of Corinth, henceforth making out its position by the stars, and went where I could never see accomplished the shameful predictions of my cruel oracles.

Taylor argues that "orientation in moral space turns out again to be similar to orientation in physical space. We know where we are through a mixture of recognition of landmarks before us and a sense of how we have travelled to get here ... ."[18] All the landmarks before the eyes of Oedipus are mistaken; he is confused because, first, he does not know who he is, and, second, because after being struck by terror in Delphi, he *forgets that he does not know who he is and he acts as if he does know.* How else can we understand *why* upon hearing the oracle at Delphi he flees Corinth, since it was in Corinth that he first suspected himself to be the bastard son of the king? The uncertainty about his identity vanishes in a split second, although without any rational foundation for his new belief. Oedipus becomes certain once more that his parents are Polybus and Merope, and he entertains this illusionary certainty for the duration of his sojourn in Thebes. The confusion has doubled now, and he has no means of regaining his orientation. The only unmistakable marks of his identity are his pierced and swollen feet, but Oedipus is not yet in a position to read this sign.

In my reading of *Oedipus Tyrannus* I follow the cycles of questions and answers[19] created by Sophocles to reconstruct, dramatically, the narrative of Oedipus' life. This approach zooms in on the self in the polis, as discussed in the previous section, for the webs of interlocution are constituted by the people of the polis, who test the protagonist's relations within it. It is here that Oedipus converses with his fellow citizens, the priest of Zeus, and the seer Teiresias; he also meets members of his own royal *oikos* (his brother-in-law, and his wife and mother, the Queen Jocasta); and he reaches the critical moments when the Corinthian messenger and the servant of Laius reveal segments of his personal history. The webs of interlocution are the wider frameworks within which the three major cycles of questions in *Oedipus Tyrannus* fall: the questions to Jocasta,

---

[18] Taylor 1989:48.
[19] "We take as basic that the human agent exists in a space of questions" (Taylor 1989:29).

who reveals the background to Laius' murder and the oracle the old king had received; with the Corinthian shepherd/messenger, who brings the news of Polybus' death and who reveals the details of Oedipus' rescue as a baby—his pierced feet and his provenance from Laius' household; and finally with the old servant of Laius (who also witnessed the affray at the junction of the three roads), who confirms that Oedipus the King is the baby the servant himself rescued and gave to the Corinthian shepherd and that this baby was the son of Laius.

Oedipus' many decisions and actions, the landmarks and the critical moments of his life, are intimately intertwined with these webs; and each of them is linked with a specific locality, a place that, in the history of the hero, becomes transformed into a moral space. As I will argue fully in the following chapter, Oedipus proves to be a strong evaluator in situations where he faces dilemmas calling for moral decisions:[20] when, on reaching adolescence, he learns that he might not be the true son of the king; upon receiving the oracle; when meeting the Sphinx; confronted by the misery of his fellow citizens stricken by the plague; and, above all others, on the realization of his true identity, which leads to his self-blinding.

I have argued elsewhere about the localities of Oedipus' story as told by Sophocles in *Oedipus Tyrannus*, and how they relate to different stages of Oedipus' realization of his identity as he sets out on a quest to find his father[21]—a quest that culminates in a gradual and painful reconstruction of himself. Moreover, each of these localities embodies spatial segments into which the story of the life of Oedipus can be divided. All these places relate to the primal question of Oedipus, "Who am I?"; they all offer part of the answer, even though Oedipus is so "disoriented" that he cannot understand them.

4.1 Cithairon: Naming the Baby

I mentioned earlier that the only unmistakable sign of Oedipus' identity is his wounded feet, whence he got his name. His name was not given to him, as expected, by his parents in the royal palace, where he was born. Since the baby was exposed to die on Mount Cithairon, he should have remained nameless. There was a parental act, however, that was linked with the naming of the baby: Laius' piercing of his son's feet, an act of unjustifiable cruelty that has always been perplexing. It is obvious, however, that this act constitutes a perverted form of naming, since the scars on the feet are an indelible mark of identity, unmissable and irrefutable, even if everything else has become unrecognizable,

---

[20] See chapter 5.3 below.
[21] Karakantza 2011b:149–164.

as with Odysseus' scar on his thigh. As the play unfolds, moving closer to the revelation of the truth, the messenger from Corinth supplies the first clue to Oedipus' identity, revealing that, when he freed the baby, his ankles were pierced and pinned together (λύω σ' ἔχοντα διατόρους ποδοῖν ἀκμάς, 1034), and he owes his name to this alone (ὥστ' ὠνομάσθης ἐκ τύχης ταύτης ὃς εἶ, 1036). Symbolically, then, Cithairon becomes not only the birthplace of Oedipus, since it ensures his physical survival, but also the place where Oedipus receives the first segment of his identity, his name. Furthermore, on a second symbolic level, Cithairon is named by the chorus as the nurse and the mother of Oedipus in the short euphoric interval of the third *stasimon* (καὶ τροφὸν καὶ ματέρ' αὔξειν, 1092); ironic, but utterly true since the mountain assumes the role of mother, as if it had nurtured the baby within its wooded glens (ναπαίαις ἐν Κιθαιρῶνος πτυχαῖς, 1026). Oedipus, shortly before this third *stasimon*, fills the gap of his identity with reference to *Tyche*, considering it as his mother (1080–1082):

> ἐγὼ δ' ἐμαυτὸν παῖδα τῆς Τύχης νέμων
> τῆς εὖ διδούσης ...
> τῆς γὰρ πέφυκα μητρός·

> I regard myself as child of the event that brought good fortune, ... /
> *she* is my mother.

Interestingly, in the renowned (if also strongly criticized) analysis of the myths of the family of Oedipus by Lévi-Strauss[22] the patrilineal line is linked through

---

[22] "The Structural Study of Myth," in the first volume of *Structural Anthropology* (1963:227–255), presents the grid of the structural analysis of the myths related to the family of Oedipus—the only Greek myth ever analyzed by Lévi-Strauss. Although very often cited, I will give here a concise résumé of the major postulates of the analysis: starting with the Spartoi Thebans through the last generation of the children of Oedipus, Lévi-Strauss breaks down the relevant narratives into the smallest possible segments, the so-called mythemes (from French *mythèmes*, *mythe* + *ème*), and locates them on four columns, in respect also to the diachronic and synchronic axis of the narratives; this is the grid the structuralist analyst has to form before the actual analysis. The first two columns comprise the mythemes denoting the positive (column I) and negative (column II) aspect of the idea of kinship ties: overrating (for example, the marriage of mother and son) and negation (the mutual killing of the brothers). The last two columns explore the idea of autochthony, similarly in its negation (column III) and acceptance (column IV); an example of the former is the killing of the autochthon dragon by Cadmus; of the latter, the swollen feet of Oedipus. The motivating question of the entire analysis is the origin of man: do we come from the union of a man and a woman (as human experience proves) or do we spring from the very earth of our native land? Myths do not give a positive answer to either possibility, Lévi-Strauss claims, but oscillate between the bipolar divisions/distinctions inherent in human societies, denoting the way that the human mind works. This last statement epitomizes the structural motto in approaching myths in general. The major criticism against structuralism is its ahistorical dimension. For ancient Greek culture, the scholarship of the French School

a serious corporal deficiency or sign. In the fourth column of the grid of his structural analysis, one can read, along the diachronic axis, the thematic thread marking the affinity between three male generations of the Labdacids: Labdacus himself (the grandfather of Oedipus and a descendant of the founder of Thebes, Cadmus); Laius, the father of Oedipus, and Oedipus himself. Of all the four columns of the grid, this last one, which, together with the third column, represents the idea of autochthony in the myth of Oedipus, arouses a certain degree of speculation, relying, as it does, mainly on etymology rather than on narratives related to the history of the family. Of course, one may rightly observe that resorting to etymology is a legitimate means for the structural analyst, for this pays tribute, so to speak, to the "father" of this methodology, Ferdinand de Saussure and his Structural Linguistics.[23]

According to the fourth of Lévi-Strauss's column, Labdacus is lame, Laius' body is maimed on its left side, and Oedipus (as we all know) has swollen feet from the old piercing of his ankles. The alleged lameness of Labdacus is based on the meaning of the letter *lambda* (or *labda*) and the similarity of his name to *Labda*, the Lame, who was the mother of Cypselus, the tyrant of Corinth and the founder of the long line of political leaders of the city, the Cypselids; the latter is well attested in Herodotus (3.50–54, 5.92).[24] The compiler of the *Etymologicum Magnum* (199.24–31) explains how the letter *lambda* (Λ) resembles a person whose legs are twisted outwardly askew. He also infers that the wife of Eëtion, and mother of Cypselus, the tyrant of Corinth, is named La(m)bda because of her resemblance to the letter whose form embodies the notion of lameness.[25] In a similar vein, Laius has a body defective on its left side ("left-sided"?), because his name is likely to derive from λαιός (= "left"). Thus, even if the original corporeal deficiency has become suppressed in the narratives related to Labdacus and Laius, it is embedded in the etymology of their names, making Oedipus the true heir to this patrilineal descent.

---

presents one response to that critique (see below). For a full analysis of the approach, its advantages and shortcomings, and its reliance on structural linguistics, see Karakantza 2004:147–178, with relevant bibliography at 220–222.

[23] Ferdinand de Saussure and his seminal book *Cours de Linguistique Générale* (*Course in General Linguistics*) published posthumously in 1916 by Saussure's students from their notes on his seminars in Geneva (1906–1911). Although not a systematic exposition of principles, the book exerted a huge influence in shaping structuralism and semiotics by introducing the notion of the linguistic sign and the precedence of the synchronic analysis of a text over the diachronic.

[24] For a detailed analysis of the Herodotian narrative by Vernant, see also chapter 4.7 below.

[25] *Etymologicum Magnum* 199.25–27: Ὁ δ' Ἐτυμολόγος, ὁ τοὺς πόδας ἐπὶ τὰ ἔξω διεστραμμένος, καὶ τῷ Λ στοιχείῳ ἐοικώς. Διὰ τοῦτο καὶ Λάμβδα ἐκαλεῖτο ἡ γυνὴ μὲν Ἡετίωνος, μήτηρ δὲ Κυψέλου τοῦ Κορίνθου τυράννου. See also Delcourt 1944:20–21. For lameness as a mythic motif, see further Vernant 1988:209–212; Delcourt 1957; and Delcourt 1986 on physical deficiencies in myth.

Furthermore, Lévi-Strauss uses his wide knowledge of Amerindian myths to advance his argument further, stating that any corporeal deficiency related to feet or impairment in walking denotes the belief that those thus afflicted are still somehow rooted in the maternal soil; that is, such men are not as yet completely detached from the ground, thus pointing to their autochthonous provenance. In Lévi-Strauss's analysis, the myths relating the history of the family, starting with Cadmus and ending with the Epigonoi (the grandchildren) of Oedipus, point to a single question that troubles members of human societies, and this is the question of origin. To this primal question (where do humans come from?) the myths offer two possible options: either human beings come from the same (from the union of two human beings) or they spring from the very ground of their native land (autochthony). In the structural vein of analysis, myths do not give a definite answer to either option; rather, they oscillate between the two binary poles of opposition, for dividing things into binary oppositions is the way that humans conceive their world. So, in this structural analysis of the Oedipus myth, the great underlying question is the origin of mankind, not just of Oedipus himself nor of human knowledge (or happiness) in general.[26]

I will not, at this point, highlight the flaws in the structural methodology and the specific results of the analysis of the Oedipus myth. I will only point out that we live in a poststructuralist era, where attempts to articulate a universal methodological tool to interpret myths and traditions across the globe (the preoccupation of the structural approach in the social sciences in the 70's and 80's) are no longer viable, for we have come to realize that any monolithic approach is bound to fail. As well, classical scholars find Lévi-Strauss's analysis highly unconventional, with its selective emphasis on some traits of the myth (the so-called *mythèmes*), at the expense of others; but above all, for its disinterest in the social and historical context of classical Greece.[27] However, from my perspective, the final results of Lévi-Strauss's analysis of the Oedipal family myths yields convincing results, to a greater extent than the widespread humanistic emphasis on the quest of human knowledge, or the Freudian attachment to the mother and envy of the father, or the other critical tendencies that I discussed at the beginning of this chapter. Lévi-Strauss, coming from another academic tradition, puts an emphasis on the "question of origin" that

---

[26]   Later, in the second volume of *Anthropologie Stucturale* (1976:31–35), Lévi-Strauss revisits the Oedipus myth and connects the riddle of the Sphinx (a question to which the answer should remain apart) with the incest (a relation in which two persons should remain apart) as two situations that bear internal and logical similarities. And, lastly, in *Mythe et oubli* (1975:294–300), he connects lameness, lisp, and oblivion as themes used by myths to express the breakdown of communication on various levels of social life. See also Karakantza 2011b:154–155 n19.

[27]   The latter was remedied by Jean-Pierre Vernant and the French School that introduced into structuralism the consideration of the polis and its 'structures' of thought, ethics, and behavior.

is a pervasive component, I argue, of Sophocles' own treatment of the myth. The difference, of course, is the universality of this interpretation; Lévi-Strauss poses the question of human origin in general, and his method, by revealing the binary oppositions embedded in this (and other) narratives, presents a general picture of the working of the human mind.

In the present argument, I will concentrate on the fourth column of the grid and claim that the etymology of the names of the three generations of patrilineal descent fits Oedipus almost seamlessly into the family tree and that he is, indeed, given his name by his father, as tradition would require. Of course, the naming of the baby is performed in the form of a distorted, perverse, and bloody ritual that would mark the disintegration of the individual *oikos* in favor of the polis. The naming of the child involves blood, physical pain, scarring for life, and, above all, exclusion, in lieu of integration, blessing, and a strengthening of family ties and continuation. Ritual cruelty, Walter Burkert argues, transposes some of the violence of pre-civilized life into the polis in an institutionalized, thus controlled, form of action.[28] But here is the reverse: a private ritual (Laius' scarring of the baby), which distorts the institutionalized form of the ritual that integrates the newborn baby into the family.[29] In a resolutely patriarchal society, typified by ancient Greece, one of the first actions after birth is to secure the attachment of the male heir to the line of the father through (indelible) naming; in *Oedipus Tyrannus* the grotesque "swollen-foot" substitutes for a proper human name. The ritual that should follow (or that corroborates the naming) is that five days after birth the head of the *oikos*, the father, child in arms, walks around the hearth, thus irrevocably embedding the child as the new member of the household.[30] That private ritual is twisted into perversion, for instead of the hearth of the *oikos* the child is "admitted" in the "wooded folds" of Cithairon (εὑρὼν ναπαίαις ἐν Κιθαιρῶνος πτυχαῖς, 1026) that, as if a surrogate mother, shelters him and saves his life. But without the individual *oikos*, of course, there is no polis, and without proper admission into the father's *oikos* there can be no possibility of assuming proper citizenship. Thus the piercing of the feet is a gross perversion of the ritual of naming the child, crippling any later capacity for acting properly as a citizen.

---

[28] Apropos of ritual flogging in the festival of Artemis Ortheia in Sparta (1985:262).

[29] It should be noted here that naming a male child after the paternal grandfather is a tradition that is still strongly adhered to in modern Greece. It is one of the symbolic gestures in social and cultural anthropology that shows remarkable conservatism through time.

[30] This is the ritual of Amphidromia, "to which a sacrifice at the hearth belongs" (Burkert 1985:255). Equally important for the right of citizenship is the three-day ancestral festival of Apatouria, during which the father, together with two witnesses from the same *dêmos*, registers the male child as a genuine descendant to the *phratria*; see Burkert 1985:255 and Parker 1996:105.

The thread of Lévi-Strauss's analysis of the fourth column focusing on lameness is taken up by Jean-Pierre Vernant in his classic study on the *Lame Tyrant: From Oedipus to Periander*.[31] Despite his objections to the anthropological model of Lévi-Strauss, Vernant accepts that the motif of lameness is alluded to in the names of Labdacus and Laius. However, he advances his argument further by introducing a more abstract notion of lameness, embracing anything that is not straight, normal, or acceptable behavior, thus betraying a mode of thinking and acting that deviates from established social norms. Of course, at moments of similar ruptures (when, for example, a "lame" person takes over political power, as in the case of Cypselids) we have a paradigm-shift, a total re-establishment and re-formulation of the existing codes and practices. This moment acquires significance for men to remember, recall, and set down in narrative form. Vernant claims that an *actual* physical deficiency is not necessary to be lame; Laius was "lame" because of his excessive, violent homosexuality, which was forced on Chrysippus, and because of the irregular sexual act that he practiced with Jocasta so as to avoid pregnancy.

Thus, if we follow Lévi-Strauss's analysis of Labdacus' and Laius' names, Oedipus is well established in the family tree through his corporeal deficiency. His name *is* his swollen feet because his father pierced and shackled his ankles together before he gave him away to be exposed to die.[32] This cruel act of permanently scarring the baby opens another critical perspective: Oedipus acquires a corporeal sign, a stigma, marking him as a dangerous social outcast, and it functions as a warning, a signal, of his propensity to bring evil in the eventuality of his surviving. He becomes stigmatized in the current meaning of the term. Erving Goffman begins his classic book on *Stigma* by stating that:

> The Greeks, who were apparently strong on visual aids, originated the term *stigma* to refer to bodily signs designed to expose something unusual and bad about the moral status of the signifier. The signs were cut or burnt into the body and advertised that the bearer was a slave, a criminal, or a traitor—a blemished person, ritually polluted, to be avoided, especially in public places.

The scars, which were inflicted on Oedipus' body from birth, make visible a "spoiled identity," marking him as a pariah to be avoided at all costs; he is ritually polluted, as Oedipus himself eloquently elaborates in the long passage on the punishment awaiting the murderer of Laius: no shelter, no food or drink, no

---

[31] See below, section 4.7, pp. 85–88.
[32] Of course, "the body is the main element of identity, a sense of the self and belonging to society" (Makrinioti 2004:27).

admittance to public or private rituals, banishment from all homes, for *he is the pollution of the city* (ὡς μιάσματος / τοῦδ' ἡμὶν ὄντος, 241–42). The plague, the horrific backdrop that evokes the doom-ridden ambience from the outset of the play, makes the pollution brought about by Oedipus visible and tangible. He is a social outcast, and his stigmatized feet bear witness to this.

Of course one can play with the assonance of the name of Oedipus with the verb οἶδα (= "I know, I have learnt"), indicating the person *who knows*; this can be linked with the intelligence Oedipus displays in solving the riddle, but it also alludes to the failure of his intelligence, since Oedipus did *not* know (nor did he understand) the clues leading to his identity. This pseudo-etymology intensifies the renowned Sophoclean "flickering irony":[33] Oedipus is a person who, above all, does not know who he is, although he is known to everybody (ὁ τοῖς πᾶσιν κλεινός, 8); he does not even realize he has carried the signs of his identity all along, the scars on his feet, for his identity is primarily a corporeal sign. Euben argues that "a person's name (say Oedipus or Pentheus) is an omen and oracle of identity, then placing them in some narrative that mentions their parents and ancestors, where they come from and now belong, and where they stand in the world."[34]

Taylor's formulation "where one stands in life" as part of one's identity, now becomes clearer, as does the ensuing disorientation and confusion when someone lacks the pieces that connect him with his origin. Laius did not give Oedipus a proper name linking him with his ancestral patrilineal line (or so he thought). He signified him by mutilating his feet in the hope his son would be indeed lost. Contrary to his intentions, the infant survived, but Oedipus was, thenceforth, disoriented.

4.2 In the Webs of Interlocution: Delphi, the Crossroads, and the Sphinx

Oedipus sets out on the road to Delphi pre-occupied with the pressing question, "who am I?" Both posing the question and expecting an answer fall into the original situation of identity formation because, as Charles Taylor claims, we form our self (among other things) in relation to the language and vision of others.[35] Or, as he puts it slightly differently, one identifies one's self in relation to "where [one] is speaking from and to whom,"[36] because "there is no way we could be

---

[33] Goldhill 2012:20, 25–37.
[34] 1990:96.
[35] Taylor 1989:36.
[36] Taylor 1989:35.

inducted into personhood except by being initiated into a language."[37] This last statement is strongly reminiscent of the Lacanian initiation into the symbolic order of society through the linguistic symbol of the Father that imposes the incest prohibition. This Law of the Father is our initiation into the symbolic order of society that produces a language-mediated order of culture; for Lévi-Strauss, it was a kinship-mediated order of culture. The Lacanian version combines both: laws of kinship *and* language, because it is through kinship nominations that the societal order is imposed through preferences and taboos. In the Lacanian vein, the confusion of generations (son and husband, mother and wife, children and siblings) represents the abomination of the Word (in the Bible as in all traditional frameworks of laws)—a situation tellingly applicable to the case of Oedipus, in whose person the "confusion of generations" is indelibly etched.[38] However, we need to advance a step beyond the Lacanian approach, which has been accused of being wholly androcentric.[39] As I will argue at length later, what is at stake here are the laws of kinship that sustain patriarchy with the denomination of women as exchangeable goods aimed at forming an extended network of relationships between families; this network, within which all kinship relations are firmly defined, also relegates women to an inferior position in society. In the narrative of Oedipus, these laws collapse, the Law of the Father becomes ineffective, and Jocasta, *the* female figure par excellence, is elevated to a stature of authority unusual for the times.[40]

Returning to the issue of identity formation in the webs of interlocution, Taylor argues that we are initiated into a language by those who bring us up when they introduce us to the meanings of key words. Later, as we engage in continual dialogue with our conversational partners, we implicitly debate our experience of the significance of these words (i.e. "anger, love, anxiety, the aspiration to wholeness etc"); we bring these "objects for *us*" into some kind of common space where their meaning is debated; we may conform or

---

[37] Taylor 1989:35.

[38] Lacan 2001:73.

[39] Across a wide spectrum of studies—ranging from feminist economics, psychoanalytic studies, and cinematic studies, to religion, literature, sociology of gender, and classics—critics have revisited and criticized the phallocentric Name of the Father, that is, the law of the phallus and male sexuality as the maker of meaning, and, consequently, the formation of the female sexed subject of difference. I will refer the reader to only a few, but significant, studies regarding the re-evaluation and reconfiguration of the Lacanian position on sexual politics: Banwell and Fiddler 2018; Cavanagh 2017; Leeb 2017; Kostikova 2013; Hook 2006a and 2006b; Hewitson 1999; Beattie 1999; Brodribb 1992; Lorraine 1990; Gallop 1982. The refutation of my own earlier reading of Oedipus, resting on the Lacanian postulate of the Law of the Father, with the mother as the seductive voice of disorder (Karakantza 2011b) can be read below, in chapter 4.5 "Questions with Jocasta: Dislocating the Origin *or* Jocasta's Body and Mind."

[40] See especially pages 71–78 of section 4.5.

innovate, but both actions presuppose a common language as a base.[41] Thus, with this activity, we become an intrinsic part of what Taylor calls the "webs of interlocution,"[42] within which we repeatedly redefine our identity, because one crucial feature of the self is that "one is a self among other selves"[43] and that "I am a self only in relation to certain interlocutors."[44] In the domains of interlocution we debate our position in the world, and this is a cardinal component of our identity. On a personal level, we cannot clarify our position in life until we talk about it; debating one's position in this world is also an abiding feature of Attic tragedy.

Consequently, when Oedipus travels to Delphi to pose his question to Apollo, he enters in the webs of interlocution, where, significantly, instead of clarity more confusion is created. The interpretation of Apollo's answer to Oedipus has been a matter of great controversy in scholarship. What sort of oracle is this? Does Apollo warn the hero? Does he simply state the facts of Oedipus' life, from which there is not escape no matter how hard he tries?[45] In relation to this last remark, a major issue in the interpretation of *Oedipus Tyrannus* arises: is the action of the hero closely predefined by divine will, as is expressed in the oracle? To what extent is the exertion of Oedipus' free will constrained? Is the divine action superimposed on the human action? If this is so, is *Oedipus Tyrannus* a tragedy of destiny, since no matter how hard Oedipus tries, he only manages to enmesh himself more inextricably in the net of a predestined life?

I will revisit the question of divine action versus human action in *Oedipus Tyrannus*—one of the most puzzling and unsettling features of the play—later. For now, I will dwell on the issue of the nature of Apollo's answer to Oedipus. Let us follow the thread of the Sophoclean narrative. In the long reiteration of his past life (771–833), Oedipus describes to Jocasta how he went to Delphi and how Apollo responded to his question (787–793):

---

[41] Taylor 1989:35–36.

[42] Taylor 1989:36

[43] Taylor 1989:35.

[44] Taylor 1989:36.

[45] I cannot present an exhaustive overview of the scholarship on the nature of oracles in *Oedipus Tyrannus*, in Sophocles, or in Greek tragedy. Oracles in Sophocles are of "labyrinthine nature" (Pucci 1994:33). In regard to the thorny issue whether (or to which extent) oracles dictate the action in a play, Kamerbeek states rightly that: "... a stronger case can be made for the oracles as interpretation of the events than for the events as the result of the oracles. And indeed Sophocles, who did not alter the main data of Oedipus' life, did alter the oracle given to Laius in a very important respect (cf. the guilt of Laius), or at least did not use Aeschylus' version of the oracle" (1965:31). A concordant idea, that of prophecy as the narratological voice of the poet himself, is articulated by Peradotto in his "Disauthorizing Prophecy." Understandably, works that deal with Apollo, and "his ways" in *Oedipus Tyrannus*, also refer to the nature and function of the oracles. For the relevant discussion and bibliography, I refer the reader to chapter 5.2 below, pp. 115–130.

λάθρᾳ δὲ μητρὸς καὶ πατρὸς πορεύομαι
Πυθώδε, καί μ' ὁ Φοῖβος ὧν μὲν ἱκόμην
ἄτιμον ἐξέπεμψεν, <u>ἄλλα</u> δ' ἀθλίῳ
καὶ δεινὰ καὶ δύστηνα προὔφάνη λέγων,
ὡς μητρὶ μὲν χρείη με μειχθῆναι, γένος δ'
ἄτλητον ἀνθρώποισι δηλώσοιμ' ὁρᾶν,
φονεὺς δ' ἐσοίμην τοῦ φυτεύσαντος πατρός.

Without the knowledge of my mother and my father I went to Pytho, and Phoebus sent me away cheated on what I had come for, but came out *with other things* terrible and sad for my unhappy self, saying that I was destined to lie with my mother, and to show to mortals a brood they could not bear to look on, and I should be the murderer of my father who had begotten me.

I have argued elsewhere that Apollo answers "as if [Oedipus] has asked a completely different question,"[46] and this is pretty much what Oedipus himself expresses in the play: "ἄλλα δ'[ε]", "Apollo came out with *other things*." I have now reached the point of revising this thesis, and suggest that Apollo's reply conforms *exactly* to what he has been asked. It *seems* that his reply is irrelevant to the question because Oedipus (and the audience for that matter) crucially fails to take a minute to complete Apollo's deliberately elliptic response: "you [are the person who] will marry your mother and kill your father." Apollo answers Oedipus' question precisely and truthfully. However, it is interesting to note the seductive power of the poetic diction here, and how Sophocles can lure us into believing what he wishes us to believe; we are as eager as Oedipus in thinking about what the oracle is about: *other things*. We share in the panic and confusion besetting Oedipus, failing to rationally process the information the oracle provides, although, as members of the audience or readers of the play, we possess superior knowledge and could easily complete the elliptic sentence.

Seen in this light, the oracle makes better sense—and need not be understood in the context of other Sophoclean prophecies. In *Oedipus Tyrannus*, the god reveals a substantial feature of the hero's identity, giving it the value of a statement rather than a warning, as in Laius' case.[47] Nor does it set a

---

[46] Karakantza 2011b:150.

[47] "The oracle has warned him not to beget a son, for the son that should be begotten would kill his father; nevertheless, flushed with wine, he had intercourse with his wife" (χρήσαντος τοῦ θεοῦ μὴ γεννᾶν (τὸν γεννηθέντα γὰρ πατροκτόνον ἔσεσθαι) ὁ δὲ οἰνωθεὶς συνῆλθε τῇ γυναικί, Apollodorus *Bibliotheca* 3.7; trans. Frazer). In line with this tradition, Euripides in his *Phoenician Women* (17–20) has Jocasta retelling the oracle after Laius inquired about his childlessness: "But

precondition needing fulfillment for a plan to materialize, as with the prophecy in *Philoctetes* concerning the bow of Heracles as a prerequisite for the fall of Troy. The oracle in *Oedipus Tyrannus* is not even cryptic, with the meaning only understood at the denouement, as with the oracles in the *Trachiniae*, where we first have the promise of a tranquil life for Heracles, signifying not the conclusion of his labors, but his death (*Trachiniae* 1169–1172); and, second, the celebrated oracle given by Zeus to Heracles that "the dead will kill the living" (*Trachiniae* 1160–1163), which is finally revealed as incriminating the dead centaur as the actual killer of Heracles.

Apollo's pronouncement in *Oedipus Tyrannus* does not fall within any of these categories. Apollo seems to state what will happen simply because of his superior knowledge. His oracle is *not* a revelation of future events, but of Oedipus' identity, since what will happen is an intrinsic part of it, as are his pierced feet, and (later) his mutilated sight. For the time being, I shall leave aside one of the contentious issues of the interpretation of this tragedy, namely Jocasta's denial of the validity of the oracles (willingly adopted by Oedipus) in the second episode.[48] In my interpretation, the doubting of the oracles is paired with the subversion produced by the gendered body of the Queen, where the established distinctions of the patriarchal society collapse. What interests me, at this point, are the webs of interlocution in which Oedipus converses. In all three important waypoints before Oedipus reaches the city of Thebes (Delphi, the crossroads of Phocis, and the outskirts of Thebes), he finds himself in dialogue with other linguistic agents (the god Apollo, his biological father, and the Sphinx). A dialogue entails a linguistic exchange that ideally leads to linguistic articulacy[49]—this is how human beings communicate and this is how a person forms and nurtures his identity as a member of a community of interlocutors. In the case of Oedipus, however, the attempted communication is broken, leading to failed articulacy; Oedipus is an eager interlocutor incapacitated by a distorted idea of his identity.

In Delphi, asking meaningful questions and expecting meaningful answers fails, because Oedipus is incapable of completing the elliptic answer of the god. At the intersection of the three roads at Phocis, Oedipus has, for his first and last time, the chance to converse with his own biological father. Interestingly,

---

Phoebus replied, 'King of Thebes, city of fair horses, do not keep sowing the child-begetting furrow against the gods' will: if you sire a son, your own offspring will kill you, and the whole house will be embroiled in bloodshed'" (trans. Kovacs). Sophocles in *Oedipus Tyrannus* gives the following account from the mouth of Jocasta (711–714): "An oracle once came to Laius ... , saying that it would be his fate to die at the hands of the son who should be the child of him and me"— this account resembles an indirect warning rather than an open prohibition by the god.

[48] Which I analyze below, in section 4.5.

[49] Taylor 1989:91–92.

the dialogue between father and son (to the point that it can be reconstructed) is about the exertion of power (paternal over filial), as the father asks his son to step back and allow free passage to the advancing carriage. The paternal authority in this narrative is implied (since neither party knows the identity of the other) by the royal insignia and the authoritative voice of the king reinforced by that of his herald. Observe how Oedipus relates the incident (804–805):

> ... κἀξ ὁδοῦ μ' ὅ θ' ἡγεμὼν
> αὐτός θ' ὁ πρέσβυς πρὸς βίαν ἠλαυνέτην

> ... and the leader and the old man himself tried to drive me from the road by force.

Oedipus does not give way to the royal father and keeps walking; and while walking alongside the carriage he strikes the driver who asked him to cede the road. This is how the debate turns into a physical assault, and Laius strikes his son's head with his double-edged scepter. In retaliation, Oedipus returns the blow with added violence[50] and kills his father. He completes the assault by massacring the royal party (810–813):

> οὐ μὴν ἴσην γ' ἔτεισεν, ἀλλὰ συντόμως
> σκήπτρῳ τυπεὶς ἐκ τῆσδε χειρὸς ὕπτιος
> μέσης ἀπήνης εὐθὺς ἐκκυλίνδεται·
> κτείνω δὲ τοὺς ξύμπαντας.

> Yet he paid the penalty with interest; in a word, this hand struck him with a stick, and he rolled backwards right out of the wagon, and I killed them all.

Turning an attempted dialogue into sheer violence proves the failure of human communication, hence the failure of the linguistic media; and even more so, if we take into account that the Father is the linguistic symbol of the Law that prohibits incest,[51] and that at this moment in Oedipus' life the Father and the father are ironically coincident. Oedipus fails to recognize the father (without the clues to do so), and the road to committing incest is now wide open and beckoning.

---

[50] Finglass ad 810–813: "... retribution that exceeds the original offense is a fundamental principle of ancient justice."

[51] Lacan 2001:73.

In the orthodox Freudian approach, this debate over the strip of land could very well signify the filial antagonism expressed in all the succession myths of the theogonic narratives. Richard Caldwell has shown how the motif of the powerful son who castrates or overthrows the father who is the ruler of the world, in the succession myths of Ouranos–Kronos–Zeus, is the reversal of the fear of castration that a son feels threatened by in his Oedipal desire for the mother.[52] Interestingly, Caldwell also detects this motif in "hidden" (not openly expressed) desires, as manifested in the mythologies of Hephaistos, Prometheus, the monster Typhoeus, and, generally, all those rebelling against the power of Zeus. Forbidden Oedipal desires and the ensuing fears of the male child turn out well for the son in the narratives, as he displaces, by castration or murder, the father, the King, or the Ruler. In Euripides' *Phoenician Women*, Laius and Oedipus coincide in Delphi inquiring about the existence of one another: Oedipus about his parents (τοὺς φύσαντας ἐκμαθεῖν θέλων, 34), and Laius as to whether his son is still alive (τὸν ἐκτεθέντα παῖδα μαστεύων μαθεῖν / εἰ μηκέτ' εἴη, 36–37). Moreover, their paths literally coincide on Phocis' Cloven Way (καὶ ξυνάπτετον πόδα / ἐς ταὐτὸν ἄμφω Φωκίδος σχιστῆς ὁδοῦ, 37–38). There, the exertion of paternal power that bears the royal insignia is condensed in the following order: "Stranger, make way for royalty" (Ὦ ξένε, τυράννοις ἐκποδὼν μεθίστασο, 40). While the son keeps walking, silently and proudly (ἄναυδος, μέγα φρονῶν, 41), the horses' hooves of the royal chariot bloody the tendons of his feet (πῶλοι δέ νιν / χηλαῖς τένοντας ἐξεφοίνισσον ποδῶν, 41–42), in a sinister repetition of the original act of parental violence at his birth. The difference is that now Oedipus can react to this act of violence, and consequently he kills his biological father and returns with the royal chariot as a prize for Polybus, his foster father (44–45).

Additionally, an Oedipal desire and the ensuing fear of castration are submerged in all accounts of the succession myth and the divine narratives that record a mortal threat posed by the birth of a son mightier than his father; once again, an Oedipal rival to paternal authority in disguise. In one of these archetypical stories, Zeus swallows Mêtis; in another, Thetis is given as a bride to mortal Peleus. The goddess Athena and the hero Achilles are the respective offspring of these unions, but they pose no threat, for the first is a female goddess who always sides with the father, while the latter is a great hero, but mortal. For Oedipus the prediction is clearly that he will kill his father, transposing the responsibility, as in the previous accounts, to the father to thwart the fulfillment of the oracle: Oedipus should not have been allowed to be born

---

[52] In *The Origin of the Gods: A Psychoanalytic Study of Greek Theogonic Myth* (1989).

in the first place; after his birth, the only solution is a death that concretizes all the nightmarish fears of the son in Oedipal rivalry with the father.

Even if we did not have any Freudian, post-Freudian, or Lacanian readings of the play, there is a passage that succinctly fuses the identity of the son with that of the father (not in rivalry but in a seemingly harmonious unity), which defies even the wildest imagination of all psychoanalytic approaches. Surprisingly, Freud did not single out this passage in the formulation of the Oedipus complex. Oedipus has just finished pronouncing the punishment awaiting the murderer of king Laius and utters the curses to fall upon his head. "I am doing this," Oedipus says, "because" (258–266):

> ... νῦν δ' ἐπεὶ κυρῶ τ' ἐγὼ
> ἔχων μὲν ἀρχάς, ἃς ἐκεῖνος εἶχε πρίν,
> <u>ἔχων δὲ λέκτρα καὶ γυναῖχ' ὁμόσπορον,</u>
> <u>κοινῶν τε παίδων κοίν' ἄν</u>, εἰ κείνῳ γένος
> μὴ 'δυστύχησεν, ἦν ἂν ἐκπεφυκότα –
> νῦν δ' ἐς τὸ κείνου κρᾶτ' ἐνήλαθ' ἡ τύχη·
> ἀνθ' ὧν ἐγὼ τάδ', <u>ὡσπερεὶ τοὐμοῦ πατρὸς</u>
> ὑπερμαχοῦμαι κἀπὶ πάντ' ἀφίξομαι
> ζητῶν τὸν αὐτόχειρα τοῦ φόνου λαβεῖν ...

> But now, since I chance to hold the power which once he held, and *to have a marriage and a wife in common with him*, and since had he not been unfortunate in respect of issue *our children would have had one mother* [κοινῶν τε παίδων κοίν' ἄν]—but as things are he has been struck down by fortune; on account of this I shall fight for him *as though he had been my father*, and shall go to every length in searching for the author of the murder ...

Sophocles' lexical double entendres, lethally loaded with psychological and mental premonitions of what lies ahead, are remarkable. In terms of narratology, this passage is a masterpiece. The underlying meaning, obscured from the speaker, is stronger than the surface meaning and is ominously ever present in the minds of the audience. Γυναῖχ' ὁμόσπορον (260) = ὁμοίως σπειρομένην, that is, ἣν καὶ ἐκεῖνος ἔσπειρε (literally, the woman who was also "sown" by Laius), is wonderfully fused with the later accusation of Teiresias (459–460): τοῦ πατρὸς / ὁμόσπορος = τὴν αὐτὴν σπείρων γυναῖκα (in the active voice this time).[53] The second point of convergence is the children, who are born of "one

---

[53] Jebb ad loc.

mother and would have made ties between he and me,"[54] as Oedipus declares. The "obvious sense of κοινά, that is, 'common to Laius and Oedipus,' has behind it a second, sinister, sense, in which it hints at a brood who are *brothers and sisters of their own sire.*"[55] Paraphrasing slightly Sophocles' diction, it is as if Oedipus said the following words: "I shall pursue this investigation on the grounds of my strong affinities with Laius (the woman and the children); and I will do it eagerly, immediately, and with great dedication, *as if Laius were my father*" (ὡσπερεὶ τοὐμοῦ πατρός, 264); this last formulation is an exquisite culmination of Sophocles' celebrated flickering irony.[56]

This passage prepares the ground for the revelations of Teiresias in the first episode, which actually name Oedipus as the killer of Laius and the incestuous husband of Jocasta. In this latter case, we have a near revelation of Oedipus' identity. One thing should be clear: Oedipus disbelieves the seer, not because the language of the seer is cryptic, for Teiresias openly accuses him of the murder of Laius (362). Oedipus, however, cannot understand, and thus rejects the accusations as the product of malign conspiracy because of the voids in his knowledge of the narrative of his life; or, to put it differently, his narrative of his own life is flawed with false elements, for although he received the oracle of impending parricide and incest, he reigns at Thebes as the son of Polybus and Merope. We have seen earlier how, upon hearing the oracle of Apollo, Oedipus, stricken by panic and fear, erases his doubts about his identity and resumes his Corinthian parentage.

We can now return, better informed by the text, to the primal question regarding identity: "where am I speaking from and to whom?" We realize that the conversation reaches articulacy only if someone knows where "he stands in life," that is, "where he speaks from, in the family tree, in social space, in the geography of social statuses and functions."[57] If a void exists there, within the webs of interlocution, communication fractures,[58] as exemplified by Oedipus. We have seen that Oedipus' pressing need to communicate with Apollo fails,

---

[54] Jebb's translation, slightly modernized.

[55] Jebb ad 261.

[56] Goldhill 2012:26–27; and especially the second part of his chapter 1 ,"Analysis of Sophoclean Irony" (25–37). See also Finglass ad 264–268: "The irony in ὡσπερεὶ τοὐμοῦ πατρός, which in other contexts might have seemed rather obvious ... , thus forms a culmination of the unusually intense dramatic irony in this passage, and of Oedipus' desire to connect himself as closely as possible to his predecessor."

[57] Taylor 1989:35.

[58] Or as Segal puts it (1981a:151): "Continually breaking down, this communication either ceases prematurely because of fears or knowledge that cannot be spoken or runs to excess because of passion and anger."

while in his second failed communication at the crossroads at Phocis, he kills his father.

The third web of interlocution is created on encountering the abrasive female quasi-human singer (σκληρᾶς ἀοιδοῦ, 36) on the outskirts of Thebes; she poses one single question, in the form of a riddle set in hexameter verses (always the same, single, fatal question), to the youth of Thebes. Failure to give a meaningful answer to the question of the Sphinx leads to death. Oedipus (a Theban youth, although he does not know it) finds himself in this "space of questions";[59] this last linguistic encounter is successful because Oedipus secures his life, clearing the path for the youth of his native land to continue their lives unhindered. The accomplishment resonates with an initiation task set to the young Prince before he can rightfully claim his throne;[60] and this is, indeed, what it is. However, the mutilated narrative of his life makes the task a mock trial for the Prince, spreading the word around about this intelligent, young man from nowhere (ὁ πᾶσι κλεινὸς Οἰδίπους καλούμενος, 8), immediately hailed as the savior of Thebes.

It is crucial for Oedipus' story that the riddle of the Sphinx refers to the identity of man:

> ἔστι δίπουν ἐπὶ γῆς καὶ τετράπον, οὗ μία φωνή,
> καὶ τρίπον, ἀλλάσσει δὲ φύσιν μόνον ὅσσ' ἐπὶ γαῖαν
> ἑρπετὰ γίνονται καὶ ἀν' αἰθέρα καὶ κατὰ πόντον·
> ἀλλ' ὁπόταν πλείστοισιν ἐρειδόμενον ποσὶ βαίνῃ,
> ἔνθα τάχος γυίοισιν ἀφαυρότατον πέλει αὐτοῦ.

> There is a creature on earth, the same very creature, that walks on two, four, and three legs; it is the only creature on land, in the air, and in the sea that changes [the way it walks]. And when it stands on four legs [or on 'three' according to the Scholiast on Euripides], then it walks the slowest.[61]

Of all the features of man, the Sphinx focuses on the legs and the ability to walk—a feature pointing directly (albeit not overtly) to the identity of Oedipus himself. Oedipus has no difficulty in understanding and correctly answering the question: the *tetrapous*, *dipous*, and *tripous* creature is a human being similar to him. He misses, however, the strong undercurrent connecting himself and man

---

[59] Taylor 1989:91.

[60] Renger 2013:9–22, 27–31; see also Edmunds 1985:13n60; Edmunds and Dundes 1983:147–173.

[61] Asclepiades in Athenaeus *Deipnosophistae* 10.83.38 (my translation). The Scholiast on Euripides (*Phoenissae* 50.8) has τρισσοῖσιν ἐρειδόμενον.

especially in the *tetrapous* and *tripous* phase of a human life: as an infant (the *tetrapous* phase) he is exposed with pierced feet on Cithairon, the signs of which are still engraved on his body (*oidipous*); and he will enter the *tripous* phase not as an old man but prematurely, after blinding himself, condemned to walk with the help of the staff of a blind wanderer; the latter, of course, will be revealed to him in the last act of this drama.

Returning now to the solving of the riddle (the heroic exploit of Oedipus), a feat of intelligence that, in the final analysis, not only seals his own fate but indirectly leads to the demise of the citizens of Thebes who, when the tragedy opens, are dying in large numbers. It also leaves the ground open for further speculation as to why Oedipus was fit to answer it. Peter Euben claims that Oedipus was able to see unity where others saw "difference and discontinuity";[62] he could see "morning, noon, and evening as one day and one life." True, in this sense, where they were *many*, he saw *one*; but this *one*, is not his selfhood, but the general and undifferentiated identity of man.[63]

My argument in this chapter has followed the webs of interlocution created before Oedipus triumphantly entered Thebes, which are only narrated after the action of the drama has begun. There were three webs in three different localities: the oracle at Delphi, the crossroads at Phocis, and the outskirts of Thebes. In the first two, the attempted communication failed swiftly and fatally. The third one, the engagement with the Sphinx, was successful. The Sphinx is overthrown and Oedipus descends to Thebes to be rewarded with his own mother as a prize for his intelligence.

4.3 In the Space of Questions at Thebes: Reconstructing Identity

As has already been argued,[64] identity does not just comprise "who we are" and "what we are," but also "where we are going," since life is a continuous process of change and evolution that molds autonomous beings who take their places in the world. We understand our lives as an unfolding story, composed of the constant movement and change we experience in life. Taylor argues that "making sense of one's life as a story is also, like orientation to the good, not an optional extra; that our lives exist also in this space of questions, which only a

---

[62] Euben 1990:113.
[63] The "one and the many" riddle as a major inconsistency of the drama is further elaborated below, in 4.6 "Contesting Human Intelligence: The One and the Many."
[64] See above, pp. 36–37, 44–45.

coherent narrative can answer";[65] individuals find themselves in this "space of questions" that gives meaning to their lives and selfhood through the exchange of linguistic articulation.

Thus, "we grasp our lives in a *narrative*";[66] and this is nowhere truer than for Oedipus: he walks in life with his mind imbued with a false narrative, and the decisions he has come to make in the course of his life have been based on this falsehood. At the end of his first quest (from Corinth to Delphi and Thebes) and in the period of his settled sojourn in Thebes, he has to recast his life into a new narrative.[67] It has been said that Oedipus continuously constructs narratives about himself,[68] and it is clear that Sophocles pivots the text of his tragedy around various narrative clusters that intentionally blur or clarify a particular aspect of the story,[69] ultimately leading to the revelation of the complete story of the hero.

Thebes is the only location of the events on stage in *Oedipus Tyrannus*, for all the previous encounters, misdirections, questions, and answers have taken place in other places and at a time long before the dramatic action. Thebes becomes this "space of questions" par excellence, where the false, and at times "broken" narrative of the life of Oedipus eventually becomes coherent—only because the questions asked in this final location (which, ironically, also saw the inception of his life) are answered in a way that provides the story with cohesion, internal logic, and causal continuity. In reality, *Oedipus Tyrannus* retells the story of Oedipus to Oedipus, constructing a narrative hitherto unknown to the hero. Cameron rightly argues: "this is not an Oedipus about whom such and such discoveries are made. ... Nor is this even an Oedipus who makes discoveries about himself. ... This is Oedipus discovered by himself."[70]

In the "space of questions" of Thebes, three major cycles of questions open: one with Jocasta, the second with the Corinthian messenger, and the third with Laius' servant. Piece by piece the painful reconstruction of Oedipus' life is unfolded before our (and his) eyes: starting with Jocasta's relation of the story of Laius' murder at the crossroads and of the oracle about the parricide, and ending with the last two encounters that tease out the details of the very beginning of the story on Mount Cithairon. We hear the story of the exposed baby and his pierced feet, the only unmistakable sign of Oedipus' identity that he has borne throughout life, retold by the Corinthian messenger; and finally, the

---

[65] Taylor 1989:47.
[66] Ibid.
[67] Taylor 1989:97.
[68] Pucci 1991:6.
[69] Karakantza 2011b:154.
[70] Cameron 1968:57.

confirmation of the kinship of the baby exposed to die on Cithairon to Laius himself retold by his servant. However, even before Jocasta, an unexpected space of questions opens between two interlocutors whose (mis)communication and distrust bring about a preview of Oedipus' identity.

4.4 Questions with Teiresias: A Preview of Identity

Teiresias is summoned on stage to assist in answering the question "Who is Laius' murderer?" Nothing in the plot or in the minds of the *dramatis personae* foreshadows this first preview of identity. Before examining this scene as the first explicit—to a certain extent—and certainly horrifying revelation of Oedipus' identity, it is worth noting the special relationship this episode has to the progressive unfolding of the rest of the play, in terms of the quest for the hero's self.

The Teiresias scene is "a masterful stroke" by Sophocles, writes Vayos Liapis,[71] a statement with which I am in total agreement. Instead of concealing facts important to the story, of which the audience is aware, Sophocles decides to "give the game away"[72] at the outset of the play. The seer is summoned to aid the search for Laius' murderer; and indeed, he fulfills the purpose for which he has been called on stage. The problem is that the murderer so revealed bears the name of Oedipus, for whom some additional disturbing pieces of information are added, explicitly or allusively: he, the king, lives shamefully with the closest of his relatives (366–367, 422–423), and will find himself embroiled in countless evils that, when disclosed, will level him with his children (424–425). This same person to be proven murderer of Laius will be also revealed as the murderer of his father and the lover of his mother (457–460).

As one might expect, the overall interpretation of the scene has deviated from investigating the murderer or the identity of Oedipus to focusing on the issue of knowledge and understanding, for we have two interlocutors conversing without establishing any level of mutual understanding. As has been noted many times, the question of verisimilitude has hovered over the scene since the time of Voltaire (at least), who contemptuously pointed out in his *Lettres à M. de Genonville* (in 1719) the many faults of "human logic" in the encounter between the seer and Oedipus;[73] the misunderstanding between the two creates an impasse. Lowell Edmunds suggests that two competing forms of

---

[71] Liapis 2012:86; Bain 1979:132–145.
[72] Liapis 2012:86.
[73] *Oedipe, tragédie par Monsieur de Voltaire.* Followed by *Lettres écrites par l' auteur qui contiennent la critique de l' Oedipe de Sophocle, de celui de Corneille et du sien;* see also Liapis 2012:89; Dawe 2006:7.

knowledge are established here, setting a cognitive framework for the rest of the tragedy. With the verb *phronein* that Teiresias uses to begin (315) and virtually end his speech in the scene (462), he focalizes the theme of knowledge that is fundamental here and in *Oedipus Tyrannus* in general.[74] The seer's knowledge regarding the truth (ἀλήθεια, and the cognitively related verb of λεληθέναι [= escape notice] used to describe Oedipus' actions in 356,[75] and 366–369)[76] contends with Oedipus' human intelligence (γνώμη); in fact, "Oedipus construes the riddle-solving as a competition in which he defeated Teiresias."[77] Steven Lattimore, before Edmunds, focuses also on intelligence and understanding; the question we should ask about the scene is not "why did Oedipus not understand Teiresias," but rather, "why is Teiresias made to tell Oedipus so much?"; because "Sophocles meant to show that the question in the following action is not the individual intelligence of Oedipus but the efficacy of all human understanding. ... The prophet of Apollo, when consulted, proves considerably more talkative than Apollo's priestess, but the amount of humanly usable information he conveys is not appreciably greater."[78]

Indeed, divine knowledge and human misunderstanding both pervade this scene; in fact, the scene could epitomize miscommunication, or rather broken communication, not because of linguistic inarticulacy or inadequate intelligence, but because of a lack of *symbola*, of clues as to the murder of Laius and its perpetrators. "Here do I stand before you all," says Oedipus to the gathering of the Theban suppliants, "a stranger / both to the deed, and to the story. What / could I have done alone, without a *clue*?"[79] (ἀγὼ ξένος μὲν τοῦ λόγου τοῦδ' ἐξερῶ, / ξένος δὲ τοῦ πραχθέντος· οὐ γὰρ ἂν μακρὰν / ἴχνευον αὐτός, μὴ οὐκ ἔχων τι <u>σύμβολον</u>, 219–221). The use of *symbola* in this investigation is succinctly brought to the interpretative fore by Michel Foucault.[80] It is not human understanding or knowledge *in general* that is under scrutiny (as the humanist

---

[74] Edmunds 2000:34–73.

[75] The famous, although controversial in translation, line containing the *vox Sophoclea* τρέφω: τἀληθὲς γὰρ ἰσχῦον τρέφω ("the truth I nurture has strength," Lloyd-Jones; "I have a champion—the truth," Kitto; "in my truth is my strength," Jebb; "I nourish the strength of truth," Finglass; "my strength lies in truth," my own).

[76] ΤΕ. λεληθέναι σέ φημι σὺν τοῖς φιλτάτοις / αἴσχισθ' ὁμιλοῦντ', οὐδ' ὁρᾶν ἵν' εἶ κακοῦ. / ΟΙ. ἦ καὶ γεγηθὼς ταῦτ' ἀεὶ λέξειν δοκεῖς; / ΤΕ. εἴπερ τί γ' ἐστὶ τῆς ἀληθείας σθένος (T.: "I say that you are living unawares in a shameful relationship with those closest to you, and cannot see the plight in which you are." O.: "Do you believe that you will continue to repeat such things and go scotfree?" T.: "Yes, if the truth has any strength").

[77] Edmunds 2000:55. Edmunds also acknowledges other functions of the scene, such as its metatheatricality, which constructs, so to speak, "today's version of the myth" (42).

[78] Lattimore 1975:106.

[79] Trans. Kitto.

[80] Foucault in his essay "Truth and Juridical Forms" (2000) interprets the whole play as a criminal investigation using *symbola*; the whole truth is possessed only by Apollo and Teiresias. See

interpretation of *Oedipus Tyrannus* would lead us to believe), but a specific case study: the investigation of the murder of Laius, obstructed by the lack of clues and relevant information.

Of course, this investigation is also related to the identity of Oedipus, for which the tokens (clues and pieces of information) are given later in the play. David Bain, in his paper "A Misunderstood Scene in Sophokles' *Oidipous* (*OT* 300-462),"[81] beautifully depicts in a chart how all relevant information about the narrative of Oedipus' life is given *later* than the scene with Teiresias and *not* in the chronological or "correct" order that we, as readers, would expect.[82] The manipulation of the information by Sophocles is what makes *this* version of the Oedipus myth so memorable and successful. In the original performance, the spectator would have had to follow the trail laid out by the poet, without "correcting" the version, as we do by turning the pages of our printed copy back and forth.[83] We should also resist the temptation to think of Oedipus as someone who fails to understand what he should.[84] Oedipus, when conversing with Teiresias, does not have in his mind the segments of his personal story, for this is not what is at stake right now, and the earlier doubts about his past have been buried for years. This is the version that Sophocles creates, and I fully agree with Bain when he claims that "one should never underestimate the manipulative power of the dramatists and the capacity of audiences of being willing victims" to this power.[85]

Therefore, one should read the scene in terms of dramatic technique and acknowledge Sophocles' audacity in disclosing the essentials right away, "setting the stage for a much more intricate plot" and the "astounding dénouement"[86] of the play. Sophocles also introduces details that are not canonical, thus novel to this version, such as the future blinding and exile.[87] This dramatic technique that ambushes the audience when least expected, brings about an extraordinary result: the truth about the murder and the identity of Oedipus (which will be gradually and painfully reconstructed in the course of the whole tragedy) "lies hidden in plain view," just like Poe's purloined letter; so well, indeed, that

---

4.7 below, "Intermezzo: Scholarship Thinks Oedipus is a Tyrant" for a detailed discussion of Foucault's approach, focusing on the interrelation between knowledge and power (pp. 93–99).

[81] 1979:132–145.

[82] Bain 1979:138; consider also: "We cannot be sure that an audience will at that stage in the play take it for granted that Sophocles is using the version he is using or that they will be aware of all the details that Sophocles is later to reveal about Oidipous' early life" (141).

[83] Bain 1979:137.

[84] Along with the other misconceptions that see Oedipus as the "guilty," the "puppet," or "in need of psychotherapy," Bain 1979:133.

[85] Bain 1979:141.

[86] Liapis 2012:86.

[87] Ibid.

"everyone (save Teiresias) fails to see the obvious."[88] The revelations and warnings, however, "must be resisted"[89] because they actually initiate the upholding of the plot: a heated conversation between Oedipus and Creon will follow, where the latter denies the allegations, which provokes Jocasta's intervention to retell for the first time the oracle of Laius and the encounter at the crossroads. In terms of the narratological technique that animates the intricate plot of the play and leads to all the fragments of evidence eventually coalescing, this scene is indeed a "masterful stroke." Questions like "why did Oedipus not understand" do not make sense; Oedipus *could* not understand because Sophocles' manipulation of the action makes the dramatic and psychological moment inappropriate for understanding. For one thing, Teiresias has remained silent for many years about the murder of Laius; second, when summoned, he charges the current king not only with the murder of his predecessor, but with a number of other hideous transgressions, as yet unproclaimed as problems; and third, since no clues or evidence has yet surfaced in relation to this murder, why should anybody believe Teiresias?[90]

Oedipus is not the only one who fails to understand. Even the chorus, who in the second *stasimon* will be so skeptical about the slurs cast on the veracity of oracles and seers by Jocasta, sides here—in the first *stasimon* immediately following the scene with Teiresias—with their king by questioning the credibility of seers (498–503):

ἀλλ' ὁ μὲν οὖν Ζεὺς ὅ τ' Ἀπόλλων ξυνετοὶ καὶ τὰ βροτῶν
εἰδότες· ἀνδρῶν δ' ὅτι μάντις πλέον ἢ 'γὼ φέρεται,
κρίσις οὐκ ἔστιν ἀληθής·

Well, Zeus and Apollo are wise and know the affairs of mortals; but when it comes to men, one cannot tell for sure that a prophet carries more weight than I.

Above all, the chorus claims that Oedipus is, in their eyes, innocent of all crimes, for he is their "sweet" king (509–512):

---

[88] See the remarks of Vayos Liapis (2012:88), who compares Edgar Allan Poe's short detective story "The Purloined Letter" (published in 1844) to the episode with Teiresias. In Poe's story an important letter was stolen by the unscrupulous Minister D and was hidden in "plain view" in his room, so as to fool the French police who searched his premises meticulously.

[89] Liapis 2012:88.

[90] Teiresias' accusations "sound as outrageous fabrications" (Liapis 2012:88).

... καὶ σοφὸς ὤφθη
βασάνῳ θ’ ἡδύπολις· τῷ ἀπ’ ἐμᾶς
φρενὸς οὔποτ’ ὀφλήσει κακίαν.

... he was seen to be wise and approved as dear to the city [ἡδύπολις];
thus shall he never be convicted of crime by my judgment.

However, we should bear in mind that this scene defines in essence
Oedipus' entire identity, for we hear, albeit in précis, all we need to know about
Oedipus: he is the murderer of Laius, a parricide, and incestuous. The elements
comprising the story of his life are laid bare in a coherent narrative that begins
with the arrival of the outsider, who, it transpires, is a native of the land, and
that projects into the future, with the vision of the impoverished mendicant,
wandering in foreign lands. The concluding passage to the scene is Teiresias'
last utterance, which, contrary to dramatic conventions, remains unanswered
by a counter-utterance from the main character,[91] because *this very* narrative
needs to be profoundly imprinted on Oedipus' (and the audience's) mind. He
stands silent, while Teiresias recounts his life (449–460):

λέγω δέ σοι· τὸν ἄνδρα τοῦτον, ὃν πάλαι
ζητεῖς ἀπειλῶν κἀνακηρύσσων φόνον
τὸν Λαΐειον,[92] οὗτός ἐστιν ἐνθάδε,
ξένος λόγῳ μέτοικος, εἶτα δ’ ἐγγενὴς
φανήσεται Θηβαῖος, οὐδ’ ἡσθήσεται
τῇ ξυμφορᾷ· τυφλὸς γὰρ ἐκ δεδορκότος
καὶ πτωχὸς ἀντὶ πλουσίου ξένην ἔπι
σκήπτρῳ προδεικνὺς γαῖαν ἐμπορεύσεται.
φανήσεται δὲ παισὶ τοῖς αὑτοῦ ξυνὼν
ἀδελφὸς αὐτὸς καὶ πατήρ, κἀξ ἧς ἔφυ
γυναικὸς υἱὸς καὶ πόσις, καὶ τοῦ πατρὸς
ὁμόσπορός τε καὶ φονεύς.

And I say this to you: the man you have long been looking for, with
threats and proclamations about the murder of Laius, that man is
here! He is thought to be a stranger who has migrated here, but
later he shall be revealed to be a native Theban, and the finding will

---

[91] Liapis 2012:86; Finglass 2018 ad 447–462.

[92] "Λαΐειον in place of an expected nominal genitive (264-8n) emphasises the solemnity of the
moment" (Finglass 2018 ad loc.).

bring him no pleasure; for he shall travel over strange land blind instead of seeing, poor instead of rich, feeling his way with his stick. And he shall be revealed as being to his children whom he lives with both a brother and a father, and to his mother both a son and a husband, and to his father a sharer in his wife and a killer.

The syntactical construction of the beginning of this passage points emphatically to "that man you have long been looking for" (τὸν ἄνδρα τοῦτον, ὃν πάλαι / ζητεῖς). The narrative of Teiresias begins with τὸν ἄνδρα τοῦτον, which is the antecedent prefixed to the relative clause that follows ὃν πάλαι / ζητεῖς ... , (attracted also into the case of the relative clause); when thus prefixed, it "marks with greater emphasis the subject of the coming statement":[93] οὗτός ἐστιν ἐνθάδε, that man [i.e., the murderer of Laius] is here. What follows are the segments of Oedipus' life: seemingly a foreigner, but in reality a native Theban; he will become blind from sighted, beggar from rich. The rest of the story is breathtaking in the immensity of the transgressions it depicts: *that man* shall be found brother and father of his children; son and husband of the woman who bore him; "sowing" the same field as his father and, finally, killer of his father. The conclusion of the narrative marks *that man* as the *agent* of the hideous acts in the words ὁμόσπορος and φονεύς; exchanging roles with his father, he actively[94] "sowed" the same woman, for ὁμόσπορος here is in an active sense, contrary to the earlier use of the word in the play (260). Oedipus sexually usurps the role of the father after having killed him (τοῦ πατρὸς / φονεύς).[95]

In Teiresias' narrative, the very first of the transgressions (the murder of the father), which set in motion everything else, comes only at the conclusion. It is like Ariadne's thread still fully rolled, with the murder as its conclusion; sticking out, inviting its unreeling, bringing a litany of evils as the thread unrolls. But at this moment, the narrative is complete and coherent only to the divine seer, along with Apollo and the servant of Laius, who are alone in possessing the whole truth. However, this is a story set in the future; as is shown in the prescriptive language of the divine (observe all the verbs in future tense: φανήσεται, ἡσθήσεται, ἐμπορεύσεται, and the final φανήσεται), whereas the story is already half accomplished (the transgressions; the blinding and the

---

[93] Jebb ad loc. with relevant examples; see also Finglass 2018 ad 449–452.

[94] Here in active form = τὴν αὐτὴν σπείρων (Jebb ad loc.).

[95] See also the very interesting remark by Finglass (2018 ad 457–460) regarding the three two-part predicates assigned to Oedipus by Teiresias (brother/father, son/husband, fellow-sower/murderer): "As if to prevent the sentence from becoming too balanced and schematic, the phrase accompanying each of these double predicates stands each time in a different syntactical relationship (dative, genitive with relative clause, genitive with definite article); the ruptures within Oedipus' family are reflected in unusually complex language."

exile loom). Everybody else in the play (Oedipus, Jocasta, and the two servants) possesses a segment of the story;[96] it will take all the magnificent artistry of Sophocles to piece the story together, while simultaneously racking up the dramatic tension beyond expectation.

The question posed at the beginning of this chapter "Who is Laius' murderer?" is answered: "You are." But even the pervasive question that haunts this play—"Who Am I?"—could have been answered here in a way that Oedipus would have been able to understand, because Teiresias told him that he knew his parents (436). This piece of information, as well as the clue that Jocasta reveals in the next episode ("you look very much alike the dead king," 743) will remain unexplored. The "I knew your parents" statement of Teiresias, also a native Theban, could point to the indigenous origin of the current king. However, nothing is meant to be taken as the consummation of the truth, for Oedipus does not have the question of his identity in the forefront of his mind; all doubts about this have been repressed since, terror stricken, he fled Delphi. Sophocles' task is to unearth the forgotten fragments and piece them together, simultaneously tracking the mental and psychological travails afflicting Oedipus as he unravels the answer to the question "Who Am I," which gradually resurfaces as the preeminent question of the play.

4.5 Questions with Jocasta: Dislocating the Origin (*or* Jocasta's Body and Mind)

The episode with Jocasta initiates the protracted revelations about Oedipus' identity, for, in her desperate attempt to assuage Oedipus' troubled mind regarding the murder of Laius, she reiterates the circumstances and locality of the deed, as well as the oracle foretelling the murder of Laius by his son. This information, hitherto unelucidated, evokes Oedipus' recollection of *his* murder of the old man at the junction of the three roads and the ominous oracle about parricide and incest. If the previous episode with Teiresias was a masterpiece of Sophocles' artistry, this one is yet more superb. Aside from her intervention to stop the fighting between Creon and Oedipus, Jocasta deflects the line of investigation, which leads perilously close to identifying Oedipus with the murderer, by questioning the validity of the oracles—by adopting, that is, a seemingly impious stance. In reality, however, she manipulates a precariously delicate psychological situation in which Oedipus has begun to be haunted by his worst

---

[96] As is beautifully shown by Foucault (2000:1–89 passim); see also 4.7 below.

fears, as the spate of terms denoting fear at the beginning of the next episode with the Corinthian messenger demonstrates.[97]

Doubting the oracles is, however, an act of impiety, in the light of which the famous second *stasimon* is composed. The equally famous line ὕβρις φυτεύει τύραννον (872) has triggered a longstanding scholarly debate about *hybris* in *Oedipus Tyrannus*, focusing mainly on Oedipus; Jocasta has always been considered a lesser candidate. I will not engage with the abiding preoccupation of scholars with Oedipus' possible *hybris*.[98] I will briefly state here that the relationship of the choral songs to the various episodes of the drama (and Sophoclean drama, in particular) is a very complex and, so far, unresolved issue. My thesis[99] is that a choral song stands in loose relation to both the preceding and following episodes, suggestive and allusive, rather than directly indicating the protagonists. The famous second *stasimon* (863–910) is a thorough study of *hybris*, arrogance, and irreverence, prompted by Jocasta's doubts regarding the validity of the oracles. In such a world, the chorus says, where arrogance prevails without fear of *Dikê* or reverence for the gods (883–895), "why should I continue honoring the gods with dances?" (τί δεῖ με χορεύειν; 896). We cannot deny the seriousness of the challenge Jocasta raises to the pious institution of the elders of Thebes with her insistence that "there is nothing mortal that possesses any of the prophetic art"[100] (οὕνεκ᾽ ἐστί σοι / βρότειον οὐδὲν μαντικῆς ἔχον τέχνης, 708–709). Her own history and that of Laius stand as a living proof of such a statement; their son was exposed to die, whereas Laius was killed by robbers at the junction of the three roads (710–722); thus prophetic voices are worthless—and should be discounted (723–724).

What Jocasta does is to first introduce, and then deflect, the line of investigation with two powerful instruments. The first, and more obvious, is the rejection of the oracles—a line of thought not easily accepted in Greek tragedy; she dares do so. The second, more insidious and subversive, is her gendered body and its standing in relation to Oedipus, who, as we all know, is both her husband and son. This introduces Jocasta as a heavily gendered subject, undermining

---

[97] See p. 104.
[98] I will consider a part of this debate below, in 4.7: "Intermezzo: Scholarship Thinks Oedipus is a Tyrant."
[99] My thinking is informed by the observations of many scholars, and especialy Sheila Murnaghan (2012:221), who remarks on the multiplicity of roles, and the fluidity of functions, of the choral singers in Sophocles: "... Sophocles used the chorus with great versatility, assigning it multiple forms of connecting to the main characters—as concerned observers, anxious dependants, sympathetic friends, or complicit allies—and taking advantage of the different types of choral participation built into tragic form: conversational exchanges ... ; discrete odes ... ; and lyric dialogues ... ." Also indispensable are Griffith 1999 ad 332–377; Goldhill 2012:81–108; Foley 2003; Budelmann 2000; Battezzato 2005; and Murnaghan 2011.
[100] Trans. Finglass 2018 ad 707–709.

the established familial relationships; in her body, all the distinctions—expected in a well-structured patriarchal society—collapse. Thus this section could have been titled "Jocasta's Body and Mind," because with both, Jocasta deflects the investigation into Laius' murder, which, at this point, has brought into perilous proximity the narratives of Jocasta and Oedipus, not only regarding the murder, but also, most significantly, the birth and origin of Oedipus. Jocasta's body is the *locus nativus* (γενέθλιος τόπος) of Oedipus, which makes it the most apt candidate to *dislocate* the question of origin; she does so intentionally (in her attempt to assuage the mind of Oedipus), and unwittingly (in the confusion of the laws of kinship she literally embodies).

I will begin with the more sophisticated part of this 'equation': Jocasta's gendered body, which constitutes part of the reception of the scene, albeit sometimes in an unspoken way. The reason *why* the dislocation can be materialized is because of *this* body, where the organizing principle of western culture (the prohibition of incest or, in the Lacanian formulation, "the Name (Law) of the Father") collapses; as has been said time and again, the mother is also the wife, the son is also the husband, the children are also brothers and sisters. The bipolar dichotomies within the "elementary structures of kinship"[101] that uphold patriarchy through the prohibition of incest, the law of exogamy, and the exchange of women, collapse in one of the most important founding narratives of the West—that of the incestuous relationship of Jocasta and Oedipus. It is worth remembering here that any strict bipolar taxonomy seeks to regulate the normative, and, because it privileges one of the two poles, it instigates exclusion and discrimination, as does the "female" in the distinction male/female. As a result, women become part of an elaborate network of exchange through marriage that consolidates patriarchy and the inferior position of women within those laws of kinship; thus special relations of power in the economy of sexual politics develop as canonical and hegemonic to control the female body and the process of reproduction.[102] In the analysis of Maria Wyke, female bodies in antiquity become:

---

[101] I am referring, of course, to Claude Lévi-Strauss's *Les Structures Élémentaires de la Parenté*, published in 1949 and translated into English as *The Elementary Structures of Kingship* in 1969. There the exchange of women between different tribes or clans in aboriginal societies constitutes a wide network establishing the laws of kinship; women are seen as exchangeable values or commodities, alongside other valuable and exchangeable products. These basic observations have been used by contemporary feminist thinkers to trace and criticize the kinship laws on which the patriarchal order is based.

[102] What Judith Butler calls the "heteronormative hegemonic practices" that establish the "heterosexual imperative" (1993:2).

privileged sites for the production, display, and regimentation of gender identity and gender differentials, and ... a visible material locus for gender's complex interactions with other claims to identity ... . [The body] is not a raw material upon which a conscious agent acts, but a semiotic system which its bearer can never fully master. Ancient bodies are, therefore, 'parchments of gender': textual skins on which gender is inscribed and on which can be traced other interconnected matrices of knowledge and power that give those bodies their seemingly legible contours.[103]

Wyke's further remark that bodies are also inscribed with "other interconnected matrices of knowledge and power" points to Foucault's and Butler's further refinements of our understanding of the gendered body. Judith Butler, in *Bodies that Matter*, claims that:

the body ... is a powerful symbolic form, a surface on which the central rules, hierarchies, and even metaphysical commitments of a culture are inscribed. ... It is also as anthropologist Pierre Bourdieu and philosopher Michel Foucault (among others) have argued, a practical direct locus of social control. Banally, through table manners and toilet habits, through seemingly trivial routines, rules, and practices, culture is 'made body'.[104]

Butler's eloquent formula that "culture is 'made body'" points to the refinement I would now like to bring into this discussion. In the Foucauldian vein of interpreting sex (that is to say, the anatomical differentiated sexual self, what we regularly call "biological sex"), sexual practices, and the sexual economy in general, bodies are not inert material upon which the culturally informed understanding of gender is inscribed. Instead, bodies are powerful dynamic *loci* witnessing the interaction of power relations, hegemonic practices, and heteronormative imperatives aiming at ultimate social control. In this sense, these things cannot be in reality *inscribed* in a fixed or static way (even within the confines of a certain chronological period), but must rather be debated, claimed, and manipulated to enforce hegemonic policies; on the gendered body, strategies and practices are being exerted rather than marking it forever. This more adequately explains how subversions and counter manipulation can take place, allowing margins to undermine, and thus renegotiate, hegemonic practices. In Jocasta's heavily gendered body, the *locus classicus* of the metaphorical

---

[103] Wyke 1998:3.
[104] Butler 1993:2; see also Athanasiou 2006:103.

language for the female body—that is, as a field for male ploughing—is overturned and subverted. For *this* ploughed field is also the body where distinctions and dichotomies collapse. As Butler says in analyzing Foucault's *Herculine Barbin*, "exploding the binary assumptions is one of the ways of depriving male hegemony and compulsory heterosexuality of the most treasured of primary premises."[105]

Jocasta's body is referred to primarily as a ploughed field: τὴν τεκοῦσαν ἤροσεν, / ὅθεν περ αὐτὸς ἐσπάρη ("he ploughed his mother, from whom he himself was sowed," 1497–1498); γυναῖκά τ' οὐ γυναῖκα, μητρῷαν δ' ὅπου / κίχοι διπλῆν ἄρουραν οὗ τε καὶ τέκνων ("the wife that was no wife, but the maternal field that saw a twofold harvest, of himself and of his children," 1256–1257); πῶς ποτε πῶς ποθ' αἱ πατρῷ- / αί σ' ἄλοκες φέρειν, τάλας, / σῖγ' ἐδυνάθησαν ἐς τοσόνδε; ("how ever, how ever were the furrows that were your father's able to endure you, wretched man, for so long in silence?" 1210–1212).[106]

The question of the last passage opens up the vast and absorbing debate I referred to in the previous section of this chapter. A woman (be it a mother or wife) is a *locus*, her body is a *locus* claimed for ploughing, fertilization, and reproduction by the male to ensure the patriarchal order of things. Jocasta's body was claimed and "sown" by two male agents: father and son. Thus, in this primary action of female objectification, something went terribly wrong, and the founding principle of kinship establishing patriarchy collapsed. We can trace this subversion more vividly if we think of Deianeira's description of the ploughing of her body as a "distant field"[107] by Heracles in her opening, agonizing speech in *Trachiniae* (32–34):

> κἀφύσαμεν δὴ παῖδας, οὓς κεῖνός ποτε,
> γῄτης ὅπως ἄρουραν ἔκτοπον λαβών,
> σπείρων μόνον προσεῖδε κἀξαμῶν ἅπαξ·

---

[105] In Judith Butler's "Variations on Sex and Gender" (1986:515). The work edited by Foucault, to which Butler refers, is *Herculine Barbin: Being the Recently Discovered Memoirs of a Nineteenth Century Hermaphrodite* (1980).

[106] Trans. Finglass 2018 ad locc.

[107] The other metaphor is, of course, the (in)hospitable harbor (*Oedipus Tyrannus* 420–423): βοῆς δὲ τῆς σῆς ποῖος οὐκ ἔσται λιμήν, / ποῖος Κιθαιρὼν οὐχὶ σύμφωνος τάχα, / ὅταν καταίσθῃ τὸν ὑμέναιον, ὃν δόμοις / ἄνορμον εἰσέπλευσας, εὐπλοίας τυχών; ("What harbour will there be for your cries, what of Cithaeron will not soon resound in accompaniment to them, when you perceive the wedding-song, the one without anchorage in your house, which you sailed into, having come upon sailing weather? [trans. Finglass 2018 ad loc.]).

> We had, indeed, children, whom he, like a farmer who has taken over a remote piece of ploughland, regards only when he sows and when he reaps.[108]

In this graphic metaphor, the body of Deianeira has become an objectified external locus of reproduction. Unlike Deianeira, however, who, in a more gendered conventional and socially sanctioned manner, seeks to regain Heracles' sexual favor and conjugal fidelity, Jocasta defies all this— even if unwillingly, for in *her* body the distinctions that sustain the sexual economy of patriarchy no longer exist. Her body blurs (and confounds) the confines of kinship: ὁμογενὴς δ' ἀφ' ὧν αὐτὸς ἔφυν (1362/3) (literally, "I am of the same *genos* with the person from whom I was sprung"); and in a more telling manner Oedipus exclaims finally (1403–1408):

> ὢ γάμοι γάμοι,
> ἐφύσαθ' ἡμᾶς, καὶ φυτεύσαντες πάλιν
> ἀνεῖτε ταὐτὸν σπέρμα, κἀπεδείξατε
> πατέρας ἀδελφούς, παῖδας αἷμ' ἐμφύλιον,
> νύμφας γυναῖκας μητέρας τε, χὠπόσα
> αἴσχιστ' ἐν ἀνθρώποισιν ἔργα γίγνεται.

> Marriage, marriage, you gave me birth, and after you have done so you brought up the selfsame seed, and displayed fathers who were brothers, children who were fruit of incest, brides who were both wives and mothers to their spouses, and all things that are most atrocious among men.

The endogamic blood (αἷμ' ἐμφύλιον) blurs the confines of all the kinship distinctions; renegotiating kinship is one of the most potent female means of resistance against the patriarchal order, as Judith Butler in *Antigone's Claim* and Bonnie Honig in *Antigone, Interrupted* advocate. The awkward moment when Antigone, moments before she dies, limits the cycle of the kin for whom she would sacrifice her life only to her brother puts the whole spectrum of kinship relations in another perspective. Butler claims that Antigone renegotiates the laws of kinship from the standpoint of the less privileged (i.e. women),[109] and Honig proposes that, through the politics of lamentation and by renegotiating

---

[108] Trans. Lloyd-Jones.

[109] "... if kinship is the precondition of the human, then Antigone is the occasion for a new field of the human, achieved through political catachresis, the one that happens when the less than human speaks as human, when gender is displaced, and kinship founders on its own founding laws" (2000:82); see also Karakantza forthcoming (a).

death, Antigone reclaims her political agency,[110] something she was deprived of by Hegelian and Lacanian readings.[111]

Without anyone realizing it, Jocasta emerges from this new kinship economy empowered. Sophocles gives her a dynamic entrance in the second episode to assertively stop the fighting between Oedipus and Creon that erupted when Oedipus accused Creon of conspiring with Teiresias to usurp his power and threatened him with exile and death (623). Jocasta's intervention is forceful, regal, and effective—the action of someone not only imbued with power, but who *is* in power. As if scolding inferior subjects, she demands both combatants, Creon and Oedipus, retire to the palace to free the public realm from their dispute. Jocasta is dressed in power. How and why do the trivial personal disputes of Oedipus and Creon take precedence over the important public calamities, Jocasta asks in authoritative manner (634–636):

τί τὴν ἄβουλον, ὦ ταλαίπωροι, στάσιν
γλώσσης ἐπήρασθ'; οὐδ' ἐπαισχύνεσθε γῆς
οὕτω νοσούσης ἴδια κινοῦντες κακά;
οὐκ εἶ σύ τ' οἴκους σύ τε, Κρέων, κατὰ στέγας,
καὶ μὴ τὸ μηδὲν ἄλγος εἰς μέγ' οἴσετε;

Wretches, why have you struck up this foolish battle of abuse?
Are you not ashamed to start up private troubles when the country
is thus sick? Will you not go indoors, and you Creon, to your house,
and not make what ought not to pain you into something big?

Jocasta subverts her gendered role regarding two important aspects: first, she uses a politically significant word to describe the quarrel of Oedipus and Creon: *stasis*, the civil strife that needs to be averted at all costs.[112] This statement

---

[110] Honig 2013:10, 21, 31.

[111] The first important reclamation of Antigone for political agency, contrary to the Hegelian and Lacanian readings, was made by Luce Irigaray in 1989, *Le Temps de la Différence: Pour une Révolution Pacifique*. Irigaray was a pupil and adherent of the Lacanian psychoanalytic circle. However, she distanced herself from the phallocentric Freudian and Lacanian theories by criticizing the exclusion of women from philosophy and psychoanalytic theory in her first major publication in 1974: *Speculum de l' Autre Femme*. This created such a controversy within the Lacanian School that she lost her teaching post at the University of Vincennes at the instigation of Lacan himself. This also caused her expulsion from the École Freudienne de Paris, founded by Lacan (see the opening remarks of her work *Je, Tu, Nous. Pour une Culture de la Différence*, 1990). Despite these tribulations, Irigaray has become an influential author in contemporary feminist theory and continental philosophy. For Antigone as political agent, see also Butler 2000:82; Honig 2013; Söderbäck 2010; Karakantza forthcoming (a).

[112] Karakantza 2011a:26–27, with notes 13–14.

would be expected from someone bearing political authority or who is at least conscious of the political exigencies besetting the city. It is in accordance with the heartfelt concern that Oedipus shows in the beginning of the play to care about the citizens of Thebes, a concern that seems to fall increasingly by the wayside in the course of the play. The second level of subversion concerns the public space that Jocasta comes to dominate. When she emerges from the palace, she authoritatively orders the two men to their homes, ridding the public space of their private quarrel. Jocasta is a suitable candidate for such a political action because in her "a whole new economy of the mechanisms of power"[113] is inaugurated, for, as claimed earlier, the founding narrative of patriarchy collapses. We have not realized how subversive the character of Jocasta is. Critics tend to think of her as a motherly figure or as a seductress. Lacan, for example, sees her as the polar opposite of the virginal and idealized Antigone.[114] Of course, Antigone is not a virginal, innocent heroine, nor Jocasta the seductive, empowered mother, as Lacan would have it. On the other hand, critics fall into modern stereotypes, such as the bipolar "motherly preoccupation with avoiding disgrace" and the "wifely 'survival philosophy,'"[115] as is expressed in the later "easy life" statement (979).

Jocasta has nothing to do with any of this; she commands the two men, initiates the cycle of questions, reveals intimate truths, and dares question the validity of the oracles. Now, this last movement touches upon deeply rooted beliefs stemming from the religious life of the time. Without entering into the long and interesting discussion about the function of the oracles in tragedy in general, and in Sophoclean tragedy in particular, I will note that at times, as in *Trachiniae*, there are multiple or obscure oracles; at other times, as in *Philoctetes*, parts of the oracle are revealed progressively by the playwright as a device to build dramatic tension. The meaning of an oracle might be obscure or misleading, but nowhere do we have persons questioning their intrinsic validity. The breach of common beliefs regarding this communication between mortals and gods is momentous here in *Oedipus Tyrannus*, and thus, understandably, the chorus in the following *stasimon* fears for the stability of the entire religious edifice: ἔρρει δὲ τὰ θεῖα (910); Jocasta has shaken it.

---

[113] To use Foucault's words from the first volume of his *History of Sexuality* (1990:5).

[114] Leonard 2006:131–132.

[115] Rick M. Newton as late as 1991 refers to the role of Jocasta in binary and socially constructed gendered terms: "Oedipus' Wife and Mother." He sees in her the "motherly preoccupation with αἰδώς" (41) and he thinks that Jocasta behaves "as a mother reprimanding her child" (40). In tune with this he argues: "in the previous episode Jocasta revealed a motherly preoccupation with avoiding disgrace. Her new emphasis on τύχη and her expressed goal of living an easy life, however, are more in keeping with the wifely 'survival philosophy' voiced by such figures as Tecmessa and Andromache" (43).

Therefore, Jocasta initiates *and* disorients the investigation; she dislocates the question of origin—because *she* is the origin, but her body has not sustained the confines of her gender. As a result, she becomes empowered, and steps into the public realm, rebuking the king and her brother, and questioning the oracles, thus misleading Oedipus. The Foucauldian concept of the body as the *locus* where the mechanisms of power are being exerted finds here an exemplar; Jocasta's body is not a static tablet where gender is inscribed, but an (inter) active *locus* where power strategies of hegemonic and counter-hegemonic acts are being played out. This, again, is much reminiscent of Butler's bodies "as a mode of dramatizing or enacting possibilities" in the process of gender constitution through performative acts.[116] The body is "materialized," and this materialization is not a static condition, as Butler claims in *Bodies that Matter;*[117] rather,

> the regulatory norms of 'sex' work in a performative fashion to constitute the materiality of the bodies and, more specifically, to materialize the body's sex, to materialize sexual difference in the service of the consolidation of the heterosexual imperative.

Jocasta defies all this; she sees that her system (comprising Oedipus) survives in a life that defies the binary confines of the gender distinctions. She suggests living, not in the way acceptable for a man or a woman, as Ajax and Deianeira in other plays of Sophocles declare,[118] but "live at random, live as best one can,"[119] articulated in the famous "easy life" statement: εἰκῇ κράτιστον ζῆν, ὅπως δύναιτό τις (979).

4.5.1 The Cycle of Questions

The cycle of questions initiating the investigation begins in 634, when Jocasta asks both Creon and Oedipus: "What has aroused this quarrel (*stasis*)?"; and again in 699 she asks Oedipus: "What is the reason for your blazing anger (*mênis*)?" Oedipus' indignant response is that he is the target of a sinister plot, since he is accused of being the murderer of Laius (φονέα με φησὶ Λαΐου καθεστάναι, 703).

---

[116] Butler 1988:525; and earlier in 1986:505–516.

[117] 1993:2.

[118] I am referring to the famous statements of Ajax (*Ajax* 479–480): ἀλλ᾽ ἢ καλῶς ζῆν ἢ καλῶς τεθνηκέναι / τὸν εὐγενῆ χρὴ ("the noble man must live with honour or be honourably dead") and of Deianeira (*Trachiniae* 721–722): ζῆν γὰρ κακῶς κλύουσαν οὐκ ἀνασχετόν, / ἥτις προτιμᾷ μὴ κακὴ πεφυκέναι ("for a woman whose care is to be good cannot bear to live and to enjoy evil repute"; trans. Lloyd-Jones).

[119] Trans. Kitto.

"How could that be possible?" Jocasta wonders, since Laius was killed at the intersection of three roads (ἐν τριπλαῖς ἁμαξιτοῖς, 716) by a stranger, although an oracle had foretold that the king would be killed by his son. It is here that Jocasta, seeking to reassure Oedipus about the doubts beginning to materialize in his mind, questions the validity of oracles and mentions the junction where Laius was murdered. The locality of τριπλῆ ἁμαξιτὸς shakes Oedipus: "Where is this place?" (732); "When did this happen?" (735); What did Laius look like?" (740); "How old was he?" (741). All the answers converge into identifying the murderer with Oedipus, since the place and time coincide with Oedipus' presence there.

In this first agonizing exchange of questions and answers a significant trait of identity is revealed: Laius looked very much like Oedipus (μορφῆς δὲ τῆς σῆς οὐκ ἀπεστάτει πολύ, 743) or *Oedipus looks very much like Laius*. This piece of information is neither evaluated nor commented upon, by Oedipus or anyone else in the play; it is virtually wasted, as if the mention of the physical similarity between Laius and Oedipus is of no importance.[120] Indeed, this crucial piece of information about physical similarity is neutralized at this dangerous point of the narrative when Oedipus is nearly convinced that he has killed Laius (744–745, 747). Thus, instead of pondering the curious similarity between himself and the former king, Oedipus moves on to ask a question that acquires enormous significance for him, as well as for the unfolding of the plot, which has also confounded readers ever since.[121] The new question that deflects the narrative, as well as the mind of Oedipus, is "how many": "was Laius travelling alone, or did he have company, and if yes, *how many*?" (I am paraphrasing the "πότερον ἐχώρει βαιός, ἢ πολλοὺς ἔχων / ἄνδρας λοχίτας, οἷ' ἀνὴρ ἀρχηγέτης"; 750–751). The mathematics of the encounter follow: they were altogether five, and one of them a herald, and a single wagon carried Laius (πέντ' ἦσαν οἱ ξύμπαντες, ἐν δ' αὐτοῖσιν ἦν / κῆρυξ· ἀπήνη δ' ἦγε Λάϊον μία, 752–753). "Alas," Oedipus exclaims, "with this piece of information everything has become clear" (αἰαῖ, τάδ' ἤδη διαφανῆ, 754), because the time, the space, the person, the numbers, all coincide. They all begin to dovetail to prove that Oedipus *is* the murderer of Laius. All but one: the number of the assailants enumerated earlier by Jocasta (ξένοι ποτὲ /λῃσταί, 715–716); *they were many and not just one*.

At this point—exactly in the middle of the play—Sophocles introduces a narratological device that first allows Oedipus the opportunity to retell *his* personal story and also, very importantly, *his* side of the story of the encounter

---

[120] See also the similar piece of information about Teiresias knowing Oedipus' parents, which is also "wasted" in the course of the narrative, and the manipulation of the information by Sophocles, in section 4.4 above, p. 70.

[121] See the relevant discussion in section 4.6.

with Laius. In his version of the story, (which we cannot contest), he *alone* killed the old man who was riding in a wagon and *all* of his attendants—κτείνω δὲ τοὺς ξύμπαντας (813).

Now, this statement is inconsistent with Jocasta's story on two points: first, that the assailant was alone and single-handedly killed Laius and his company; second, that there was one survivor from the assault, a slave of the royal household (οἰκεύς τις, ὅσπερ ἵκετ᾿ ἐκσωθεὶς μόνος, 756). Two points of divergence that come down to one, the only one that provides a glimmer of hope: if the assailants were many, since Jocasta has talked about robbers in the plural (the famous lines: λῃστὰς ἔφασκες αὐτὸν ἄνδρας ἐννέπειν / ὥς νιν κατακτείναιεν, 842–843), it cannot be the same incident. "Because I was alone," claims Oedipus, "and there is *no way that one equals many*" (οὐ γὰρ γένοιτ᾿ ἂν εἷς γε τοῖς πολλοῖς ἴσος, 845). The entire passage runs as follows (842–847):

> λῃστὰς ἔφασκες αὐτὸν ἄνδρας ἐννέπειν
> ὥς νιν κατακτείναιεν. εἰ μὲν οὖν ἔτι
> λέξει τὸν αὐτὸν ἀριθμόν, οὐκ ἐγὼ 'κτανον·
> <u>οὐ γὰρ γένοιτ᾿ ἂν εἷς γε τοῖς πολλοῖς ἴσος·</u>
> εἰ δ᾿ ἄνδρ᾿ ἕν᾿ οἰόζωνον αὐδήσει σαφῶς
> τοῦτ᾿ ἐστὶν ἤδη τοὔργον εἰς ἐμὲ ῥέπον.

> You said that he told you that robbers had killed him; so if he still gives the same number, I was not the killer, *for one is not the same as many*. But if he speaks unmistakably of one solitary man, then at once the balance tilts towards me.

We know (as members of the audience and readers of the play), and Oedipus comes to realize at the end of the play, that the incident was one and the same. However, how is this logical inconsistency solved? In fact, the play reaches its denouement without this impossible equation ever being solved, as will be shown in the following section.

One last word, before examining the impossible equation that Oedipus poses: "one does *not* equal many." I shall return briefly to the original statement of this chapter about "dislocating the question of origin," in the double function that I have stated earlier. Doubting the oracles delays the finding of the truth for another 400 lines of action. When Oedipus finally finds out the truth, he resorts to Jocasta's body—now lifeless—which becomes the source of Oedipus' final blow; for it is the pins holding her garments that become the instruments of his blinding. The erotic symbolism of the act is obvious, not only because in the Freudian vein of interpretation, self-blinding equals castration, but because the female body gets symbolically undressed in a manner invoking Deianeira, who, laying on her nuptial bed, uncovers her breasts before striking the fatal blow (*Trachiniae* 924–926). But even before that, when Jocasta enters the conjugal chamber, she invokes the nuptial bed (1242–1243), the sperm of Laius (1246), and Laius himself, who, with his death, "left" her to sleep with her son (1248). She weeps and wails over the bed where from her husband she engendered her husband, and from her son her sons and daughters (γοᾶτο δ' εὐνάς, ἔνθα δύστηνος διπλῆ / ἐξ ἀνδρὸς ἄνδρα καὶ τέκν' ἐκ τέκνων τέκοι, 1249–1250). It is Jocasta's body where the utterly "impossible equations" materialize, for all the distinctions sustaining the patriarchal order of things have disintegrated.

4.6 Contesting Human Intelligence: One and the Many

It should come as no surprise that in a play such as *Oedipus Tyrannus*, the major contrivance used to assuage the doubts that unsettle the mind of Oedipus and to divert the action of the play contradicts human logic. Oedipus is an exemplar of the intelligent hero par excellence, and a playwright wishing to undermine his protagonist's confidence in his own powers of intellect and to perplex his self-assurance would choose to do so in the field the hero believes he excels in. Yet, this is little comfort for a modern readership, which, since the time of Voltaire's attempt to remedy the major inconsistencies of the play in his own *Oedipus*,[122] has felt uneasy with this impossible equation: in our world (and in coherent narratives) *one* does not equal *many*; or, are there any circumstances under which one *does* equal many?

Many proposals have been made to solve this problem: the suggestion, for example, that this inconsistency lies within the framework of the elimination of the differences pervading Oedipus' story (father-son, mother-wife, children-brothers/sisters, etc.).[123] Segal claims that for Sophocles, as for Plato, "the relation of the One to the Many is the focal point for man's understanding of himself and the universe."[124] Kamerbeek remarks that not "the one to the many," but the "reverse is to become true: for Laius' son, Laius' murderer and Laius' successor will prove to be one and the same person. On the other hand this peremptory statement sheds light on the repeated ambiguous shifts from singular to plural and *vice versa* wherever the murderer or murderers are alluded to."[125] Surely,

---

[122] Voltaire 1719 (see section 4.4 above, p. 64n73).

[123] For the relevant bibliography, see Karakantza 2011b:157n25.

[124] Segal 2000:158.

[125] 1963 ad 845.

the "mistaken numbers" combine to form a nexus of misleading mathematical equations upon which the whole tragedy is built: the equating of the oracles to reality, of a person to Oedipus the just king, and to Oedipus the accursed.[126] In an era when human intelligence was celebrated as the prime mover of anthropological progress and Protagoras contended that *man is the measure for all things*, it seemed fitting to resort to mathematical methods, such as "calculation of time, measurement of age and number, comparison of place and description"[127] to resolve the riddles of *Oedipus Tyrannus*. Of course, as Lévi-Strauss puts it, some things in *Oedipus Tyrannus* should have been left unanswered or apart; in other words, the certainty apparently provided by mathematical equations proves unavailing in this play. In the second volume of the *Anthropologie Structurale*, when Lévi-Strauss revisits the Oedipus myth, he states that the riddle of the Sphinx is a question to which the answer should remain apart, and he connects the riddle with the incest, a relation where the two persons involved should have remained apart; these are two situations that bear internal and logical similarities.[128]

Indeed, equations presenting inconsistencies (the number of the attackers is but one of them) require resolution by an internal logic supported by the text itself. Let us see how this textual logic is built. In line 842, the ληστὰς ἔφασκες ἄνδρας that Oedipus singles out from the narrative of Laius' murder is in accordance with other references to the story scattered throughout the text. In the prologue of the play (in line 122), Creon refers to the murder, using again the ληστὰς ἔφασκε ("it has been said that they were robbers"), highlighting first the villainy of the action (who would think that it was simply a dispute over a strip of land and not a robbery?) and second (and most importantly) the number of the assailants. The number is corroborated again in lines 107 (τοὺς αὐτοέντας, "the assailants"), 292 (πρός τινων ὁδοιπόρων, "[to have been killed] by people on the road"), and 308 (τοὺς κτανόντας, "the killers"), and this piece of information was uttered in front of the entire city by the only survivor (πόλις γὰρ ἤκουσ', οὐκ ἐγὼ μόνη, τάδε, 850). It is certain, then, that the robbers were many and not just one; but in order to be sure, Oedipus summons the sole witness to confirm his testimony. When the herdsman finally arrives, no one asks him to verify it, for the issue at stake at that crucial moment has become the verification of the identity of the baby given to his Corinthian fellow-herdsman.[129] In other words, *it does not matter anymore* how many assailants were involved. So, did Sophocles use false information solely to misdirect our attention? Is it just a

---

[126] Knox 1957:154, 157; Karakantza, 2011b:158.
[127] Knox 1957:150; Karakantza 2011b:158.
[128] 1973:31–35; Karakantza 2011b:154n19.
[129] See also section 4.9 below, pp. 110–113.

flaw of the narrative? The other possibility is that the servant of Laius had been lying all along out of fear or shame, as has been suggested.[130] But nowhere in the play is his version discredited. Or alternatively, Oedipus knew the truth all along about the single assailant, something betrayed in two passages where, although the interlocutor speaks about many robbers, Oedipus contradicts him by stating only one was involved, as if he was recalling past knowledge (139, 293). This could be a Freudian slip of the tongue regarding an action known to, but long forgotten by, Oedipus.

In both hypotheses (the servant lies, Oedipus knows unconsciously) I am reluctant to ascribe an intention to the author: neither the servant nor Oedipus ever acknowledge what *we* try to detect in their wording. The fact that Sophocles uses a narrative that contradicts the broad schema of human logic remains an issue of great puzzlement—the formulation of Oedipus is simple and eloquent (845): οὐ γὰρ γένοιτ' ἂν εἷς γε τοῖς πολλοῖς ἴσος, *one does not equal many*; unless, of course, human logic becomes redundant under certain circumstances, as will be explored shortly.

Following the path of rationality and determination, Oedipus summons the servant. However, when the servant finally arrives (in the fourth episode) the only question that matters anymore is "Was I the baby that you gave to the Corinthian herald?" because at that moment Oedipus needs only this last piece of information, the only piece still missing to complete the puzzle of his identity. It is obvious that we (audience and readers) confront discursive forces that create their own meaning contrary to other narratives in the play. In this case, the narrative potentially exculpating Oedipus (the *many* robbers) is suspended in favor of another discursive force that imposes itself through the anticipation raised by the original oracle about the guilt of Oedipus. Rationality becomes ineffective, as the coherence of events becomes secondary to the coherence of the discourse, which exposes a fresh meaning and brings about the revelation of the truth.[131] It has been stated, rightly, that "one arbitrary fiction comes to assume the value of the truth."[132] It is the "oracular logic"[133] and not the concrete factual evidence that condemns Oedipus.

One last remark before concluding this section: this impossible equation that the playwright introduces in the play challenges human logic; but in terms of potency, is it not overshadowed by the other impossible equation that we have seen formulated in the previous section in the body of Jocasta. If human logic is contested in this emblematic play of Sophocles, so are the laws of kinship, both

---

[130] Segal 2000:90–91; Dawe 2006:7; Bollack 1990 ad 122.
[131] Culler 1981:172–175; Karakantza 2011b:158.
[132] Goodhart 1978:67.
[133] Goodhart 1978:67.

of them fixed points of reference of our cultural paradigm; and yet, Sophocles dares introduce these shaken mathematics in a narrative that imposes its own principles in defiance of the expected equations.

At the end, Oedipus needs to recast his life in a new and coherent narrative, so as to straighten out the hitherto fragmented and discontinuous tale with its impossible equations. This is progressively reconstructed within the spaces of interlocution in which Oedipus finds himself on his quest to establish who he is. The cycles of questions for Oedipus, triggered in Thebes by the investigation of the murder of Laius, have just been opened; the second cycle of questions begins with the Corinthian messenger.

4.7 Intermezzo: Scholarship Thinks Oedipus Is a Tyrant

At the risk of frustrating the reader by digressing from the flow of my argument about the webs of interlocution and the configuration of the identity of Oedipus (we were about to follow on the heels of the Corinthian messenger), I shall offer a short excursus on the issue of Oedipus as a tyrant. The reasoning behind this is multifarious: starting with Vernant's much acclaimed essays on "The Lame Tyrant" and "Ambiguity and Reversal" (with Oedipus in the latter oscillating between a tyrant and a *pharmakos*),[134] every scholar of *Oedipus Tyrannus* has encountered the issue of Oedipus' suggested proclivity for tyrannical authority; a tendency clearly discernible, according to some, in his dispute with Creon and Teiresias. Related to this is the issue of his alleged *hybris*, stemming from the famous second *stasimon* that unequivocally introduces, so it seems, this notion into the consideration of the play.[135] Even if one remains skeptical about the extent, or even the existence, of his tyrannical disposition, we can at least take up the arrogance on an intellectual level that has made Oedipus popular with

---

[134] The first is "The Lame Tyrant. From Oedipus to Periander" and the second is "Ambiguity and Reversal: On the Enigmatic Structure of Oedipus Rex"; also renowned are "Oedipus Without the Complex," and Vidal-Naquet's "Oedipus in Athens"—all of these essays are now published in the collection *Myth and Tragedy in Ancient Greece.*

[135] My intention in this chapter is *not* to tackle the issue of the tentative *hybris* of Oedipus, nor to get into the long, so far unresolved, discussion about whether the second *stasimon* refers Oedipus as *hybristes* or tyrant. The disparagement of divine laws and practices expressed in this *stasimon* is a response to Jocasta's call to discredit the divine oracles in the preceding episode; *her* intention is to appease the tormented mind of Oedipus. In section 4.5 above, I have dealt at length with the doubting of the oracles as part of a wider undermining of the patriarchal order; the prohibition of incest, one of the founding principles of patriarchy, as well as faith in oracular voices, collapse in Jocasta's body and mind.

the philosophers[136] and the humanizers.[137] Oedipus is the person who, at one and the same time, knows too much and too little, who disdains to ask for divine help in solving the riddle of the Sphinx, and takes pride in his intelligence. In short, to what extent, and in which vein, is Oedipus a tyrant?

Of course, all the above are closely entwined with the question of identity; in a sense, I need to clear the path for my interpretation by addressing some of the most popular and widespread views about *Oedipus Tyrannus*. Even if one intends to refute, or at least contest, some aspects of pervading opinions, significant lessons can always be gleaned from revisiting important scholarship on the matter.

I will begin with Vernant's "Lame Tyrant." In section 4.1 I argued that Lévi-Strauss's approach, in which the common theme of lameness links the three generations of the Labdacids, yields insightful results as we follow the patrilineal line of the family of Oedipus, fettered together in the form of a corporeal deficiency that is embedded in their names: Labdacus, Laius, and Oedipus. Thus the naming of the exposed baby—driven by the seemingly incomprehensible cruelty of the father in mutilating the feet of his son—binds the forsaken infant to the family, instead of excluding and destroying him. The theme of lameness is taken further by Vernant in the exploration of the motif that connects lameness with tyranny (in his own words "tyranny is a lame royalty"[138]); lameness has not only a physical manifestation, but a symbolic form of serial defects and distortions, such as misunderstandings, blocked (or broken) communication, forgetfulness, perverted sexuality, sterility, monstrosity, and the like. Of course, the "equivocal aspects of lameness [are] its ambivalence,"[139] not only denoting a defect, but also a special status, potentially "a sign or promise of a unique destiny."[140] This equivocation is evident in the stories of both Oedipus

---

[136] Thomas Gould's essay, extending to three parts (published between 1965–1966), titled "The Innocence of Oedipus: The Philosophers on Oedipus the King," presents the views of the ancient philosophers (mainly Aristotle's) on Oedipus. See also Miriam Leonard's chapter on "Oedipus and the Subject of Philosophy" from her *Athens in Paris* (2005:22–32), where she claims: "The question of when Oedipus becomes a figure of philosophy cannot stand in isolation. Oedipus' re-entry into the tradition of the Western thought is inextricably linked to the emergence of a philosophical preoccupation with 'the tragic' and the wider question of how the reception of the Greeks came to play such a determining role in the development of European philosophy" (23).

[137] Segal argues that there are two principal classes of interpreters of *Oedipus Tyrannus*: the "humanists" and the "theologizers" (2001:168). The "humanists" see in Oedipus the incessant quest for human knowledge, often performed with a certain arrogance bordering on *hybris* (see the argument in the present chapter).

[138] Vernant 1988a:222.

[139] Vernant 1988a:209.

[140] Ibid.

and Periander, which Vernant sees as exemplifying the Greek conception of the tyrant.

The thread tying Oedipus to Periander lies through Labdacus and Labda, both lame. Labda's lameness disbarred her from the direct line of descent in the family of the Bacchiads, an elite oligarchic group that ruled Corinth for a long time, as reported by Herodotus (3.50–54 and 5.92). To sustain the purity of their lineage, the Bacchiads intermarried within their family (ἐδίδοσαν δὲ καὶ ἤγοντο ἐξ ἀλλήλων, 5.92.3), with the exception of Labda, who was rejected due to her corporeal deformity. Her husband Eëtion, a Corinthian from the *dêmos* of Petra, and a descendant of the Lapith Caineus (who was allegedly an androgynous creature), received an oracle that he would beget a son, who, like a rolling stone (ὀλοοίτροχον, 5.92.12), would descend upon the princes of Corinth and execute justice (ἐν δὲ πεσεῖται / ἀνδράσι μουνάρχοισι, δικαιώσει δὲ Κόρινθον, 5.92.12–13).[141]

The story of Cypselus, the son of Labda, bears structural similarities with the story of Oedipus, with his near execution by the Fathers of the Bacchiads, and his unexpected survival, concealed by his mother in a container used as a beehive (hence his name). With Cypselus, the direct line of the rulers deviates, and, following the instigation of the oracle, Cypselus, on reaching adulthood, marches against Corinth and overwhelms it. Now, Cypselus and his son Periander help us configure the Greek idea of a tyrant, also reflected in the works of contemporaneous Athenian tragedy. Herodotus in this narrative (5.92.6–7) has the Corinthian Socles reply to the Lacedaemonians (who attempt to reinstate Hippias in Athens) that there is nothing more unrighteous (ἀδικώτερον) and bloodthirsty (μιαιφονώτερον) than the *tyrannis*. Both Cypselus and Periander were profligate in such excesses but the son surpassed the father in many respects,[142] not least in the outrageous act of stripping naked all the Corinthian women in the temple of Hera and burning their garments to placate his dead wife Melissa (5.92.19–22). Abusing and humiliating other people's women is a common characteristic of historical tyrants, as is the case of Hipparchus, the brother of the tyrant Hippias, who insulted the sister of Harmodius, who had been chosen, then later rejected, to bear a basket in a ritual procession in honor of Athena. Harmodius and his lover Aristogeiton conspired to kill Hippias at the Panatheneia, resulting, instead, in the murder of Hipparchus, thus ensuring

---

[141] The oracle received by Eëtion reads as follows (5.92.11–13): Ἠετίων, οὔτις σε τίει πολύτιτον ἐόντα. / Λάβδα κύει, τέξει δ' ὀλοοίτροχον· ἐν δὲ πεσεῖται / ἀνδράσι μουνάρχοισι, δικαιώσει δὲ Κόρινθον ("Eëtion, worthy of honor, no man honors you / Labda is with child, and her child will be a millstone / which will fall upon the rulers and will bring justice to Corinth"; trans. de Sélincourt/Burn).

[142] Ὁ τοίνυν Περίανδρος κατ' ἀρχὰς μὲν ἦν ἠπιώτερος τοῦ / πατρός, … , / πολλῷ ἔτι ἐγένετο Κυψέλου μιαιφονώτε- / ρος (5.92.5).

that the regime of Hippias was spurred to greater violence and bloodthirstiness.[143] In tragedy, the abuse of ritual and the murder of kin frequently appear as characteristics of the figure of the tyrant.[144] In *Oedipus Tyrannus* abuse and perversion are reflected in the practice of extreme endogamy, for in Oedipus' story the generations are fused (instead of being kept strictly apart): mother and wife, sons and brothers, daughters and sisters.[145] For Richard Seaford, Oedipus is a tyrant, a man of money, who suffers extreme isolation from kin and gods alike because of his absolute autonomy and self-sufficiency, resulting from the widespread monetization of Athens in the sixth century BCE. Money is used by tyrants to organize the religious festival and dramatic contests within the festival of the Great Dionysia and to accumulate wealth. Money homogenizes its users (historical and tragic tyrants are typically associated with excess in their desire for money) and can incite conflict between generations.[146] In *Oedipus Tyrannus* there is no conflict but the "confusion of generations," which is due to an economic dimension detectable in the retelling of the story by Sophocles and hitherto neglected, as Seaford claims:[147] "the two functions of the household, wealth and procreation, are both susceptible to introverted self-sufficiency, and seem to interpenetrate."[148]

Returning to the lame tyrant of Vernant, we read: "tyranny, a lame royalty, cannot succeed for long."[149] In the very oracle that Cypselus receives to conquer Corinth there is also the prediction of the fate of the following generations: his children will be happy, but *not* his children's children (5.92.6–9).[150] Periander's children enact a "broken communication" between the generations: the eldest son, though very fond of his father, is weak in mind and memory; the youngest son, intelligent, determined, and possessed of an implacable memory, detests his father so much (on learning of his father's murder of his mother) that he refuses to say another word to him. When Periander attempts to pass the power over Corinth to his estranged son (now living in exile in Corcyra), that son, Lycophron, is murdered by the people of Corcyra to avoid being ruled by the

---

143 Thucydides (1.20; 6.56–57) in his narrative "corrects" the motives of Harmodius and Aristogeiton from political to personal; see also Aristotle *Athenaiōn Politeia* 18.

144 Beautifully shown at Seaford 2008:49–65.

145 Seaford 2007:26–27.

146 Seaford 2007:27.

147 Seaford 2007:23.

148 Seaford 2007:26–27.

149 Vernant 1988:222.

150 Ὁ δὲ χρησμὸς ὅδε ἦν· / Ὄλβιος οὗτος ἀνὴρ ὃς ἐμὸν δόμον ἐσκαταβαίνει, / Κύψελος Ἠετίδης, βασιλεὺς κλειτοῖο Κορίνθου, / αὐτὸς καὶ παῖδες, παίδων γε μὲν οὐκέτι παῖδες ("the prophesy went like this: 'Fortunate is he who steps down into my house / Cypselus, son of Eetion, lord of famous Corinth: / Fortunate he and his sons, but not the sons of his sons'"; trans. de Sélincourt/Burn).

father, as the agreement between father and son was for a mutual exchange of positions in power. The lame lineage of Labda, like that of Labdacus, is "obliterated instead of carrying on the direct line through successive generations."[151]

In Herodotus' historical account we can easily detect a tendency to mythologize; the lameness of the Labdacid's line is "derailed" in the Cypselids as forms of disruptive marriage, endangered survival, and broken communication between the generations—all elements equally present in the story of Oedipus. Vernant concludes his analysis as follows:[152]

> The tyrant despises the rules that control the ordering of the social fabric and, through its regularly woven mesh, determine the position of each individual in relation to all the rest, in other words—to put it more crudely, as Plato does—he is perfectly prepared to kill his father, sleep with his mother, and devour the flesh of his own children. Like both a god and a wild beast, he is, in his ambivalence, the very incarnation of the mythical representation of lameness with its two contrary aspects: Because his progress is superior to human gait in that, as it rolls, it encompasses every direction at once more quickly and with more agility, he overcomes the limitations that affect a straight way of walking, but at the same time his gait falls short of the normal modalities of locomotion in that, mutilated, unbalanced, and wavering as it is, he stumbles along in his own particular fashion only to fall the more definitively in the end.

In this fascinating analysis after Lévi-Strauss, the lameness of the Labdacids is linked to the real (that is, historical) tyrants and to all the perverse ways in which abusive power is exercised. It is obvious that the Herodotean narrative incorporates non-historical (that is, mythical or fictional) discursive modules to elaborate on the notions of the tyrant (and his deviations); to a great extent, all those are also detectable in the myth of Oedipus' family. However, at this point I will raise two questions. First, to what extent does the existence of a mythical/narratological motif predetermine the overall meaning of the new version of the story? That is to say, does the motif of lameness in the myths of the Labdacids necessarily evoke the figure of the tyrant in the new version of the story of Oedipus, as told by Sophocles in this particular tragedy?[153] Lameness, in any form, in the Sophoclean version is completely suppressed, appearing only

---

[151] Vernant 1988a:226.

[152] Vernant 1988a:227.

[153] Among the specialists in the study of classical myth, it is unanimously accepted that every retelling of a traditional narrative is a new version of the story; for details on this scholarship, see Karakantza 2004:32–33, 201–205.

in the scarring of the baby as an unmistakable sign of identity. On the other hand, abuse of power *is*, indeed, one of the salient characteristics of a historical tyrant, and it can take many forms. Does this *necessarily* entail killing of kin, incest, and confusion of generations? Or if we follow the reverse order: does the killing of kinfolk, incest, and confusion of generations in *Oedipus Tyrannus* *necessarily* point to the person of the historical (or else political) tyrant, as the Greeks understood it?

In response to the above, I will adduce some simple facts frequently overlooked when identifying the tyrannical characteristics of Oedipus.[154] The extreme endogamy and the killing of his father, were not *intended* by Oedipus; in reality, he did everything he could to avoid both. We normally use this simple remark to dispute the psychoanalytic interpretation of the Oedipus story, but we forget it when referring to the various abuses of power or transgressions of the tyrant. Moreover, the abuse of ritual—again characteristic of historical tyrants—is a permanent trait of the whole of Attic tragedy, *not* exclusively of *Oedipus Tyrannus*. And the suspicion of conspiracy that we detect in Oedipus' behavior makes us lose sight of the other fact, pervasive throughout the play, that Oedipus is considered a good and just ruler, beloved and esteemed by his people; they address him with respect (not fear) and at times even tenderly (as he does them); they support him and feel pity for him, until the very end of the play (1199–1202, 1321–1322).

Another issue refers to the underlying emphasis in the analysis on the *pharmakos* interpretation of the narrative, which could be seen as clashing with the political or economic dimension of the retelling of the story. The fall of the tyrant, stumbling along in his own unbalanced fashion, with which Vernant concludes his analysis, points to the idea of the *pharmakos*, the indelibly polluted individual, who is expelled from his polis, bearing the collective *miasma* of his citizens. Vernant himself, in another, equally renowned essay titled "Ambiguity and Reversal: On the Enigmatic Structure of *Oedipus Rex*,"[155] suggests that Oedipus embodies the two ends of the two polar extremes: the sacred king and the polluted *pharmakos*. Of course, this line of thought points to a long line of thinkers, starting with James Frazer and his sacred king, who is dethroned every

---

[154] In 2002 Lowell Edmunds in his paper titled "Oedipus as Tyrant" identifies several of the characteristics we have mentioned earlier in the paper with Athenian and panhellenic ideology about the tyrant and his regime. However, there are extra or heterogeneous ingredients in the tyranny of Oedipus that differentiate it from the expected parabola of the regime: his intelligence, the plague, and the curse. As for the fall of the tyrant, this is "oddly inconclusive" (97).

[155] Vernant 1988b:113–140. Observe the following formulation: "It is this axis on which the divine king occupies the highest point and the *pharmakos* the lowest that governs the whole series of reversals that affect the figure of Oedipus and turn the hero into a 'paradigm' of ambiguous, tragic man" (125).

year only to be reinstated to his position to bring renewed vigor and fertility to the people and the land. This model is very relevant to the opening scene of *Oedipus Tyrannus*, with the land lying desolate and barren, the animals dying, and the women of the city bearing stillborn offspring. What is described in the opening of the play is a pervasive sterility, embodying the nightmare beset-ting any primitive society unable to control the means of reproduction (of the plants, animals, and humans). Death in this context signifies the total physical demise of human society.[156] Frazer's sacred king is echoed in the *eniautos daimon* (the god who dies and is reborn annually) of Jane Harrison and the Cambridge Ritualists.[157] But most importantly for our case, the sacred king who is degraded, humiliated, and expelled (in order to symbolically re-acquire his vigor again and with it to reinvigorate the community) is beautifully formulated in René Girard's interpretation of Oedipus (in his classic book *La Violence et le Sacré*), as being the epitome of *pharmakos*. From the zenith of kingship, beloved and respected by the Thebans, Oedipus plunges to the other end of the spectrum, for he is not simply the scapegoat of Thebes attracting and removing the pollution from the society; he is himself the source of the pollution.[158] The fusion of the extremes of this polarity in the story of Oedipus is absolute. But if we take this interpretative path, then the *tyrannus* cannot be accused of abuse of power, but rather praised as a benefactor to his community in cleansing it.

Bernard Knox historicizes the figure of the tyrant in his *Oedipus at Thebes*, where he suggests that Oedipus stands primarily for a hegemonic Athens, a polis that is democratic for its citizens but tyrannical to the dependant poleis; so Athens becomes a *polis tyrannus* (and Oedipus instantiates this polis):

> The individual *tyrannus* had receded into the past to become a bitter memory, but he had been succeeded by the *polis tyrannus*, Athens, which had the resources and the skill, as it undoubtedly had the ambi-tion, to become supreme master of the Greek world. In these circum-stances, and the climate of feeling which they produced, the title which Sophocles has so repeatedly conferred on his hero served to provide not a historical framework, nor even a moral criterion, but a

---

[156] This is a symbolic plague, *not* a mirroring of the plague of the Peloponnesian War as is often suggested. Of course, the historical plague, as was vividly described by Thucydides and expe-rienced by Sophocles himself, could provide imagery that could be grist to the playwright's mill (provided, of course, that the staging of the play post-dates the outbreak of the plague in Athens). And again, the imagery does not relate so much to the physical symptoms (which were very diverse), but rather to the bleak picture of widespread death and the general disruption of civic life.

[157] Karakantza 2004:79–84.

[158] On René Girard, see Karakantza 2004:103–105; Girard 1972:143–144.

vital contemporary reference which enabled him to appeal directly to the hopes and fears of his audience not only as individuals but also as Athenians. ... Oedipus's peculiar *tyrannis* is a reference to Athens itself ... .[159]

Oedipus, Knox claims, does not present the most egregious features of the characteristics of the tyrant in his person: "he does not defy ancestral laws, outrage women, or put men to death without trial. He does not plunder his subjects, distrust the good and delight in the bad, or live in fear of his people."[160] Knox proceeds to elicit affinities between Oedipus and Pericles, the character of the Athenians, and their polis, as drawn by Thucydides. The affinities with Pericles—the "first" citizen, but in reality the πρώτου ἀνδρὸς ἀρχή—are further corroborated by the "hereditary curse on his family through the sacrilegious murder of Cylon by his ancestors."[161] What is more interesting, though, are the many parallels drawn between Oedipus and the collective character of the Athenians, as shown mainly in the "Funeral Oration" and the Corinthian speech at the Congress of the Peloponnesian allies in Thucydides' history. Oedipus' virtues and defects resemble those of the Athenians: magnificent vigor, faith in action, courage, speed of decision and action, combined with careful reflection, intelligence, self confidence, adaptability and versatility, devotion to the city; on the debit side, one can note the suspicion of a political conspiracy against him and his anger.[162] In all cases Knox draws a parallel from the contemporary action or decision-making of the Athenian policies during the Peloponnesian War.

Knox' scholarship and that of his contemporaries draws one-to-one correspondences between contemporary historical events and the work of Sophocles, without questioning the methodology dedicated to seeing literary works as a mirror in which contemporary reality is reflected. But, as Pierre Vidal-Naquet has elegantly shown, this mirror is "broken" (*le miroir est brisé*) and the reflection of reality is refracted, through the countless fragments of the mirror, into a multitude of images that are often not even recognizable as corresponding to historical persons and events. What are reflected in the fragments of the mirror are the various intermingled codes and structures of social and political reality: spatial, temporal, social, financial, gendered, and age-ranked categories.[163] To limit the work of an artist, such as Sophocles in *Oedipus Tyrannus*, to a mere holding–the-mirror function is to blatantly ignore the function of tragic

---

[159] Knox 1957:61.
[160] Knox 1957:59–60.
[161] Knox 1957:63.
[162] Knox 1957:67–77.
[163] Vidal-Naquet 2003:46.

art and of any art in general. The correspondence between historical reality and the tragic play is subtle and sophisticated, referencing codes of thought and behavior, structures of cultural assumption, collective concepts of the self and of identity; in any work of art (tragedy being a prime example), we see reversals and distortions, subversions and reconfigurations, of the socio-political reality of its time. Greek tragedy, in its very essence, is itself a liminal passage,[164] and it studies the destruction of *any* confining limits.

We have seen thus far the lame tyrant, the king and the *pharmakos*, the man of money, a reflection of the historical tyrant of the hegemonic Athens. In another, wide cycle of interpretations, Oedipus veers towards tyranny: that is to say, to deviancy and excess, through intellectual arrogance and his capacity for philosophical reflections.

Jean-Joseph Goux claims that Oedipus, by solving the enigma of the Sphinx, breaks away from the ritualistic world of cyclic repetition to initiate a new process, one of reason; eradicating the Sphinx "marks the entrance into the world of linearity, progress, and knowledge."[165] However, a prerequisite for performing this intellectual feat is the prior elimination of paternal authority. The removal of the father ensures the autonomy of the son, thus giving birth to philosophy, paving the path for "the beginning of the formation of the philo-sophical thought."[166] The son, freed from domination by any tutelage, proceeds to an individualistic search for the truth (time and again, Oedipus reassures us that he himself understood and solved the riddle of the Sphinx without the help of any external authority) that is analogous to Socrates' conduct in philosophy: autodidactic, accountable only to his inner voice, his *daimon*. Socrates finds the truth "by himself and in himself."[167] For Oedipus, precisely as for Socrates, "no father, no master, no hierophant taught him a thing."[168] This process marks, in a sense, "a developmental stage" in the history of philosophy,[169] which is placed "at the moment of deprojection that brings back to the subject what had first been attributed to external reality or excepted from the accomplishment of rites."[170] However, there is always the danger of excess, even in philosophical thinking, or overweening confidence in one's own intellectual powers. Oedipus has precisely that, as well as having inherent in his mythology the defining characteristics of a

---

[164] Vidal-Naquet 2003:46.

[165] Taxidou argues that eradicating the Sphinx "signifies the end of ritual repetition" (2004:49).

[166] Goux 1993:141.

[167] Goux 1993:142.

[168] Hegel, as quoted by Goux (1993:142), records another exception to the Athenian rule for Socrates: his non-initiation into the Eleusinian Mysteries.

[169] Taxidou 2004:45.

[170] Goux 1993:143. "Deprojection" is the reverse process of a projection in which the original figure is reproduced.

tyrant: excess in "frenetic impulses" (his anger and murder) and giving free rein to illegitimate pleasures (sleeping with the mother).[171] He thus moves from the Platonic philosopher-king to the perverse tyrant, who succumbs to his impulses and desires; "the perverse tyrant is an Oedipus, but a willful Oedipus."[172] In the person of Oedipus, the "enlightened tyrant" (with his confidence in human reason) is fused with the "perverse tyrant" (with his impulses and desires); what could have been the two opposite poles of an antithesis, becomes a dangerous synthesis in tragedy; and this is our Oedipus.

Interestingly, a special type of human knowledge (an Oedipus-who-knew-too-much) in conjunction with Oedipus as tyrant is the focus of Michel Foucault's interpretation of Oedipus, in a work that has been largely ignored by classicists.[173] Foucault's reading of Oedipus is in the second of the four Brazilian lectures he gave at the Pontificia Universidade Catolica in Rio de Janeiro in 1974 on "Truth and Juridical Forms," which are in a sense a "variant working draft for the book *Surveiller et Punir: Naissance de la Prison (Discipline and Punish: the Birth of the Prison)* published in France a year later."[174] The perspective of Foucault's approach to Sophocles' *Oedipus Tyrannus* is the special connection between power and knowledge within his attempt to rework the theory of the subject, subjectivity, and domains of knowledge. Contrary to theories based on economic/Marxist postulates about the human subject or on perspectives that view the human subject as pre-formed by economic, social, and political conditions, Foucault radically questions the position of the subject and his relative connection with truth. He claims, and sets out to prove, in the course of these lectures:

> how social practices may engender domains of knowledge that not only bring new objects, new concepts, and new techniques to light, but also give rise to totally new forms of subjects and subjects of knowledge.

---

[171] Goux 1993:148.

[172] Ibid.

[173] Foucault 2000:31–89, "Truth and Juridical Forms." I am deeply indebted to Miriam Leonard for bringing this lecture of Foucault's to my attention through her book *Athens in Paris* (2005). Her assessment on this "forgotten" reading of Oedipus is as follows (2005:71): "It is not only integrally part of Foucault's intellectual biography, it also reveals a fascinating moment in the encounter between 'French theory' and post-war French Hellenism. From its sustained dialogue with the work of Vernant, to its re-evaluation of the anti-psychoanalytic project of Deleuze and Guattari's *Anti-Oedipe*, [*La Vérité et les Formes Juridiques*] charts a period in French intellectual history which, despite its rooting in a dialogue with antiquity, has largely been ignored by classicists."

[174] James D. Faubion in his Introduction to Foucault 2000:3.xii; see also Leonard 2005:73. This period of intellectual activity coincides with Foucault's intense activity as a political militant; in 1971 he co-founded (with Pierre Vidal-Naquet and Jean-Marie Domenach) the Groupe d'Information sur les Prisons (GIP) in his attempt to break the penal system open to criticism and reform.

[For] the subject of knowledge itself has a history; the relation of the subject to the object; or, more clearly, truth itself has a history.[175]

In this series of lectures, the social practices, which Foucault saw as engendering a new type of subject and knowledge, were control and supervision [*surveillance*], which of course fall into his wider engagement with the penal system as a mechanism for turning petty criminals into hardened delinquents, resulting in his great work *Surveiller et Punir* in 1975. The notions of individuality, normality, and deviation are all politically constructed concepts, enforced by social practices that produce domains of knowledge and types of individuals, "and consequently, relations between man and truth."[176] Since in western philosophy the subject *is* the core of all knowledge, Foucault undermines the very core of this intellectual edifice. *His* subject, and consequently *his* knowledge, is not a given, even if influenced by particular conditions at any given place and time, but it is "established and reestablished by history."[177]

Foucault sets his analysis of *Oedipus Tyrannus* within this framework of reconsidering subjectivity and the social practices that engender it: first, the play itself introduces a new method of criminal investigation to attain the truth, and, second, there is a special connection between power and knowledge exemplified in the person of the king. For reasons that will be clarified shortly, *Oedipus Tyrannus* marks a curious episode in the history of knowledge and the emergence of inquiry in Greek thought.[178]

I quote the very words of Foucault in the programmatic statement of his analysis of Oedipus:

> I want to show how the tragedy of Oedipus, the one we can read in Sophocles ... is representative and in a sense the founding instance of a definite type of relation between power and knowledge [*savoir*], between political power and knowledge [*connaissance*], from which our civilization is not yet emancipated. It seems to me that there really is an Oedipus complex in our civilization. But it does not involve our unconscious and our desire, nor the relations between desire and the unconscious. If there is an Oedipus complex, it operates not at the individual level but at the collective level; not in connection with desire and the

---

[175] 2000:2.

[176] Foucault 2000:4; and see, too: "There cannot be particular types of subjects of knowledge, orders of truth, or domains of knowledge, except on the basis of political conditions that are the very ground on which the subject, the domains of knowledge, and the relations with truth are formed" (15).

[177] Foucault 2000:3.

[178] Foucault 2000:5.

unconscious but in connection with power and knowledge. That is the 'complex' I want to analyze.[179]

So, it is the power relations instantiated in the manipulation of knowledge in the first criminal investigation ever recorded in the West and the types of subjectivity that this manipulation engenders that Foucault scrutinizes. The Foucauldian Oedipus complex speaks about power relations, not our individual unconscious. As Foucault claims:

> if I were asked what I do and what others do better, I would say that we don't study structures; indulging in wordplay, I would say that we study *dynasties*. Playing on the Greek words *dunamis dunasteia*, I would say that we try to bring to light what has remained until now the most hidden, the most occulted, the most deeply invested experience in the history of our culture—power relations.[180]

Foucault then proceeds to lay bare the mechanism of establishing the truth in this investigation, which moves along by the rule of the "halves." The story of the killer of Laius, which is also the story of the exposed infant Oedipus, is broken into two, and then, in turn, each fragment is further broken into two halves, and so on. Only the god possesses the whole truth, but this is presented in the form of the future.[181] The fragmented parts are rejoined together ("all these fragments parceled out among different hands"), and it takes the meeting between the god and his seer, Jocasta and Oedipus, and the Corinthian and Theban servants "for all these halves, and the halves of halves to match up, align themselves, and fit together to form the whole pattern of the story."[182] The broken and rejoined parts represent the technique of *symbolon* (the Greek word for "symbol"),[183] which is the bearer of power—religious and political. At a practical level, the holder of a secret or of power breaks a ceramic and keeps the one half, while entrusting the other to an individual who would share and validate the truth. The *symbolon* becomes an instrument of power, and its overall configuration, when the separate fragments yield the unique object, is the manifest form of power. The Oedipus story is the fragmenting (and reassembling) of that token. In the handling of the story by Sophocles, the first halves of the story

---

[179] Foucault 2000:17.

[180] Ibid.

[181] Foucault 2000:20.

[182] Foucault 2000:22.

[183] Indeed, Oedipus declares himself unable to set out on the path of investigation for lack of a *symbolon*, a token that can be used to initiate it (οὐ γὰρ ἂν μακρὰν / ἴχνευον αὐτός, μὴ οὐκ ἔχων τι σύμβολον, 220–221).

are held by the god and the prophet, the religious (or quasi-magical) world; the next series by Jocasta and Oedipus, the royalty; and the final, and decisive for the enunciation of the truth, by the slaves. The prescriptive type of the divine discourse is taken up by the retrospective, by evidence of the mortal world. Thus this tragedy "establishes a symbolic world in which the memory and the discourse of men are like an empirical margin around the great prophecy of the gods."[184]

Returning to the *symbolon* mechanism of the progress of truth, Foucault writes, "Oedipus is not the one who did not know, but, rather, the one who knew too much."[185] He also possesses a certain type of power, which, conjoined with the special type of knowledge, produces the figure of the tyrant of sixth- and fifth-century Greece. Throughout the play, Foucault claims, Oedipus' problem is about his power, and not about his innocence; he dreads the moment he might fall from power. "Don't try to hold on to your power" (πάντα μὴ βούλου κρατεῖν, 1522) is the final exhortation of Creon to the fallen Oedipus, who even at the last minute tries to manipulate his punishment. The special power of Oedipus recalls the pattern and power of the historical tyrants: extreme alternations of fortune in their personal history, as well as a full identification with the power of the city (in the heated debate between Creon and Oedipus in the second episode, Creon indignantly protests, claiming that "I belong to this city as well, it's not yours alone," 630)[186] and replacement of the city's laws "with his whims and his orders" (when Creon condemns his decision to banish as unjust, Oedipus answers: "No matter if it's just or not, it will have to be obeyed all the same").[187]

The interesting point that Foucault raises in the context of this analysis is that the tyrant is the person who, not only seized power in a certain (not institutionalized) manner, but also possessed a particular knowledge, superior to others, and was solitary. The case of Oedipus is a prime example: he succeeds in solving the riddle with his own intellectual powers aided by neither the gods nor mortals. His special knowledge is characterized by the Greek words *euriskein*, *eureka* ("I have found"):

---

[184] Foucault 2000:24.

[185] Ibid.

[186] Translation as found in the text of Foucault (2000:28). The entire passage (*Oedipus Tyrannus* 628–630) is rendered by the philosopher as follows: "You're wrong; you identify with this city where you were not born, you imagine that you belong to this city and that it belongs to you; I belong to this city as well, it's not yours alone." The rendering is more explanatory of the thesis of Foucault than a literal translation. The Greek runs as follows: ΚΡ.: εἰ δὲ ξυνίης μηδέν; ΟΙ.: ἀρκτέον γ᾽ ὅμως. /ΚΡ.: οὗτοι κακῶς γ᾽ ἄρχοντος. ΟΙ.: ὦ πόλις, πόλις. / ΚΡ.: κἀμοὶ πόλεως μέτεστιν, οὐχὶ σοὶ μόνῳ (Cr: "But if you understand nothing?" Oed: "Nonetheless, I have to rule." / Cr: "Not if you rule badly!" Oed: "Think of the city, the city!" / Cr: "But I too have a share in the city, not you alone.")

[187] Foucault 2008:28.

Finding is something done by oneself. Finding is also what one does when one opens one's eyes. And Oedipus is the one who says repeatedly: "I asked questions, and since no one was able to inform me, I opened my eyes and my ears, and I saw." The verb *oida*, which means at the same time 'to know' and 'to see,' is frequently employed by Oedipus. *Oidipous* is the one who is capable of that activity of knowing and seeing. He is the man of seeing, the man of gaze, and he will be that to the end.[188]

This special knowledge is the "autocratic knowledge of the tyrant who can govern the city through his own abilities."[189] This is the special relation between power-and-knowledge, and knowledge-and-power that Foucault detects in the story of Oedipus: tyrannical power combined with solitary knowledge. "With his tyrannical power, Oedipus could do too much; with his solitary knowledge, he knew too much."[190] While establishing "the junction between the prophecy of the gods and the memory of men," he is also "the man of excess, the man who has too much of everything—in his power, his knowledge, his family, his sexuality. Oedipus, the double man, was excessive with regard to the symbolic transparency of what the shepherds knew and what the gods had said."[191] In the end, and this is the important "lesson" of the Sophoclean Oedipus, the form of the political power he stands for, "privileged and exclusive,"[192] is fundamentally devalorized, and thus contributing to creating the "great myth" of the West, "according to which truth never belongs to political power."[193] But this great myth needs to be demolished, for "behind all knowledge [*savoir*], behind all attainment of knowledge [*connaissance*], what is involved is a struggle for power."[194] In the myth of Oedipus, therefore, one can detect forms of power implemented by forms of knowledge; or to put it slightly differently, knowledge possessed by men in power is used to further their own whims and predilections, to bypass other forms of collective power. Oedipus in this respect is a tyrant; the democratic body and his empirical knowledge demolish the privileged position of power and knowledge exemplified in Oedipus' person. The people gain

---

[188] Foucault 2000:29.
[189] Ibid.
[190] Foucault 2000:30.
[191] Ibid.
[192] Ibid.
[193] Foucault 2000:32; both in Sophocles' *Oedipus Tyrannus* and Plato's *Republic*.
[194] Ibid.

"the right to judge, the right to tell the truth, to set the truth against their own masters, to judge those who govern them."[195]

Returning to the original framework of Foucault's inquiry into "how social practices may engender domains of knowledge ... that give rise to totally new forms of subjects and subjects of knowledge,"[196] one can confidently assume, after his analysis, that the new type of knowledge instigated by socially inferior persons destroys the existing political structures of the privileged manipulation of knowledge and power; in the penal system of classical Athens, new forms of attaining the truth are inaugurated and implemented. The autocratic, solitary knowledge of the tyrant is no longer viable. Of course, a change in the ideology of the penal system reflects wider ideological changes in society; the profound democratic system is based, as we have seen in earlier chapters,[197] on the transfer of knowledge of the local to the master networks of power: the experience of managing the political affairs on the level of the *dêmoi* is transferred onto the master network for managing the central system of democratic Athens. One of the major components of this transformation is the collection of individual domains of knowledge, and its consequent diffusion from individual to collective structures. The sophisticated design of the master network could not have been implemented without the new type of knowledge, neither autocratic nor privileged nor exclusive. Neither could it have been implemented without a new type of subject, or the forms of subjectivity whose emergence we have witnessed in the process of a "new creation" in the Castoriadian vein at the turn of fifth-century Athens.

---

[195] Foucault 2000:33. I do not share Leonard's reservations about Foucault not mentioning the structures of democratic Athens and the ideology and rhetoric of the polis; and consequently, making his Oedipus "as historically indeterminate as his Freudian counterpart" (2005:85). In addition, Leonard charges that in his analysis of Oedipus as tyrant, contrary to the Vernant's tyrant who is well rooted in the historical reality of ancient Athens, Foucault has in mind the analyst "who works at the service of our 'carceral society'" (2005:88), thus aligning himself with the anti-Oedipus of Deleuze and Guattari, who point at analysts as a bourgeois/capitalistic mechanism to control and "discipline" the individual. However, as I have been arguing in these pages, Foucault does not mention explicitly (or in terminology familiar among Hellenists) the polis and its ideology; *but*, he describes succinctly in his analysis the very transition from the autocratic, solitary knowledge of the tyrant (who consequently controls and governs using this knowledge), to the knowledge acquired by experience of members of "lower" classes who gain the right to judge and to tell the truth. This is a huge difference between the previous autocratic tyrannical rule and one that is easily recognized as democratic. Foucault's tyrant might not be as well rooted in the Greek polis as Vernant's, but he is well rooted in what the philosopher calls the power relations that change exactly at that very moment that the new concept of Athens and Athenians is consolidated through the reforms and institutionalized actions that brought about the Athenian radical democracy.

[196] Foucault 2000:2.

[197] Chapters 2 and 3.

My intention in this chapter has not been to produce a new theory on the notion of the tyrant in *Oedipus Tyrannus*. From my perspective, the individual characteristics adhering to one form or another of the figure of the tyrant offer complementary readings in the quest for identity. My personal assessment, however, is that alongside the influential "Lame Tyrant" of Vernant lies the Foucauldian political reading. It is very important for contemporary critical thinking about Hellenic culture to comprehend the philosopher's motto: "I do not study structures; instead, I study 'dynasties', the power relations of our culture"; and consequently, to reconceptualize our approach accordingly. Foucault rightly claims:

> The economic structures of our society are better known, more thoroughly inventoried, more clearly defined than the structures of political power. In this series of lectures I would like to show how the political relations have been established and deeply implanted in our culture, giving rise to a series of phenomena that can be explained only if they are related not to economic structures, to the economic relations of production, but to the power relations that permeate the whole fabric of our existence.[198]

If there is a tyrant in *Oedipus Tyrannus*, I am compelled to accept that this is the tyrant of Foucault. Even if not explicitly stated by the philosopher, or in the same terminology that I have been using throughout this book, the way that power relations are reconsidered and reconfigured in his reading reflects the paradigmatic moment of the creation of radical democracy, which I have been considering as a milestone for the new concept of Athens and the Athenians; the Sophoclean tragedy stands as the "broken" mirror in which this radical moment is reflected.

4.8 Questions with the Corinthian Messenger: The Baby with the Pierced Feet

Simon Goldhill remarks that the messenger enters the stage as an "instant answer"[199] to the prayer of Jocasta, who at the outset of the third episode prays for a λύσιν εὐαγῆ (921), a "solution that would shake off the pollution"[200] and

---

[198] Foucault 2000:17.

[199] Goldhill 2012:14.

[200] I suggest this translation if we focus on the negative meaning of the second component ἄγος (see the discussion later this chapter). There is a general agreement among critics on translating the passage: Jebb translates as "riddance from uncleanness," Goldhill (2012:13) "holy release" and

simultaneously "release" the fear-fraught mind of Oedipus. He also claims that the pervasive word *lusis*, and its cognate vocabulary, is "a marked term, a promise of release," and that it "becomes a sign in Sophoclean theater for the failures of human control and, ultimately for the only release that is inevitable and sure, that of death."[201] The *lusis* of this very episode will be the death of Jocasta, but the overall *lusis* of the drama is more convoluted and painful than death.

Starting with Goldhill's thesis, we should bear in mind the double meaning implied in the word εὐαγῆ. If we focus on the negative meaning of the second component ἄγος—that is, the sense of pollution—then we can immediately think of the widespread plague in Thebes and of Oedipus himself as the source of this pollution. In this case, the adverb εὖ would point to the wish to turn the ἄγος into its opposite or to shake it off altogether. If, on the other hand, we understand ἄγος as an expiation, then the adverb εὖ intensifies its meaning, hence a notion of a "double" cleansing arises. Both meanings are embedded in Jocasta's use of the word, in the context of her (now) pious offerings and prayer to Apollo. This piety, however, stands on shaky foundations given her repudiation of the validity of oracles at the end of the preceding episode and the moral desolation of the following, equally famous second *stasimon* (863–910), with its bleak portrayal of a world devoid of divine oracles, divine justice, and human piety. As argued earlier, Jocasta's relationship with Apollo is seriously compromised. How could one evince pious reverence to the god, but reject his servants, bearers of his will to mortals? This piety is laced with skepticism, even renunciation of one of the most important channels of communication between the gods and mortals. *Oedipus Tyrannus* is not only about the breakdown in communication between Oedipus and his interlocutors; it is also about the rupture in Jocasta's communication with Apollo.[202]

Crucially, the messenger arrives as a surrogate of Apollo, not simply as the divine response to Jocasta's prayer. The wording used in the communication with him comprises the marked terms σημαίνω and σημεῖα, which are known descriptors of the ways of Apollo, who, in his oracles, rather than predicting, gives signs, σημαίνειν. In the dialogue that follows, the cognate words σημῆναι

"an undefiled solution," Lloyd-Jones "cleansing solution," Kitto "delivery and peace," Finglass "blessed release."

[201] Goldhill 2012:15; the telling title of the relevant chapter is "Undoing *Lusis* and the Analysis of Irony."

[202] Of course, as I argued in section 4.5, Jocasta's impiety is a side effect of her attempt to manipulate a precariously delicate psychological situation when Oedipus begins to be haunted by his worst fears, as the outpouring of terms denoting fear at the beginning of the third episode with the Corinthian messenger demonstrate.

and σημάντωρ γενοῦ (or σημήνας γενοῦ)[203] articulate the questions addressed by Jocasta and Oedipus to the messenger in exhorting him to deliver his message. "Tell me what you wish to say, indicating with signs," says Jocasta (ἀλλὰ φράζ' ὅτου / χρῄζων ἀφῖξαι χὤτι σημῆναι θέλων, 932–933), while Oedipus, some twenty lines later, repeats the question (957): "What are you saying stranger? You yourself be the indicator," (or, "be the informant of the signs of the event" (σημάντωρ γενοῦ);[204] or, if we accept the variant σημήνας γενοῦ, "stranger, tell me with signs." The periphrasis σημήνας γενοῦ is legitimate[205] and preferred by both Pearson and Lloyd-Jones and Wilson in their editions. I think, however, that the semiotic connotations in the σημάντωρ γενοῦ (preferred by Jebb, Dawe, and Finglass) from the Homeric usage are strong and exciting:[206] σημάντορες are the commanders of subdivisions of the army who give the signal to join battle, but, most importantly, to maintain the order of the formation: when they are absent, disorder, fear, and transgression hold sway (*Iliad* 15.325, *Odyssey* 19.314). Consequently, the absence of a σημάντωρ engenders fear, for the army or groups of people are left without guidance. When Apollo looked the Greeks full in face, in *Iliad* 15, they lost their nerve, as if they had become a herd of cattle or a flock of sheep, left without a σημάντωρ (*Iliad* 15.323–327):

οἱ δ' ὥς τ' ἠὲ βοῶν ἀγέλην ἢ πῶϋ μέγ' οἰῶν
θῆρε δύω κλονέωσι μελαίνης νυκτὸς ἀμολγῷ,
ἐλθόντ' ἐξαπίνης σημάντορος οὐ παρεόντος,
ὣς ἐφόβηθεν Ἀχαιοὶ ἀνάλκιδες· ἐν γὰρ Ἀπόλλων
ἧκε φόβον, Τρωσὶν δὲ καὶ Ἕκτορι κῦδος ὄπαζεν.

And as two wild beasts drive in confusion a herd of cattle or a great flock of sheep in the darkness of black night when they have come on them suddenly, and a herdsman [σημάντορος] is not by, so were the Achaeans driven in rout with no valor in them; for on them

---

[203] The first hand in L wrote σημήνας, a corrector has changed it to σημάντωρ. Jebb, Dawe, and Finglass prefer the σημάντωρ γενοῦ, while Pearson, Bollack, and Lloyd-Jones and Wilson the σημήνας γενοῦ; Kamerbeek also claims that σημάντωρ has to be rejected (ad 957).

[204] Finglass 2018 ad 957: "the grand nominal phrase σημάντωρ γενοῦ suits a message of high importance." He translates: "What are saying stranger? You yourself be the signifier to me."

[205] According to Dawe 2006 ad 957; for the counter-arguments, see Finglass 2018 ad 957.

[206] I wrote this part of my argument based on my preference for σημάντωρ γενοῦ rather than σημήνας γενοῦ, before Finglass's commentary on *Oedipus the King* was published. When I was able to consult it, I was happy to realize that we both agree on σημάντωρ γενοῦ. It is interesting to see the other route through which I have reached the same conclusion: semantics and Homeric tradition. This latter corroborates my firm belief that Homeric diction and ideology were well rooted in the minds of the poets and spectators of classical drama; both of the latter were in constant dialogue with the Homeric tradition.

Apollo had sent panic, and to the Trojans and Hector was he giving glory.[207]

A σημάντωρ signals, indicates, instills coherence, dispels fear, and maintains order. The exhortation to the messenger to become a σημάντωρ encompasses all these meanings so sought after by the troubled mind of Oedipus and the increasingly anxious mind of Jocasta. Both urge the messenger to deliver his message, but in reality they seek signs and guidance to clarify their dire situation. Initially, it is hard to understand why the royal couple resort to this wording, replete with cognates of σημαίνειν, until just before the end of the episode when Oedipus realizes that the various pieces of information given by the messenger are nothing other than signs to aid in discovering his origin (1058–1059):

> οὐκ ἂν γένοιτο τοῦθ', ὅπως ἐγὼ λαβὼν
> <u>σημεῖα</u> τοιαῦτ' οὐ φανῶ τοὐμὸν γένος.

> It cannot be that when I have obtained such *indications* [σημεῖα] I shall not bring to light my birth.

"For the time has come," Oedipus said to the members of the chorus a little earlier, "to learn who I am. So, please indicate to me [σημήναθ'[ε], 1050] whether you know the shepherd of whom the Corinthian messenger speaks."[208] It cannot be coincidental that in this episode the use of the verb σημαίνειν and its cognate σημεῖα converge, for it is in this episode that Jocasta attempts to re-establish communication with Apollo and Oedipus discovers the first indications of his origin. Apollo responds immediately by providing all the signs needed for Jocasta to understand clearly who Oedipus is. By the end of the episode she has killed herself, while the downfall of Oedipus is only minutes away. The λύσιν εὐαγῆ, the "solution to shake off pollution," for which Jocasta prayed, sustains its double meaning: beneficial for the community, while expunging entirely the sources of the pollution.

It has been said that "no play is more about language than the *OT*";[209] that it continually deconstructs the certainties created by the diction of the

---

[207] Trans. Murray/Wyatt.

[208] Free rendering of the lines 1047–1050: ΟΙ. ἔστιν τις ὑμῶν τῶν παρεστώτων πέλας / ὅστις κάτοιδε τὸν βοτῆρ' ὃν ἐννέπει, / εἴτ' οὖν ἐπ' ἀγρῶν εἴτε κἀνθάδ' εἰσιδών; / σημήναθ, ὡς ὁ καιρὸς ηὑρῆσθαι τάδε.

[209] Segal 1981b:151; see further Pucci 1988:131–154; Pucci 1991:10; Peradotto 1992:6; Calame 1996:31; lastly, Budelmann's *The Language of Sophocles* (2000) and Goldhill's *Sophocles and the Language of Tragedy* (2012) corroborate this fact.

protagonists. The λύσις εὐαγής is but one example. I would proceed further in suggesting that language in Sophocles "possesses a double power" (δύναμιν διπλῆν, 938). I transpose the meaning of this phrase, describing in this episode how the news about Polybus' death can bring both sadness and joy to the entire play. The literal "double power" of the language is exquisitely manifested in line 928 when the chorus signifies Jocasta as γυνὴ δὲ μήτηρ θ᾽ ἥδε τῶν κείνου τέκνων ("this lady is his wife and the mother of his children").[210] What if the actor delivering the line lingers for a while in the first two metrical feet, γυνὴ δὲ μήτηρ ἥδε, pausing purposefully *after* ἥδε and not after δὲ (which he probably did)? "*This is his wife and mother,*" the chorus is heard to say;[211] at the end of this episode, this is exactly what is going to be confirmed in the wake of a series of revelations, as we enter a new space of questions with the messenger breaking the news of Polybus' death.

"What have you said?" asks Jocasta, "is Oedipus' father dead?" (πῶς εἶπας; ἦ τέθνηκε <Πόλυβος>; 943). The news triggers such an outpouring of relief that for the next fifty lines Jocasta and Oedipus exult over their riddance from the fear of parricide that has burdened the life of Oedipus. The exultation is intertwined with an unshakable (so they think) proof of the invalidity of the oracles of Apollo and the signs conveyed by the birds (964–972):

> φεῦ φεῦ, τί δῆτ᾽ ἄν, ὦ γύναι, σκοποῖτό τις
> τὴν πυθόμαντιν ἑστίαν, ἢ τοὺς ἄνω
> κλάζοντας ὄρνεις, ὧν ὑφ᾽ ἡγητῶν ἐγὼ
> κτανεῖν ἔμελλον πατέρα τὸν ἐμόν; ὁ δὲ θανὼν
> κεύθει κάτω δὴ γῆς· ἐγὼ δ᾽ ὅδ᾽ ἐνθάδε
> ἄψαυστος ἔγχους, εἴ τι μὴ τὠμῷ πόθῳ
> κατέφθιθ᾽· οὕτω δ᾽ ἂν θανὼν εἴη 'ξ ἐμοῦ.
> τὰ δ᾽ οὖν παρόντα συλλαβὼν θεσπίσματα
> κεῖται παρ᾽ Ἅιδῃ Πόλυβος ἄξι᾽ οὐδενός.

> Ah, ah, lady, why should one look to the prophetic hearth of Pytho, or to the birds that shriek above us, according to whose message I was to kill my father? But he is dead, and lies deep below the earth; and I am here, not having touched the weapon, unless he died from missing me; in that way I might have caused his death. But still Polybus lies in Hades, and with him have gone the oracles that were with us, now worth nothing.

---

[210] Goldhill 2012:14.

[211] Also Finglass (2018 ad 927–928): "The word order of 928 allows the sense 'this woman is his wife and mother' until the final three words clarify the significance of the 'mother'."

In lieu of insolence in the rejection of oracles, I read an immense feeling of relief experienced by someone who has just been liberated from the fetters of fear. Jocasta described at the beginning of the episode the state of Oedipus' mind, convulsed with every kind of grief (λύπαισι παντοίαισιν, 915), and how he is carried away by whoever incites fear by what he says (εἰ φόβους λέγει, 917). In cases such as this, a person becomes disoriented: first, he is no longer subject to rational thought: ... οὐδ' ὁποῖ' ἀνὴρ / ἔννους τὰ καινὰ τοῖς πάλαι τεκμαίρεται, ("... and he is not interpreting new happenings by means of earlier ones like a rational man," 915–916); and, second, he can seriously undermine the system within which he lives and in which he formerly wholeheartedly believed. Oedipus agrees with Jocasta in her questioning (and rejection) of the oracles (973–974):

> ΙΟ. οὔκουν ἐγώ σοι ταῦτα προὔλεγον πάλαι;
> ΟΙΔ. ηὔδας· ἐγὼ δὲ τῷ φόβῳ παρηγόμην.

> J.: Did I not foretell this to you long ago? O.: You told me but I was led along by fear.

Oedipus is sincere in his desire to see the oracles refuted, but he is neither impious nor insolent, for he has proven his loyalty to the system from the outset of the play; he is merely a person transfixed by fear. With the father dead, the fear for the mother remains; the diction of the passage is replete with words related to fear for both parricide and incest (ὀκνεῖν, 976, 986; φοβοῖτ', 977; φοβοῦ, 980; φόβος, 988; ἐκφοβεῖσθ', 989; φόβον, 991; ὀκνῶν, 1000; φόβου, 1002; ταρβῶν, 1011; φοβεῖ, 1013; τρέμων, 1014). The Corinthian messenger has come to release him from his fears (1002–1003):

> τί δῆτ' ἐγὼ οὐχὶ τοῦδε τοῦ <u>φόβου</u> σ', ἄναξ,
> ἐπείπερ εὔνους ἦλθον, <u>ἐξελυσάμην</u>;

> Why, since I have come in friendship, do I not *release you* [ἐξελυσάμην] from this *fear* [φόβου], my lord?

Now, these two lines combine everything that matters now in *Oedipus Tyrannus*, and they seem to be the direct answer to the λύσιν εὐαγῆ of the prayer of Jocasta. There is often a moment of high optimism in the Sophoclean plays when a happy resolution seems within reach; the incipient euphoria it brings only briefly precedes the unfolding of the plot leading to the catastrophic descent into the inevitability of destruction and death. Therefore, the ἐξελυσάμην of the messenger in line 1003, instead of releasing Oedipus from the fetters of fear, becomes ironically a textual sign to initiate the crucial cycle of questions that follow, leading to the gradual reconstruction of Oedipus' identity. In this episode, Jocasta understands; but for Oedipus a fourth and final cycle of questions is needed (with Laius' servant) to complete the puzzle of his self.

The barrage of questions triggered by the announcement of the death of the foster father runs as follows:

> "What are you saying? Was not Polybus my father?" (πῶς εἶπας; οὐ
>   γὰρ Πόλυβος ἐξέφυσέ με; 1017).
> "But why did he call me his son?" (ἀλλ ἀντὶ τοῦ δὴ παῖδά μ'
>   ὠνομάζετο; 1021).
> "Did you buy me or find me before you gave me to him?" (σὺ δ'
>   ἐμπολήσας, ἢ τυχών μ' αὐτῷ δίδως; 1025).
> "Why were you travelling in those regions <in Cithaeron>?"
>   (ὡδοιπόρεις δὲ πρὸς τί τούσδε τοὺς τόπους; 1027).
> "So you were a shepherd, wandering about in your servitude?"
>   (ποιμὴν γὰρ ἦσθα κἀπὶ θητείᾳ πλάνης; 1029).
> "<You said you saved me.> What trouble was I suffering from when
>   you took me in your arms?" (τί δ' ἄλγος ἴσχοντ' ἐν χεροῖν με
>   λαμβάνεις; 1031).

The investigation into Oedipus' suffering (ἄλγος) leads to the only concrete feature of identity that is recognizable and unmistakable: "your ankles would bear witness to it" (ποδῶν ἂν ἄρθρα μαρτυρήσειεν τὰ σά, 1032), replies the messenger; "Ah, why do you speak of that ancient grief?" (οἴμοι, τί τοῦτ' ἀρχαῖον ἐννέπεις κακόν; 1033), exclaims Oedipus. "When I released you, your ankles had been pierced" (λύω σ' ἔχοντα διατόρους ποδοῖν ἀκμάς, 1034). "Yes, it was a dreadful brand of shame that I had from my cradle" (δεινόν γ' ὄνειδος σπαργάνων ἀνειλόμην, 1035). "So that it was from that occurrence [τύχης] that you got the name you bear" (ὥστ ὠνομάσθης ἐκ τύχης ταύτης ὃς εἶ, 1036).

With these last sentences, the identity bound up with Oedipus' name has been established: he is the baby whose ankles were pierced at birth. As argued earlier,[212] this cruel and seemingly unjustifiable act of physical branding is an indelible, unignorable, and irrefutable way to establish one of the traits of his identity; if everything else becomes unrecognizable, the scarring of the feet bears witness to the origin of the baby. Furthermore, the allusion in his name to Oedipus' lameness links him with his forbears, Laius and Labdacus, in the renowned analysis of Lévi-Strauss, who sees the patrilineal descent in

---

[212] See section 4.1, pp. 46–52.

terms of a corporeal deficiency. It seems that Laius unwittingly, and ironically, fitted Oedipus, with his swollen feet, seamlessly into his family tree. Moreover, piercing the feet as an act of naming the baby is a gross perversion of the ritual performed in all individual *oikoi* to include the baby in the family a few days after birth. If, instead of inclusion, the father attempts to ensure the exclusion and destruction of the child, the child's later capacity of acting properly as a citizen is crippled forever. Lastly, we should not forget that branding someone with cuts or burns on the body has been widespread since antiquity to indicate a social outcast. A person is stigmatized (in the current meaning of the term) to function as a warning or signal of his propensity to bring evil. The stigma gives the person a "spoiled identity" that accompanies him forever. The messenger indicated (σημαίνειν) the signs of this identity he was aware of, but in reality Oedipus' pierced feet already signified a social outcast; this was the dreadful shame (δεινὸν ὄνειδος) that he carried from birth.

"Ah, why do you speak of this ancient evil [ἀρχαῖον κακόν]?" asks Oedipus in line 1033. Ἀρχαῖον is not a puzzling term; it is a common word found in abundance in all extant classical literature with unambiguous meaning. However, I feel that it needs further clarification, as my discussion on the ἀρχαίου θηρός, characterizing Nessus in *Trachiniae* (555–556), will show.[213] There, the ἀρχαίου causes some puzzlement: why is Nessus ἀρχαῖος, since it belongs to the narrative of the life of Deinaeira, who is surely not ancient? Malcolm Davies goes as far as correcting the ἀρχαίου to ἀγρίου, suggesting that ἀρχαίου is a copyist's error made under the influence of the previous παλαιόν. He thinks that ἀγρίου is a plausible restoration of the meaning.[214]

However, the ἀρχαίου is probably what Sophocles intended, for the playwright "has an uncanny ability to suggest the horror lurking in mundane language."[215] In my opinion, not only do plentiful grounds exist to support ἀρχαίου, but it also imbues the passage with a dark, sinister quality. Nessus, emerges from the remote past, as an ἀρχαῖος θήρ; not just from Deianeira's past, following the tendency in modern commentaries and translations when explaining the ἀρχαίου / θηρός,[216] but from the Stygian depths of mythical narratives from the primitive past. Nessus is a centaur living on the outskirts

---

[213] In a forthcoming (b) publication "Beauty and the Beast: A Reading of Sophocles' *Trachiniae*."

[214] Davies 1999 ad 555–556.

[215] Goldhill 2012:26.

[216] Jebb ad 555: "ἀρχαίου because he lived long ago; the emphasis on the past is natural in one who is looking back sadly to the days of her youth, and speaking to young maidens for whom Nessus is only a legendary name." Easterling 1982 ad loc: "Nessus is described as ἀρχαῖος because to D's audience he is a figure of the past." Lloyd-Jones translates: "I had an ancient gift from a monster long ago" transposing the meaning of ἀρχαίου to the gift and that of παλαιοῦ to Nessus. Jebb's translation is closer to the original text: "I had a gift, given to me long ago by a monster of olden time ... ."

of cultured life, carrying travelers across the ravaging waters of the torrent Evenus, "one of the fiercest and most treacherous torrents in Greece,"[217] using his body as the means of transportation. Thus, the "ancient" quality of the beast is a textual sign of the uncivilized, primitive, and violent character inherent in Nessus' actions. Likewise, in Oedipus' story the evil is ancient because, first, it is lost in the depths of his personal history; but more significantly, it is ἀρχαῖον because it refers to the primal act of his birth that entails violence and rejection.

Neither the birth, nor the scars can be understood by Oedipus; it all seems cruel and unjustified. Thus his next question is "who did that to me? My mother or my father?" (ὦ πρὸς θεῶν, πρὸς μητρὸς ἢ πατρός; φράσον, 1037). The answer contains yet another pun on the name of Oedipus (1038): οὐκ οἶδ'· ὁ δοὺς δὲ ταῦτ' ἐμοῦ λῷον φρονεῖ ("I do not know; the man who gave you to me knows it all better than I did"). And thus, with the participle ὁ δοὺς (which ironically here holds the position of the second component of the name Οἰδίπους) the servant of Laius is introduced, "suddenly and casually":[218] "then did you not find me, but received me from another man?" (ἦ γὰρ παρ' ἄλλου μ' ἔλαβες οὐδ' αὐτὸς τυχών; 1039). And then, a fusillade of questions follows:

> "Who was that man?" (τίς οὗτος; 1041).
> "<A servant of Laius?>. The same Laius, who was the king of this
> land?" (ἦ τοῦ τυράννου τῆσδε γῆς πάλαι ποτέ; 1043).
> "Is the shepherd still alive?" (ἦ κἄστ' ἔτι ζῶν οὗτος … ; 1045).
> "Is there one among you who are standing by who knows the shep-
> herd of whom he speaks?" (ἔστιν τις ὑμῶν τῶν παρεστώτων
> πέλας /ὅστις κάτοιδε τὸν βοτῆρ' ὃν ἐννέπει, 1047–1048).
> "Tell me, since it is time these things were found out!" (σημήναθ, ὡς
> ὁ καιρὸς ηὑρῆσθαι τάδε, 1050).

This last exhortation seals both Oedipus' determination to pursue his quest for his origin and his resolve to read the long forgotten signs of his birth. One more time Jocasta tries to protect him, urging him: "don't desire even to remember these words, spoken in vain as it were" (τὰ δὲ / ῥηθέντα βούλου μηδὲ μεμνῆσθαι μάτην, 1056–1057).[219]

Oedipus emphatically rejects this prospect (1058–1059):

> οὐκ ἂν γένοιτο τοῦθ', ὅπως ἐγὼ λαβὼν
> σημεῖα τοιαῦτ' οὐ φανῶ τοὐμὸν γένος.

---

[217] Jebb 1892 ad 559; also, "the older name of the river, Λυκόρμας, expressed the 'wolf-like' rush of the river" and "the name Nessos symbolizes the roar of the angry torrent" (ad 557f).

[218] Finglass 2018 ad 1038.

[219] Emendation and translation by Finglass 2018.

It cannot be that when I have obtained such *indications* (σημεῖα) I
shall not bring to light my birth.

Now is the moment to uncover "who I am" (1050). Jocasta despairingly tries to
dissuade him from the quest of his identity; however, since every quest is a quest
for meaning,[220] Oedipus can no longer prolong his life without discovering the
only question that is meaningful to him: "you will never persuade me not to find
out the whole truth" (οὐκ ἂν πιθοίμην μὴ οὐ τάδ' ἐκμαθεῖν σαφῶς, 1065). Not
uncovering the truth, not knowing who he is due to his acceptance of mistaken
advice, has hurt him for a long time (μ' ἀλγύνει πάλαι, 1067). Jocasta now knows
and wishes only one thing for Oedipus: "that you may never find out who you
are" (ὦ δύσποτμ', εἴθε μήποτε γνοίης ὅς εἶ, 1068).

The ironic misunderstanding of this scene by Oedipus is distilled in his
misapprehension of Jocasta's extreme chagrin:[221] "but she, for she has high
thoughts as a woman can, feels shame of my low birth"[222] (αὕτη δ' ἴσως, φρονεῖ
γὰρ ὡς γυνὴ μέγα, / τὴν δυσγένειαν τὴν ἐμὴν αἰσχύνεται, 1078–1079) muses
Oedipus aloud. Everything for him is now reduced to the question of his birth
and origin: "even if it is lowly, I desire to learn my origin" (τοὐμὸν δ' ἐγώ, / κεἰ
σμικρόν ἐστι, σπέρμ' ἰδεῖν βουλήσομαι, 1076–1077; literally: "I desire to learn the
seed I come from, however base").

Oedipus, at the end of this episode erupts into a euphoric, and blissfully
utopian, delineation of his genealogy—an ironic preamble to the euphoric
choral song that will follow. This genealogy consists of *Tyche* as the mother, and
the months as his relatives who raised him to greatness (1080–1085):

> ἐγὼ δ' ἐμαυτὸν παῖδα τῆς Τύχης νέμων
> τῆς εὖ διδούσης οὐκ ἀτιμασθήσομαι.
> τῆς γὰρ πέφυκα μητρός· οἱ δὲ συγγενεῖς
> μῆνές με μικρὸν καὶ μέγαν διώρισαν.
> τοιόσδε δ' ἐκφὺς οὐκ ἂν ἐξέλθοιμ' ἔτι
> ποτ' ἄλλος, ὥστε μὴ 'κμαθεῖν τοὐμὸν γένος.

> But I regard myself as child of the event that brought good fortune,
> and shall not be dishonored. *She* is my mother; and the months that
> are my kin have determined my smallness and my greatness. With

---

[220] Taylor 1989:35–38.

[221] The Elders of the chorus remark that the Queen left the stage driven by "wild" chagrin: ὑπ'
ἀγρίας /... λύπης, 1073–1074.

[222] Trans. Finglass 2018.

such a parent, I could never turn out another kind of person, so as
not to learn what was my birth.

The members of the chorus reiterate the happy speculation about Oedipus'
origin. In the very short choral song that follows (third *stasimon*), they refer to
Cithaeron as the mother, nurse, and (most of all) as the fellow-native of Oedipus
(1089–1091). Oedipus, the once celebrated king and the father of all the Thebans
at the outset of the tragedy (note the very first line of the play, ὦ τέκνα, Κάδμου
τοῦ πάλαι νέα τροφή; and again, τέκνα in line 6) has now become an infant bereft
of parents (1098–1099): τίς σε, <u>τέκνον</u>, τίς σ᾽ ἔτι- / κτε ("who bore you, child")?
His paternal and authoritative status has been diminished to an infantile powerlessness. It takes some time to arrive at a conclusion regarding his origin that
seems to be both promising and felicitous; and the chorus, now relieved, can
reiterate the dances in honor of Apollo that were "interrupted" in the second
stasimon (καὶ χορεύεσθαι πρὸς ἡμῶν [1093] vs. τί δεῖ με χορεύειν; [896] of the
second *stasimon*).

There is, however, a crack in the narrative from which a plague of evils will
burst forth. Jocasta's silence as she rushes off stage is an omen and a token of the
impeding catastrophe, a silence pregnant with evils. Sophocles has a penchant
for these moments of silence, gravid with the menace of imminent catastrophe;
they are usually attributed to women (Jocasta, Deianeira, and only exceptionally
to Ajax), and they mark a complete collapse in communication. Silence fills the
void when language fails to furnish the bridge between meaningful questions
and meaningful answers. Jocasta has relinquished her desperate attempts to
deter Oedipus because for her the narrative of his birth and life is now complete
and coherent. She has no words left other than to pity him (1071-1072):

ἰοὺ ἰού, δύστηνε· τοῦτο γάρ σ᾽ ἔχω
μόνον προσειπεῖν, ἄλλο δ᾽ οὔποθ᾽ ὕστερον.

Ah, ah, unhappy one! That is all that I can say to you, and nothing
any more!

Communication with Jocasta in this web of interlocution is irrevocably broken.

4.9 Questions with the Servant of Laius: Articulating the Truth

> After all, even what happened before I was born might on one reading be seen as a part of the process of my becoming. Isn't birth itself an arbitrary point?
>
> Charles Taylor, *The Sources of the Self*

In the short space of the fourth episode (1110–1185), Oedipus learns who he is. Jocasta's silence on leaving the stage now breaks and a spate of evils bursts forth, as fearfully predicted by the chorus. The servant of Laius, now on stage, is asked by the Corinthian messenger the only meaningful question, into which all previous questions are now subsumed (1142–1145):

> ΑΓ. φέρ' εἰπέ νυν, <u>τότ' οἶσθα παῖδά μοί τινα</u>
> <u>δούς</u>, ὡς ἐμαυτῷ θρέμμα θρεψαίμην ἐγώ;
> ΘΕ. τί δ' ἔστι; πρὸς τί τοῦτο τοὔπος ἱστορεῖς;
> ΑΓ. ὅδ' ἐστίν, ὦ τᾶν, κεῖνος ὃς τότ' ἦν νέος.

> M.: Tell me now, *do you remember giving me a child,* so that I could bring it up as my own? S.: What? Why are you asking me this question? M.: This man, sir, is he who was once that child.

Laius's servant implores the Corinthian messenger to silence (οὐ σιωπήσας ἔσῃ; 1146). However, silence is no longer an option. The inexorable point has arrived when Oedipus' understanding of himself and his history will be recast into a new narrative. The whole episode is organized around two narrative modules; the infant (παῖδα, 1150, 1156) and his story (ἔπος / ἐννέπων / ἱστορεῖν, 1144, 1150, 1156, 1165). The fearful reluctance of the servant to become the instrument of reconstructing the last shreds of Oedipus' life is confronted by the determination of the king to extract this last remaining piece of information, the missing link in his whole story. The central question around which the episode, the entire play, and finally the narrative of Oedipus' life pivots is now articulated (1156):

> τὸν παῖδ' ἔδωκας τῷδ' ὃν οὗτος ἱστορεῖ;

> Did you give to this man the child he is asking about?

The answer is a "one-word admission";[223] the single piece of information that Oedipus yearned for is now irrevocably uttered (1157):

ἔδωκ<α>

I did.

A barrage of questions follows in order to clarify this simple statement, since the kinship connection to Laius has yet to be established:

> Where did you get it from? Was it your own, or someone else's?"
> (πόθεν λαβών; οἰκεῖον ἢ 'ξ ἄλλου τινός; 1162)
> From which of these citizens, and from which house?" (τίνος
> πολιτῶν τῶνδε κἀκ ποίας στέγης; 1164)
> Was it a slave <of the house of Laius>, or one of his family?" (ἢ
> δοῦλος, ἢ κείνου τις ἐγγενὴς γεγώς; 1168)

At this point all further questions and answers freeze. It is futile to pretend Oedipus has not understood, or that the servant can longer delay uttering this one phrase that seals Oedipus' understanding of his origin. However, before the servant speaks and Oedipus hears the implacable κείνου παῖς—it was *his* child (1171)—there is a suspended moment of prolonged expectation, when full revelation of the truth hangs imminent over all present, but as yet unvoiced. The condition of linguistic articulacy is strongly set here in the sense that nothing exists (as yet) until it is spoken.[224] Moreover, this is the *telos* of Oedipus' obstinate endeavour to establish and finally re-assemble the scattered fragments of his identity in his quest to make sense of his life at last. At this moment in the Sophoclean narrative, the final resolution of this long process looms; we stand

---

[223] Finglass 2018 ad 1157.

[224] Taylor (1985:24–25) writes about linguistic articulacy as a necessary part of the process of evaluating our preferences in life: "There is the beginning of a language in which to express the superiority of one alternative, the language of higher and lower, noble and base, courageous and cowardly, integrated and fragmented, and so on"; a strong evaluator is capable of a reflection that is more articulate. Taylor also supports the necessity of linguistic articulacy for the good to exist (1989:91). He also argues that "the obvious point to begin with is that the goods ... only exist for us through some articulation. ... A vision of the good becomes available for the people of a given culture through being given expression in some manner. The God of Abraham exists for us (that is, belief in him is a possibility) because he has been talked about, primarily in the narrative of the Bible but also in countless other ways from theology to devotional literature. And also because he has been talked *to* in all the different manners in liturgy and prayer. Universal rights of mankind exist for us because they have been promulgated, because philosophers have theorized about them, because revolutions have been fought in their name, and so on." And finally, articulacy is about depth: "where there is articulacy there is the possibility of a plurality of visions which there was not before" (Taylor 1985:26).

on the verge of the final articulation. The very last question "was the child a slave of Laius house, or one of his family?" invites it, but it also creates a frozen moment when both the slave and Oedipus reflect on the power of this very articulation presaging the terrible consequences to come (1169–1170):

> ΘΕ. οἴμοι, πρὸς αὐτῷ γ' εἰμὶ τῷ δεινῷ <u>λέγειν</u>.
> ΟΙ. κἄγωγ' <u>ἀκούειν</u>· ἀλλ' ὅμως <u>ἀκουστέον</u>.

Jebb's comment on line 1169 is "I am close on the horror—close on uttering it," while his translation reads as follows: "Ah me; I am on the dreaded brink of speech." Similarly, Finglass translates: "*Oimoi*. I am on the brink of the perilous point in my telling."[225] If we dissect the syntax of line 1169, we realize that it is constructed around "this horror" (αὐτῷ τῷ δεινῷ) towards which (πρὸς) the servant approaches; but he is not there yet. For the *deinon* to be fleshed out (although already present in the minds of those on stage and in the audience), we need the actions of *legein* and *akouein*, the fundamental and indispensable actions of articulation.[226] The words of the impeding utterance will thus become part of the public discourse: they will acquire a material form and become part of the collective truth supplanting all other truths of the preceding narratives of the play. "I will say it," implies the servant; "and I will listen to it," would have been the line of Oedipus: "for I have to listen to it."

Oedipus now listens to the final touches of the recasting of the narrative of his life: "it was said to be his child" (κείνου γέ τοι δὴ παῖς ἐκλῄζεθ', 1171); "ask your wife indoors, for she could best tell you" (ἡ δ' ἔσω / κάλλιστ' ἂν εἴποι σὴ γυνὴ τάδ' ὡς ἔχει, 1171–1172). At this moment, the line-for-line exchange breaks down into even smaller units, "in the arrival of *antilabê*" (1173–1176);[227] half a verse, at one point one single word, bears the momentous burden of the whole revelation.

> "Was it she who gave it to you?" (ἦ γὰρ δίδωσιν ἥδε σοι; 1173)
> "Yes, my lord" (μάλιστ', ἄναξ, 1173)
> "For what purpose?" (ὡς πρὸς τί χρείας; 1174)
> "So that I could kill it." (ὡς ἀναλώσαιμί νιν, 1174)
> "Her own child, the wretch?" (τεκοῦσα τλήμων; 1175)

---

[225] 2018 ad 1169. To which Oedipus replies: "And I in my hearing, but nevertheless I must hear" (Finglass 2018 ad 1170).

[226] Taylor 1989:91–97; Taylor 1985:24–26, 59. If we wish to advance this argument further, we should note that classical Greek thought sees reason in the notion of "linguistic articulacy," for it considers *logos* as part of the *telos* of human beings. This is an ethical question in its broader sense, since it relates to the issue of making sense of one's life (Taylor 1989:92).

[227] Which normally signals "a tightening of emotional tension," Finglass 2018 ad 1173–1176.

"Yes, it was for fear of evil prophecies" (θεσφάτων γ᾽ ὄκνῳ κακῶν, 1175)

"What prophesies?" (ποίων; 1176)

"It was said that it would kill its parents." (κτενεῖν νιν τοὺς τεκόντας ἦν λόγος, 1176).

Everything falls into place: the two prophecies, the exposure of the infant, the mother's complicity. Now all the past events become comprehensible: the swollen feet, the killing of the father. All the illusions of the past collapse: the foster parents along with the false identity. At the end of the previous *stasimon* the question of birth was raised; now it is resolved: "if you are who he says you are, know that you were born to misery" (εἰ γὰρ οὗτος εἶ / ὅν φησιν οὗτος, ἴσθι δύσποτμος γεγώς, 1180–1181).

With this last movement, the questions once floating in dislocated space suddenly cohere to form the new, terrifying narrative of Oedipus' life. Pieces of information or signs hitherto misunderstood or ignored now coalesce to recast his life into this new narrative. Other plays about Oedipus existed before Sophocles, and many followed after his, as we all know,[228] but *this* Oedipus is different in one essential point, as Alister Cameron aptly puts it: "this is not an Oedipus about whom such and such discoveries are made. ... Nor is this even an Oedipus who makes discoveries about himself. ... This is Oedipus discovered by himself."[229] Oedipus' identity is finally reconstructed, and with this revelation his very name acquires a whole new meaning.

The *before* of the life of Oedipus is fully illuminated now and the line of events (previously ignored or misunderstood) become instantly coherent with Oedipus learning who he is and where he comes from. The *after* of the hero is still to be constructed, the *after* that follows on the heels of the revelation regarding his identity (1180 and onwards). Now the original question "who am I?" is answered with what seems to be a simple statement: "I am Oedipus." Being Oedipus, however, is as convoluted (and painful) as was the process of reconstructing the scattered and cryptic fragments of his past. From line 1180 until the very end of the play things happen, decisions are made, and the action unfolds inexorably to culminate in two acts of new horror: the suicide of Jocasta and the self-blinding of Oedipus. The "I am Oedipus" now contains new elements that constitute his newly found identity: the very act of the self-blinding seals the Sophoclean Oedipus as we know him.

I cannot help thinking at this point of Foucault's Don Quixote, whose existential metamorphosis happened in the "narrow gap between the two volumes"

---

[228] Edmunds 1985:47–57; Segal 200:24–32; Jebb 1887:xi–xix.
[229] 1968:57.

of the book of his wondrous adventures.[230] The hero's life is divided between *before* and *after*: *before* (in the first volume of his adventures) he is a "sign wandering through a world that did not recognize him"; *after*, in the second volume (during which Don Quixote meets people who have read the first volume of his adventures), the hero becomes the recognizable sign of his own narrative containing his truth.[231] Thus although "he is constantly under the impression that he is deciphering signs," in reality he resembles closely "all those signs whose ineffaceable imprint he has left behind him."[232] Don Quixote's narrative is manipulated by Cervantes as he interlaces the threads of the story in and out of the textual story of the two volumes; and so, too, Sophocles in *Oedipus Tyrannus*.

The *after* of Oedipus forces him to confront Jocasta (although he finds only her lifeless body) and blind himself; and then, in tortured lamentation, he engages in an excruciating dialogue with the members of the chorus, explaining why he has mutilated himself and how he sees his life as an accursed and stigmatized person in his polis. Despite the temptation, I will *not* consider *Oedipus at Colonus* as the *after* of *Oedipus Tyrannus*. For one thing, *Oedipus at Colonus* was staged some twenty-five years later. More importantly, however, Sophocles wishes us to consider the story he narrates within the short contours of a single tragedy. More often than not, the playwright ends his plays with an open ending,[233] not defining in any concrete way what is expected beyond the end of his play (with the exception of *Philoctetes*). Exile for Oedipus remains as yet unconfirmed at the end of *Oedipus Tyrannus*, for Creon sends an envoy to consult the oracle once more to resolve the situation. Of course, we have the prediction of Teiresias in the first episode (454–456) that Oedipus will end up as an impoverished wanderer in foreign lands. But nothing is fixed yet, and we need

---

[230] Foucault 1974:48.

[231] Ibid.

[232] Foucault 1974:49, 48.

[233] More often than not, Sophocles leaves the end of his plays open; that is to say, without a definite closure according to the programmatic statements of the beginning, and the consequent unfolding, of the play. Pietro Pucci, in reference to *Oedipus Tyrannus*, wonders whether this is due to "the vagaries of *tuchê* or to the drifting of Sophoclean writing" in combination "with Sophocles' intention to leave the ending of the play open" (1991:3). My belief is that the playwright intentionally leaves the ending of his plays "suspended"; in *Ajax* the hasty and unheroic burial of Ajax simply saves the body from defilement; in *Electra*, the spectators (and the readers) wonder whether there are more evils to fall on the house of Atreus (and when?); in *Antigone,* there is not any foreseeable solution to the play (all protagonists are either dead or mentally and psychologically destroyed); lastly, in *Oedipus Tyrannus*, nothing is decided at the end: Oedipus goes back to his palace, and whether he will be exiled or condemned to death (as the original oracle dictated, 100–101) remains to be decided after a new consultation of the oracle. The end of *Oedipus Tyrannus* is so inconclusive that scholars athetize lines (or a group of lines) from the *exodos* of the play (see Kovacs 2009a:53–55; further on the end of *Oedipus Tyrannus*, see Budelmann 2006:43–61).

no projections into the future to delineate the *after* of Oedipus; this has been all too well established in our tragedy. Oedipus has been transformed into a sightless outcast within the confines of his own polis; his close family and the citizens of Thebes recognize him as the embodiment of the truth of his own narrative, which now, finally, makes sense.

5

I Am Oedipus
Reframing the Question of Identity

Πάντες ἄνθρωποι τοῦ εἰδέναι ὀρέγονται φύσει. σημεῖον δ᾽
ἡ τῶν αἰσθήσεων ἀγάπησις· καὶ γὰρ χωρὶς τῆς χρείας
ἀγαπῶνται δι᾽ αὐτάς, καὶ μάλιστα τῶν ἄλλων ἡ διὰ τῶν
ὀμμάτων. οὐ γὰρ μόνον ἵνα πράττωμεν ἀλλὰ καὶ μηθὲν
μέλλοντες πράττειν τὸ ὁρᾶν αἱρούμεθα ἀντὶ πάντων ὡς εἰπεῖν
τῶν ἄλλων. αἴτιον δ᾽ ὅτι μάλιστα ποιεῖ γνωρίζειν ἡμᾶς
αὕτη τῶν αἰσθήσεων καὶ πολλὰς δηλοῖ διαφοράς.

Aristotle *Metaphysics* 980a22–28

All men naturally desire knowledge. An indication of this is our esteem
for the senses; for apart from their use we esteem them for their own
sake, and most of all the sense of sight. Not only with a view to action,
but even when no action is contemplated, we prefer sight to practically
all the other senses. The reason for this is that of all the senses sight
best helps us to know things, and reveals many distinctions.[1]

The "who am I?" has now been answered. The *after* in the reconstitution of
the hero's identity culminates in the new horror of Oedipus' self-blinding. As
we embark on defining the "I am Oedipus" several questions arise.[2] Why does
Oedipus blind himself? Is the motivation for his action consistent with his
character, in keeping with the man we have come to know as "our" Oedipus?
Additionally, is this an act of violent impulse, or does it result from a calculated
appraisal of what the future holds for him? Does Oedipus clarify his action in

---

[1] Trans. Tredennick.

[2] The self-blinding occurs also in Aeschylus, but it is attributed to the family curse, which is
emphasized in the Aeschylean trilogy—the curse that follows Laius' rape of Chrysippus and that
becomes a family Erinys (Segal 2001:26; for the various versions of the self-blinding in ancient
and later traditions, see also Edmunds 1985:15–16).

a manner consonant with the renowned intelligence and determination that characterized his previous life? It is obvious that, in the light of this barrage of questions, the issue of identity has shifted focus. From line 1180 onward Oedipus emerges in full command of his powers to face a difficult new question: how do I now proceed in the knowledge that I have committed parricide and incest? He enters again the moral public space of all difficult decisions, where we act as social beings. He also repositions himself in the webs of interlocution—where this time *he* is questioned, and where he responds with a lengthy justification of his actions.

5.1 Self-Blinding

[ANTIGONE]:
WE BEGIN IN THE DARK
AND BIRTH IS THE DEATH OF US

Anne Carson, *Antigonick*

I agree with Alister Cameron's view that the self-blinding is *the* central act of the denouement of the play, the transformation through which Oedipus becomes the "actor of his own fate," and that it "is made to represent and somehow contain all the other acts which have gone before it."[3] Oedipus declares himself to be the sole agent[4] of the blinding (1331–1332):

ἔπαισε δ' αὐτόχειρ νιν οὔτις, ἀλλ' ἐγὼ τλάμων.

And no other hand struck my eyes, but my own miserable hand!

The decision to shut himself off from the light of the day is confirmed the moment Oedipus understands the whole truth. The connection between the inner knowledge and the external light, as well as the symbolism of the reversal of this analogy, has become a commonplace in almost all analyses of the play. I shall only remark on how this reversal (a *topos* in the Sophoclean corpus) is exquisitely captured in Ajax' apostrophe to darkness: that it is his own light (σκότος, ἐμὸν φάος, *Ajax* 394) that allows us room to see Oedipus' apostrophe to light (ὦ

---

[3]   1968:105 and 116.

[4]   To preempt any objections to my ignoring the immediately previous lines (Ἀπόλλων τάδ' ἦν, Ἀπόλλων, φίλοι, / ὁ κακὰ κακὰ τελῶν ἐμὰ τάδ' ἐμὰ πάθεα, 1329-1330) that indicate Apollo's complicity to the act, I would state here that this issue will be dealt with at length in the following section (5.2, pp. 125-133), where the entire passage is discussed.

φῶς, τελευταῖόν σε προσβλέψαιμι νῦν, 1183) as a possible statement of death. Thus we may understand why Oedipus, in a fit of fury, asks for a sword from the palace servants who witnessed Jocasta's retreat to the nuptial chamber—is the victim to be Jocasta or himself?[5] However, death by the sword is not how Sophocles envisages the climax of his narrative. The lifeless body of Oedipus' wife and mother is already hanging there when he rushes in; all that remains for him is to release her body from the noose, and lay it upon the ground before putting his eyes out with the golden pins of her garment.[6] Everything is decided and executed within a split second. Then and there, we learn for the first time why Oedipus mutilates himself, as reported by the messenger (1271–1274):

> ... ὁθούνεκ' οὐκ ὄψοιντό νιν
> οὔθ' οἷ' ἔπασχεν οὔθ' ὁποῖ' ἔδρα κακά,
> ἀλλ' ἐν σκότῳ τὸ λοιπὸν οὓς μὲν οὐκ ἔδει
> ὀψοίαθ', οὓς δ' ἔχρῃζεν οὐ γνωσοίατο.

> ... that they should not see his dread sufferings or his dread actions, but in the future they should see in the darkness those they never should have seen, and fail to recognize those he wished to know.

He seems to decide on purely moral grounds. His transgressions are so egregious that Oedipus is impelled to act with the same determination and clarity of thought that he had in the past; he cannot bear to look upon the people he shamed, nor to be seen by them. He needs to exist in total darkness, not just because his human sight failed him by not recognizing his parents, but because the act of seeing brings him only shame. The eyes of others will forever reflect his crimes and, thus, the re-enactment of the shameful acts. Shame becomes materialized in a sense, acquiring a physical quality when seen.[7] When Taylor discusses the multifaceted nature of identity, he points out that one of its essential features is "how [one] moves in public space commanding respect or failing to do so."[8] Failing to do so, as Oedipus does now, results in his having to face irredeemable shame, instead of the esteem and respect he has striven for all his life.

---

[5] Segal 2001:124; Edmunds 1985:15n75.

[6] See also chapter 4.5 above (pp. 80–81) about the erotic/sexual connotations of this act over the body of Jocasta.

[7] Sorabji 2006: "As for participation in community, I stress ... , in opposition to Descartes, that the infant acquires its idea of 'what *I* am looking at' only in a social exchange and hand in hand with the idea of what *another* is looking at, and I commend analogous insights in the Greeks" (49; emphasis the author's).

[8] Taylor 1989:15.

Unable to extirpate the shame brought on others and on himself, he chooses to witness it no more; the only path open to him is to mutilate his sight.

These considerations evoke the notion of sight and the action of seeing in their cultural, social, and ideological context. Oedipus is overwhelmed with the dread of seeing others and witnessing how he is seen by them. The culturally informed way of seeing and being seen fits into an exploration of the constructed notion of the "gaze." This notion is widely explored by feminist critics, who point to the male gaze directed toward women and their bodies that transforms them into objectified sources of erotic pleasure. Starting from Freud's scopophilia, introduced in *Three Essays on Human Sexuality*, which depicts the pleasure derived from looking at erotic objects,[9] and moving to Lacan, who gave theoretical force to the gaze (*le regard*),[10] contemporary cinema studies[11] explore the male gaze as the active power that looks.[12] Of course, this "male gaze" and "erotic pleasure" have no part here.[13] But the "gaze," that is, the culturally specific way of looking at things and persons, and the way we understand people looking at us, falls into social categories that interest me in the *Oedipus Tyrannus*; "a gaze can never be neutral and ... every act of seeing involves a 'way of seeing.'"[14] We should also bear in mind that even before the proliferation of cinema studies—from the 1970s onward—and feminist criticism, the notion of "gaze" could be detected in works on classical literature. I take the classic work by Bruno Snell, *The Discovery of the Mind*, especially the chapter on "Homer's View of Man," as a case in point.[15] In this much-cited study, the author makes us "see" the many

---

9 "Scopophilia" ("pleasure in looking") is coined to translate Freud's term *Schaulust* (*Three Essays on the Theory of Sexuality* in *The Penguin Freud Library*, vol. 7 (1977 [1905]), 69–70), and it is used in the case of his patient known as the "The Rat Man," who has a "burning and tormenting curiosity to see the female body" (*Notes on a Case of Obsessional Neurosis*, in *The Penguin Freud Library*, vol. 9.2 (1991 [1909]), 41–42).

10 One of the four sexual drives, according to Lacan, is the scopic drive (the erogenous zone is the eyes, the partial object is the gaze, and the verb is to "see"), linking scopophilia with the appreciation of the other (Lacan 1978:183, 1990:86).

11 The advent of the seminal paper by Laura Mulvey "Visual Pleasure and Narrative Cinema," published in *Screen* (16.3:6–18) in 1975, opened the way for "gaze" studies in their cinematic and other artistic contexts to flourish.

12 Salzman-Mitchell 2005:7.

13 Unless we consider the Freudian equation of self-blinding to self-castration, see George Devereux's classic paper in 1973 "The Self-blinding of Oidipous in Sophocles' *Oidipous Tyrannos*," *Journal for Hellenic Studies* 93:36–49.

14 Mary Devereaux, as cited by Salzman–Mitchell 2005:11.

15 Pages 1–22 of the English translation. In this seminal study, originally published in 1946, we hear of the many ways that a Homeric person "sees" because of the great variety of verbs denoting vision, and the operation of sight: ὁρᾶν, ἰδεῖν, λεύσσειν, ἀθρεῖν, θεᾶσθαι, σκέπτεσθαι, δέρκεσθαι, παπταίνειν, some of which had gone out of use in classical Greek (1–2). The interesting thing is that most of the verbs do not describe the function of sight as such, but the specific way of

different ways that Homeric heroes "look": the "fixing gaze"[16] of a warrior, the uncanny deadly stare simulating that of a dragon,[17] and the gleam in the eyes that somebody else sees in us.[18] So it comes as no surprise that Helen Lovatt's 2013 book focuses entirely on *The Epic Gaze*.[19]

The special quality of the gaze positions it in a clearly social context; we "look at" others in an ideologically informed manner and, in return, we "receive" the gaze of others.[20] We can be either recipients or agents. The lack of respect that Oedipus will see reflected in the eyes of the citizens of Thebes will corroborate the ruin of his social status; similarly, the gazes of Jocasta and Laius, when he meets them in Hades, will reflect his hideous transgressions. Of course, seeing and being seen is an interactive process. Oedipus' gaze toward others will be irrevocably changed. The benign, intelligent, empowered king will be transformed into what he has now become: a social outcast doubly mutilated. Oedipus refuses to be the agent of such a gaze; blindness will protect him from the visible manifestations of shame. As public space is also a moral space, a blind Oedipus will not witness his own ethical ruin or his social degradation. In the reciprocal network of power relations that the polis engenders, things have now been reversed, for "men do not simply look; their gaze carries with it the power of action and of possession."[21] As Oedipus becomes ethically and socially disempowered, so does his gaze. Self-blinding is a very conscious decision.[22]

---

looking at something, or the specific quality of a certain glance or gaze, a perspective that has become in later studies the notion of "gaze."

[16] Observe the telling titles of chapters 2 and 3 of the book by Salzman–Mitchell *A Web of Fantasies*: "Intrusive Gaze" and "Fixing Gaze."

[17] The Homeric verb is δέρκεσθαι, cognate with δράκων, denoting a "visual attitude, and does not hinge upon the function of sight as such" (Snell 1946:3). "Δέρκεσθαι is also used with an external object; in such a case, the present would mean: 'his glance rests upon something,' and the aorist: 'his glance falls on an object,' 'it turns toward something,' 'he casts his glance on someone'" (2–3). Of course, the petrifying gaze of the Gorgon is also much explored in contemporary scholarship.

[18] Such is one of the meanings of δέρκεσθαι: "the gleam of the eye as noticed by someone else" (Snell 1946:2), as well as the verb λεύσσω, cognate to λευκός as "gleaming," "white," meaning "to see something bright" (3). When the verb is accompanied by expressions of joy (χαίρων, τερπόμενοι), then "it is clear ... that this term too derives its special significance from a mode of seeing; not the function of sight, *but the object seen, and the sentiments associated with the sight*, give the word its peculiar quality" (3–4, my emphasis).

[19] Some of Lovatt's chapters have the following telling titles: "The Divine Gaze," "The Mortal Gaze," "The Female Gaze," and on warriors especially, "The Assaultive Gaze." The Roman gaze is explored by Brian Krostenko in *Cicero, Catullus and the Language of Social Performance* (Chicago, 2001), especially in chapter V.2 "Looking down from the inside: the Roman Gaze."

[20] Revermann 2010:69–97.

[21] Salzman–Mitchell 2005:7. I transfer the meaning from the gender power relations to which the quote refers, to power relations in general.

[22] See also Finglass (2018 ad 1369–1415) commenting on the passage as a "closely reasoned justification for his self-blinding."

We may understand now why Oedipus declares his sole agency for the self-blinding, despite the anxiously repeated question of the chorus: "who was the *daimon* who inflicted this on you?" There is, in addition, another dimension to this act, which I will consider now by examining the notion of the human agent as a "strong evaluator"—that is to say, "a person who strongly evaluates his desires" and thus "is capable of a reflection which is more articulate."[23] The result is a moral decision whose motivation goes deeper still; the strong evaluator "has articulacy about depth."[24] It is obvious that Oedipus meets all these prerequisites. Faced with an extreme situation, he acts as a human agent and can indeed be seen as a strong evaluator, for he makes a difficult decision and articulates his motives in great depth. He does this with the same responsibility, lucidity, and determination he has demonstrated all his life. Such an evaluation is not even a choice; it is an *articulation* of what one considers "worthy, or higher, or more integrated, or more fulfilling."[25] In this sense, the self-blinding "is made to represent and somehow contains all the other acts which have gone before it."[26] It seems credible to assume that Oedipus, at this critical juncture of his life, examines all his possible actions, including suicide—an option he rejects.

The depth of this decision escapes the perception of the chorus (and perhaps also our common human understanding). Since the crimes are so intolerable, the chorus seems to ask, *why not kill yourself?* Self-mutilation is more extreme than committing suicide (1367–1368):

οὐκ οἶδ' ὅπως σε φῶ <u>βεβουλεῦσθαι</u> καλῶς.
κρείσσων γὰρ ἦσθα μηκέτ' ὢν ἢ ζῶν τυφλός.

I do not know how I can say that you *deliberated on the matter well;*[27]
for you would have been better dead than living but blind.

Oedipus' following justification of the act is lengthy (1369–1415), leaving no room for doubts about his motivation. The blinding could have been

---

[23] Taylor 1985:25.

[24] Ibid. 26.

[25] Ibid. 35: "On the contrary they are articulations of our sense of what is worthy, or higher, or more integrated, or more fulfilling, and so on. But as articulations, they offer another purchase for the concept of responsibility."

[26] Cameron 1968:105.

[27] Edith Hall begins her analysis on the importance of human deliberation in Sophocles' Theban plays (2012) with this very utterance by the chorus, and Oedipus' response (313): "don't give me any more advice" (μηδὲ συμβούλευ' ἔτι, 1370). She concludes the chapter stating that even Teiresias, the intermediary between gods and mortals, "can say to Creon in *Antigone*, with full conviction, that, for humans in difficult situations, "good counsel is the most potent of assents" (1050).

characterized as an act of passion, but this would presuppose an impulsive reaction to extreme emotions. Obviously, Oedipus is filled with pain, sorrow, and shame as he enters the palace and the nuptial chamber; his self-blinding, however, appears well-calculated and is clearly reasoned in his reply to the chorus (1371–1378):

ἐγὼ γὰρ οὐκ οἶδ' ὄμμασιν ποίοις βλέπων
πατέρα ποτ' ἂν προσεῖδον εἰς Ἅιδου μολών,
οὐδ' αὖ τάλαιναν μητέρ', οἷν ἐμοὶ δυοῖν
ἔργ' ἐστὶ κρείσσον' ἀγχόνης εἰργασμένα.
ἀλλ' ἡ τέκνων δῆτ' ὄψις ἦν ἐφίμερος,
βλαστοῦσ' ὅπως ἔβλαστε, προσλεύσσειν ἐμοί;
οὐ δῆτα τοῖς γ' ἐμοῖσιν ὀφθαλμοῖς ποτε·

For I do not know with what eyes I could have looked upon my father when I went to Hades, or upon my unhappy mother, since upon them both I have done deeds that hanging could not atone for. Then, could I desire to look upon my children, since their origins were what they were? Never could these eyes have harboured such desire!

I take these words at face value. Death, a solution entertained by the chorus, could not erase Oedipus' dread of the moment of looking, sight intact, upon his parents in Hades. Nor is it a lesser surrogate for death, for even death does not expunge his deeds. Oedipus clearly says that he wants to shut himself off from the world; mutilating the senses connecting him to this world is his method. Sight is the paramount sense, but he would also willingly destroy his ears so as to block the hearing as well (1386–1388):

... ἀλλ' εἰ τῆς ἀκουούσης ἔτ' ἦν
πηγῆς δι' ὤτων φραγμός, οὐκ ἂν ἐσχόμην
τὸ μὴ ἀποκλῇσαι τοὐμὸν ἄθλιον δέμας,
ἵν' ἦ τυφλός τε καὶ κλύων μηδέν·

Why, if there had been a means of blocking the stream of hearing through my ears, I would not have hesitated to shut off my wretched self, making myself blind and deaf.

Oedipus wishes to reduce himself to a mutilated body, nurturing his wounds in the isolation of a blindness safeguarded by a blockading of his senses. Thus

Oedipus' body becomes doubly mutilated: the original "act" was performed by Laius, the second by Oedipus himself in full consciousness of his action. This last corporeal scarring is equivalent to Oedipus' giving himself the second feature of his identity, with which he will be known around the world: in a sense, one can discern a "cyclic" formation in Oedipus' life, which results in a consolidation of the corporeal "dimensions" of his identity.[28] Performing the second mutilation is the only way to make his earthly existence bearable, and also a way to transport himself to a place where sorrow can no longer touch him, as he himself declares (1389–1390): τὸ γὰρ / τὴν φροντίδ' ἔξω τῶν κακῶν οἰκεῖν γλυκύ ("it is a joy to live with one's thoughts beyond the reach of sorrow"). Oedipus languishes, disconnected from the world, while awaiting the announcement of his punishment.

The tendency to consider the blinding as self-punishment is tinged with a Christian morality that observes the self-inflicted punishments of the sinner as acts of remorse and repentance involving deprivation of earthly pleasures, infliction of physical pain, and the like. The martyrdom of saints has familiarized us with physical suffering in the name of piety or of a noble moral or metaphysical cause. In classical thought, however, committing a crime and suffering the appropriate punishment needed to be publicly proclaimed. My argument for Electra's prolonged lamentation as a means of publicly proclaiming the penalty for the unredeemed murder of her father speaks for the case.[29] The penalty to be paid for Oedipus' crimes remains as yet unclear, as Creon sends messengers once more to Delphi to consult the oracle. We know that Oedipus asks to be exiled (ἀπάγετ' ἐκτόπιον ὅτι τάχιστά με, / ἀπάγετ', ὦ φίλοι, 1340–1341); we are also aware of the harsh punishment announced at the outset of the play by the selfsame Oedipus for regicide (236–251). However, in the light of the new events, regicide is but one of many crimes, for the guilty party is king and has also committed parricide and incest. This calls for a modification of the penalty, and so Creon seeks oracular advice.

The play ends without any sentence being pronounced. Tradition records several options with or without punishment: in the *Iliad* Oedipus dies in battle; in the *Odyssey* he outlives his wife and continues to reign. In Euripides' *Phoenician Women* he is shut in the palace, blinded, while Jocasta witnesses the death of her two sons and then commits suicide over their bodies.[30] As I said earlier, I

---

[28] I owe the remark on the double mutilation as part of Oedipus' identity to my former student, Marietta Kotsafti, formulated in one of our numerous discussions on Oedipus, in and out the classroom.

[29] 2013:69–72; see also chapter 3, pp. 33–36 above.

[30] For the several endings of the story of Oedipus as recorded in various ancient sources, see Jebb 1887:xii–xxi; Segal 2001:24–32; Edmunds 1985:6–17, 47–57; Finglass 2018:13–27.

will not consider *Oedipus at Colonus*, where Oedipus is a blind exiled wanderer, as a "sequel" to *Oedipus Tyrannus*. In 430/420 BCE when *Oedipus Tyrannus* was staged, *Oedipus at Colonus* had probably not even been conceived as a dramatic piece; but even if it had, it is never alluded to in *Oedipus Tyrannus*. Sophocles, I argue, wanted us to see *Oedipus Tyrannus* (as he did with all his plays) as a self-contained entity of autonomous drama,[31] where the punishment has yet to be pronounced. The playwright in the excruciating austerity of his art leaves the end of Oedipus suspended.

5.2 Who Is To Blame? Apollo, Oedipus, or Shared Responsibility?

> It is said that whosoever the gods wish to destroy,
> they first make mad. In fact, whosoever the gods wish
> to destroy, they first hand the equivalent of a stick with
> a fizzing fuse and Acme Dynamite Company written
> on the side. It's more interesting, and doesn't take so long.

> Terry Pratchett, *Soul Music*

Any student of *Oedipus Tyrannus* is bound to stumble upon the thorny issue of the life of Oedipus as determined by the divine oracle that was already pronounced before he was even born. This determinism leaves little scope for Oedipus to shape his own life; free will thus seems impossible, or so one would think.[32] Since there is such a constricting divine strait jacket, how can one consider Oedipus to be a human agent who deliberates vigorously on his options in life, as I have argued in the previous chapter? Is the life of Oedipus not a continuous struggle against a destiny, in which he becomes ever more enmeshed even as he struggles to evade it? Are we to assume a "shared responsibility" between Apollo (as the source of the oracle *and* as an agent in the action of the drama) and Oedipus himself?[33] And if we do make this assumption, to which side does the balance tip?

---

[31] As I have argued also in chapter 4.9 above, p. 114.

[32] The notion of free will and its controversy when used in the context of classical texts of the fifth century BCE is discussed at great length in the next chapter.

[33] The "division of responsibility between Apollo and Oedipus is purposely imprecise" (Finglass 2018 ad 1329–1333). At any rate, it is common in ancient thought to combine "divine and human explanations for an event, even if overlapping and apparently mutually contradictory" (ibid.).

It hardly needs to be said that critics have responded to these issues so diversely that their conclusions cover a disparate spectrum, from one deterministic pole that sees Oedipus as a puppet, a victim trapped in the net of a cruel destiny, to the opposite pole where the protagonist has substantial command over his own life choices; in the latter, divine action remains closeted in the background or is identified with authorial intentions. The scope of the present chapter does not allow for this diversity to be tackled individually or even an attempt at broad summarization. However, I will engage in a dialogue with some of the most influential recent critical approaches, for I think we need to reframe not only the old questions but the new answers as well.

I will begin with the famous analogy used by Kovacs to graphically delineate his thesis that, while all of Oedipus' actions in the play are free, the superior intelligence of Apollo brings them to completion according to his master plan. The analogy is taken from a chess game where an ordinary chess player contends against a grand master:

> All of [the ordinary player's] moves in the game are freely chosen, and [he is] in every sense the author of them, yet the grand master can beat [him] easily—indeed, can confidently predict the result of the match beforehand ... . All of Oedipus' actions are free, but because Apollo knows more than Oedipus and because he can withhold information from him when he wants and supply it where it will be most misleading, he easily engineers the result.[34]

These sentences introduce the critic's second thesis, which sees tragedy as a "two-decker affair," since "the action happens on the human plane, but there is always a divine background"; "Apollo ... is still visibly at work in the course of the play,"[35] aiming to destroy the hero as retribution for Laius' transgressions in the case of Chrysippus. To my mind, this is a moderate stance that attempts to reconcile the freedom of Oedipus, who chooses his own actions, with his simultaneous outwitting by the god with superior knowledge. As for the family guilt, I truly doubt that this is discernible in Sophocles' treatment of the myth in *Oedipus Tyrannus*.

In order to approach the vexing problem of the co-existence of Oedipus' freedom of choice and the active involvement of Apollo in the fulfillment of predefined conclusions in the play, we need to return to Oedipus' self-blinding (1331–1332), which I discussed in the previous section. My reading there stressed the active involvement of the hero as the sole agent of the act. The full passage,

---

[34] Kovacs 2009b:359–360.
[35] Kovacs 2009b:363.

answering the agonized questioning of the chorus regarding the self-blinding, "which of the gods set you on?" (τίς σ' ἐπῆρε δαιμόνων;, 1328), runs as follows (1329–1335):

Ἀπόλλων τάδ' ἦν, Ἀπόλλων, φίλοι,
ὁ κακὰ κακὰ τελῶν ἐμὰ τάδ' ἐμὰ πάθεα.[36]
ἔπαισε δ' αὐτόχειρ νιν οὔ-
τις, ἀλλ' ἐγὼ τλάμων.
τί γὰρ ἔδει μ' ὁρᾶν,
ὅτῳ γ' ὁρῶντι μηδὲν ἦν ἰδεῖν γλυκύ;

It was Apollo, Apollo, my friends, who accomplished these cruel, cruel sufferings of mine! And no other hand struck my eyes, but my own miserable hand! For why did I have to see, when there was nothing I could see with pleasure?

This is a celebrated and much cited passage of the play. Critics who deal with the divine and human action and their interrelation in the play cannot avoid considering it, since it gives Oedipus' genuine response to evaluating who is responsible for the sufferings of his entire life (if indeed the τάδ' ἐμὰ κακὰ πάθεα refers to his entire life),[37] and for his self-blinding in particular.

Analyzing this reply of Oedipus to the chorus, as well as many other passages in the play, Douglas Cairns argues, from the active involvement of Apollo in Oedipus' downfall, that "it is Oedipus' *moira* to fall at the hands of Apollo, and Apollo is seeing to it that this will in fact happen."[38] This last remark refers, of course, to the indignant remark of Teiresias to Oedipus in the prologue of the play (376–377):

Οὐ γάρ σε μοῖρα πρός γ' ἐμοῦ πεσεῖν, ἐπεὶ
ἱκανὸς Ἀπόλλων ᾧ τάδ' ἐκπρᾶξαι μέλει.

---

[36] Note the multiple repetitions in the lines of Ἀπόλλων, κακά, and ἐμὰ marking the "passionate exclamation" of Oedipus. At first, it might seem that Apollo's role is conceived "on a greater scale," referring to the entire life of Oedipus. But since the participle τελῶν has an object (that is, τάδ' ... πάθεα), we may infer a divine involvement in the actual action of self-blinding. Whatever the case, the roles of both Apollo and Oedipus "receive considerable emphasis" in the passage (Finglass 2018 ad 1329–1333).

[37] The question of the chorus is very specific and refers to the self-blinding. Of course, it can be assumed that the κακά could be an all-encompassing term that extends to all the sufferings of Oedipus' life.

[38] Cairns 2013:128.

No, it is not at my hand that you are destined to fall, since Apollo,
who has it in mind to bring this about, will be sufficient.

Cairns's argument is elaborated at great length. There are two postulates
(at least) upon which his further reasoning is based. First, that "in *OT* the
existence of the gods and their influence on human affairs is a given;"[39] and,
second, that the divine foreknowledge, enabled by the omniscience of the god
and the pronouncements of his prophets, delineates the fact that human affairs
are divinely willed or caused. Both "maxims" point in the direction of human
subjection to a divine will. In *Oedipus Tyrannus* the parricide and incest are
divinely initiated and, as such, manifest an inherent divine order,[40] for neither
action would have happened if the god had not misled Oedipus by means of his
oracle. In short, the entire plot of the play is set in motion by the god who "initiated [the] search of which [Oedipus] is the object."

When dealing with the self-blinding in particular, Cairns approaches the
relevant passage by stating that "Oedipus sees divine influence in human
actions that are adequately motivated by human reasons; in doing so he sees
Apollonian influence in an outcome which Apollo's priest predicted," and "this
outcome is part of the downfall" of Oedipus.[41] The critic refers to Teiresias'
explicit pronouncement, made in the *prologos*, that time will turn Oedipus' life
upside down, from rich to poor, from citizen to exile, from seeing to blindness
(452–456); and so, if the self-blinding was predicted (454), that makes it part of
Apollo's wider plan that he intentionally imposes upon Oedipus. So far, it has
been obvious that the scale tips toward the side of Apollo.

However, when we come to the passage in question (1329–1332), a notion
of "shared responsibility" shapes Cairns's analysis, for the self-mutilation
in Sophocles' text implies the view that the action "is something that Apollo
causes; but it is also something that Oedipus himself causes."[42]

I will interrogate Cairns's argument by pointing to an interesting feature of
Sophocles' diction here, often ignored by commentators; in typical Sophoclean
fashion, in just two lines (1331–1332) we have accumulative terms denoting full
agency for the action of self-blinding. Oedipus takes full responsibility of the
action per se, with the words αὐτόχειρ (= with my own hand), οὔτις (= no one),
and ἀλλ᾽ ἐγώ (= no one else but me). The obdurate repetition of the idea "no
one else but me" seems to consolidate a fully-fledged αὐτοχειρία, thus making
Oedipus the conscious agent of the action. Thus we can talk about a "shared

---

[39] Ibid.
[40] Cairns 2913:129.
[41] Cairns 2013:135.
[42] Cairns 2013:136.

responsibility" implied in the phrases Ἀπόλλων τάδ᾽ ἦν and αὐτόχειρ νιν οὔ / τις, ἀλλ᾽ ἐγώ. This is undermined, however, by Cairns, who argues that the self-blinding (as well as the parricide that is connected with the blinding via the word αὐτόχειρ) "are of the same order, carried out by a human being acting for intelligible human reasons but simultaneously fulfilling prophecies whose logic entails that these aspects of the future, at least, are necessary and unavoidable. These prophecies, moreover, are presented not merely as objects of divine knowledge but *"projects of divine intervention."*[43] So, even if Oedipus (hypothetically) did not want to blind himself (as with the actions of parricide and incest, which he committed unwillingly), Apollo would have ensured "that it should still happen despite human opposition."[44] In this sense, the self-blinding becomes part of a "grand design" that encompasses all divine interventions.

Moreover, the argument goes, the "degree of freedom" possessed by mortals that nonetheless cannot "frustrate" the consummation of the divine plan points to the direction of the "over-determination" of an action, a prime example of which is the death of Patroclus in Book 16 of the *Iliad*. Even if Patroclus had wanted to remember the advice of Achilles not to press the Trojans beyond the defensive line of the Achaeans and threaten the very walls of Troy, Zeus "intervenes to ensure that he does not."[45] So "the human agents may will the means, but not the ends; … and even the means are more truly the gods' than the humans'."[46] The critic argues that "human freedom is drastically limited"[47] in the action of *Oedipus Tyrannus*, and consequently, "'free agency' is not a notion that adequately encapsulates Oedipus' career, onstage or off."[48]

I have outlined, thus far, the major points of Cairns's argument in this important exposition of the divine and human action in *Oedipus Tyrannus*. It is obvious that Cairns deprives Oedipus of the agency for which I have advocated in the previous section of this chapter. This 'minimal' human action is depicted even more graphically and vividly in Cairns's modification of Kovacs's well-known analogy of the chess game:

> … the analogy is less that of a grand master against a novice but of a grand master against a rather basic chess-playing computer programme in whose design the grand master has himself participated and in whose moves he is able directly to intervene.[49]

---

[43] Cairns 2013:136; my emphasis.
[44] Cairns 2013:138.
[45] Cairns 2013:140.
[46] Ibid.
[47] Cairns 2013:142.
[48] Ibid.
[49] Cairns 2013:138.

With this formulation, the scale tips entirely towards Apollo.

Cairns's line of argument seems plausible. After all, a similar remark is routinely addressed by students in university classes. How do we allow room for free human action in *Oedipus Tyrannus*, when we know that Oedipus' life was predetermined even before he was born? I will begin my critique of Cairns's formulations by referring first to the notion of the "over-determination" detected in the action of the self-blinding, then to the comparison he makes with Patroclus' death. I have argued extensively elsewhere about the over-determination of Patroclus' death in *Iliad* 16.[50] In this Iliadic incident, one may argue, Apollo is so dominant that he physically pushes Patroclus back from the walls of Troy, and progressively disarms him minutes before he is killed.

However, this is one of the final acts in the prolonged course of the dramatic action leading to Patroclus' death: a number of causes, each sufficient on its own to bring about Patroclus' death, converge in a complex interrelation throughout Book 16. Homer himself attributes a portion of responsibility to the hero in the conditional sentence: "for, if he had observed the word of the son of Peleus, he would surely have escaped the evil fate of black death"[51] (εἰ δὲ ἔπος Πηληϊάδαο φύλαξεν/ἦ τ' ἂν ὑπέκφυγε κῆρα κακὴν μέλανος θανάτοιο, 16. 686–687). This conditional comment by the poet explicitly acknowledges the "actorial motivation"[52] of Patroclus (he dies after ignoring the instructions of his friend Achilles), and allows, explicitly again, a certain margin for evading death.

It is obvious that Patroclus pursues his own *kleos* and acts on the battlefield not as Achilles' proxy but on his own motivations. When Patroclus has forced the panicking Trojans back from the ditch protecting the Greek camp and towards their walled city (16.293, 366–367), he intercepts them and presses them back towards the ships once more (16.395). This instigates the intervention of Sarpedon, which will trigger a series of causally related deaths—Sarpedon will be killed by Patroclus, Patroclus by Euphorbus and Hector, Hector by Achilles—because the clear objective of Book 16 is to rouse the disengaged Achilles back into the battle.[53] It is obvious that what we read here is the poet's plan, the narratological plan that overrides the plan of Zeus. I shall remind you here that what we consider "the plan of Zeus," which was formulated in the promise to Thetis, is a rather general condition indicating that Zeus will temporarily favor the Trojans to force the Achaeans to realize Achilles' importance and beseech him to return to battle. This condition has been already met in Book 9 when the members of the Embassy (following the orders of Agamemnon) offer him a

---

50   Karakantza 2014:121–140.
51   Translated by Murray/Wyatt.
52   Attributing a clear motivation of his actions to the hero, de Jong 2001:xi.
53   Karakantza 2014:122–123, 129–130.

full recompense and entreat his return. It is then that Achilles, adding a further condition, "modifies" the plan of Zeus: he will relent his anger and return to the fray only when the fire reaches his own ships. By Book 15, the parallel plans of Zeus and Achilles have reached an irresolvable impasse (for Achilles remains inactive, despite the proximity of the fire to his own ships) that will be broken only by Patroclus' intervention, which triggers an inevitable chain of events leading to his own death, to that of Hector, and finally, to the *homilia* of Priam and Achilles that forms the closure of our *Iliad*.[54]

The poet thus sets aside the two plans—of Zeus and of Achilles—and contrives his own narratological plan that defies both. He conjures up a sophisticated nexus of decisions and events in which Patroclus is inextricably enmeshed before dying as a double of Meleager;[55] and, in dying, Patroclus mobilizes the inactive Achilles, who can now return to battle with his honor fully restored, and brings about the micro-perspective of the end of the *Iliad* and the macroperspective of the fall of Troy.[56] It has been argued that "the poet's metaphor [for his determination of the plot] is the will of Zeus," and that "[the poet] claims his own originality by taking the traditional *boulê Dios* and altering it to fit his own story and provide not merely the plot of the epic, but a mechanism for the poet to enter into the story."[57]

The prediction of Patroclus' death by Zeus in Book 8 (473–477) and, even more so, the lengthy foretelling of the whole sequence leading, from Achilles' lending the armor to Patroclus, to the deaths of Sarpedon, Patroclus, and Hector, and the fall of Troy (15.64–72), occupy a different category than Zeus' and Achilles' plans. They portray the divine foreknowledge that is of the same order as Teiresias' foretelling of Oedipus' self-blinding. However, this foreknowledge does not prove a "divinely willed or caused" human action, as Cairns claims; both, I argue, belong to the foreknowledge of the poet/narrator.[58] Thus

---

[54] Karakantza 2014:122.

[55] I have argued that Patroclus assimilates the negative paradigm of Meleager and "saves" Achilles from the embarrassment of going back to battle without receiving the honorary presents from the Achaeans. Scholarship thus far has compared Patroclus with Cleopatra, the wife of Meleager, for they are both suppliants to angry heroes, one persuading Meleager to fight, the other receiving permission to fight in Achilles' stead. The essential common point of their stories, however, is that "the peril to his own chamber, that forced Meleager to return to fighting without honor (as Phoenix points out), has also reached the ships of the Achaeans and now threatens—one may assume—the ships and tents of the Myrmidons. ... If it were not for Patroclus, the fire would have forced Achilles to resume fighting in a less-than-honorable return to battle" (Karakantza 2014:127; see also 127nn14–15).

[56] Karakantza 2014:125.

[57] Wilson 2007:152–153; Karakantza 2014:125.

[58] From the standpoint of archaic ethics we have another factor that contributes to the death of Patroclus, and this is the temporal mental malfunction that is inferred in the notion of ἄτη (*atê*). The hero is seized by *atê* at that critical moment when he could have decided differently, not

Patroclus bears the responsibility for unraveling a complicated narratological plan that starts as the will of Achilles, moves to the petition of Thetis, is consolidated by the promise of Zeus, and transformed again by Achilles, only to be manipulated in its entirety by the poet;[59] in short, this is the narratological plan of the *Iliad*.

Along the same lines, in the vein of narratology and semiotics, John Peradotto in his "Disauthorizing Prophecy" approaches the oracle of Apollo in *Oedipus Tyrannus*:

> Prophecy is not conceivable apart from the narrative. It *derives from* narrative, from the representation of causal continuity in time. It is, I believe, less accurate to say that a narrative represents a prophecy than to say that prophecy represents the narrative, and does so by *pre-presenting* it, the frame paradoxically embedded in what it frames. Prophecy derives from the narrator's foreknowledge ... .[60]

Given that the oracle represents the narrative, then "the actions of Apollo are identical to the constitutive actions of the author, while those of Oedipus, Jocasta, and the rest are but *products* of those constitutive actions."[61] Furthermore, "what Apollo 'does' in the *OT*," the author argues, "is something that the poet does *directly*; what Oedipus 'does' is something the poet does *indirectly*." The divine activity in *Oedipus Tyrannus* is reflected in the "*direct* operation of the poet on the plot," for which no motivation resembling the way humans act is required.[62] It can also help us to explain, in my view, the trouble we experience in attributing an act of *hybris* to Oedipus that would conveniently and theologically justify his fall. The many and controversial analyses of the second *stasimon*, which introduces the notion of the tyrant and his *hybris*, as well as the many attempts to find Oedipus at fault either in his aggressive attitude to Teiresias and Creon, or in his intellectual pride, point to the futility of any attempt to construct a clear and unobstructed course leading from an "angry," "offended," or simply "revengeful" deity to the fallen mortal.[63]

---

to pursue the Trojans further, where the poet allows explicitly a margin of free action. In that instant when Patroclus could still have the command of his own fate, a temporary mental blindness confuses his mind. There is a long debate about whether *atê* is due to divine intervention or describes a human error. In my paper I argue that the semantic spectrum of the word spans from describing divine intervention (in the two instances of the personified Ἄτη) to mainly human decision-making (as is later reflected in the *nêpioi hetairoi* and suitors in the *Odyssey*). Patroclus' *nêpiotês* falls in the second category (Karakantza 2014:121, 131–134).

[59] Karakantza 2014:122.
[60] Peradotto 1992:10–11; emphasis by the author.
[61] Peradotto 1992:9; emphasis by the author.
[62] Quotations from Peradotto 1992:10.
[63] See chapter 4.7 above, pp. 84–89.

My argument thus far has depicted Oedipus as a conscious human agent and a strong evaluator who takes full responsibility for his actions. The self-blinding is the conscious attempt to mutilate his sight, rendering the socially constructed way of seeing and being seen impossible; he cannot endure the gaze of the others, be it his family or his fellow citizens. At the same time, he cannot endure the complete change of his own gaze. The superiority of a socially accepted benign king is forever destroyed, for he can no longer command respect in the public space. Oedipus has been transfigured from a respected king into a social outcast. In the actions of seeing and being seen, his transgressions and the ensuing public shame will be constantly re-enacted. The decision to blind himself is truly his own.

Thus, in the famous lines Ἀπόλλων τάδ' ἦν and αὐτόχειρ νιν οὔ/τις, ἀλλ' ἐγώ, I attribute to Oedipus his own clear share of responsibility. It remains to be seen how a person, such as the Sophoclean Oedipus, can act freely as a human agent and exert his own will in the context of the entire tragedy from within the circumscribed confines of his story given by the tradition. This will be addressed in the next section by revisiting the influential article of J.-P. Vernant, "Intimations of Will in Greek Tragedy" and moving on to re-evaluate the notions of will, agent, and the self, which—to my mind—are highly applicable to Oedipus. Sophocles has produced a play where he confronts the ultimate challenge of depicting a person with strength of will and remarkable determination despite the inflexible confines of the tradition that engendered his story.

5.3 Oedipus as a Human Agent

ἔοικε δή ... ἄνθρωπος εἶναι ἀρχὴ τῶν πράξεων

it seems that it is the human being who is the origin of his actions

Aristotle *Nicomachean Ethics* 1112b31–32

Up until now, critics have been at great pains to prove the degree of divine intervention in human affairs in *Oedipus Tyrannus*. I suggest taking the reverse course in our critical thinking; what if, instead of trying to determine how much the divine influences the course of events in the play, we examine the opposite perspective and try to establish the degree of human agency manifested in the play? In doing so, we should take the existence of the gods, together with the theological system they comprise, as an indispensable and constitutive part of the tradition within which Sophocles and his contemporary Athenians lived, breathed, and wrote. Sophocles composes a play that acknowledges this tradition; how could he do otherwise? Nevertheless, within this tradition, he creates a play that studies the boundless limits of human action. Sophocles constructs *his* Oedipus as an intelligent human being making decisions after intense deliberation, despite the circumscribed boundaries of his life; here, the playwright faces a challenge greater than in any other traditional narrative.

In what follows, I suggest a different perspective for interpreting the divine and human actions in *Oedipus Tyrannus*. In doing this, I shall revisit and re-evaluate the influential approach of Vernant regarding "Intimations of the Will in Greek Tragedy," where he examines the manifestation of the will in Greek tragedy as a culturally determined notion also linked to the categories of action and agent.[64] Here the emphasis is put on the judicial reforms and institutions of fifth-century Athens that explain, according to the critic, the emergence of the human subject as a discrete entity, and their decision-making and consequent actions, as we move from the "objective crime" (of the Homeric poems) to the "subjective responsibility" for transgressions as formulated by Aristotle a century later.[65] So the individual in fifth-century Athens emerges as "subject to the law,"[66] a political subject. Seductive as this idea might be, it is the first point to attract my criticism. The second is related to the way that Vernant sees the tragic agent as "still limited, indecisive, and vaguely defined,"[67] presenting "internal inconsistencies" due to the incomplete transition between older and newer concepts of justice, between Homer and the tragic genre. I will argue, on the contrary, that Oedipus can be seen as "an embodied individual," whose particular ethical role is realized within his social and political context, and is neither "fragmented" nor "incomplete," but a unitary entity, a bound self.[68] This is largely connected with the notion of identity, and "what it is to be a human agent,"[69] which has been the line of my argument throughout this book.

As I proceed to discuss the notion of the self as a non-fragmented individual, well established by the fifth century BCE (which, to my mind, should be considered as the foundation upon which Greek tragedy is formed), many collateral, but significant, issues will emerge and be tackled. First, the notion

---

[64] Vernant 1988:150–151.

[65] Vernant 1988:54–59. For the reference of the relevant Aristotelian sources, regarding this and other related issues, and the ensuing discussion, see the following pages of the current chapter.

[66] Vernant 1988:82.

[67] Ibid.

[68] All the issues related to the notion of the self, and how it is connected to the polis are tackled at great length in chapter 3 above, pp. 25–37. I shall only reiterate here the definition of the self by Richard Sorabji (2006:32): "an embodied self plain to see, which *has* or *owns* both psychological and bodily characteristics." He also argues that "I see no incompatibility between our interests in our own selves from the first-person perspective and an interest in our social duties and our objective existence as human beings" (49).

[69] Taylor 1989:ix.

of the "will," which is a highly problematic term when applied to ancient texts before the Stoics—let alone the notion of the "free will." Equally problematic is to impose later assumptions about the will on the ancient notion (or better, on the notions that fall within the spectrum of our contemporary concept of the will), thus creating confusion and misunderstandings, to the extent of seriously undermining the concomitant notions of human agency and decision making in classical Greek thought, especially when a contemporary reader seeks to identify a sequence of events purely human in attribution. Second, I will discuss the interconnection between, and transition from, the "objective crime" of the Homeric poems to the "subjective responsibility" of the tragic genre, thought by Vernant to be an "incomplete transition." I will raise the issue that, in cultural history, the coexistence of "old" and "new" structures of thought can be explained not as a deficiently resolved process needing consummation, but as a moment of creation (as Castoriadis defines it), when the old and new coexist in variable proportions and relations, positing a new *eidos*, a new "form" in the strongest and fullest sense.[70] Finally, this strand of the argument will conclude that Oedipus' actions in *Oedipus Tyrannus* are better explained by exploring the notion of the self and the concomitant dimensions of human agency that present a remarkable consistency, determination, and independence despite the constraints imposed by the divine oracle.

Before criticism, however, one should do justice to Vernant's influential approach by stating that one of the major benefits inherent in it is the realization that a modern reader of Greek tragedy considers the notion of the will as universal and pervasive throughout human history,[71] and consequently seeks to detect in the plays a fully-fledged modern category of the will. However, as the scholar remarks:

> ... the will is not a datum of human nature. It is a complex construction whose history appears to be as difficult, multiple, and incomplete as that of the self, of which it is to a great extent an integral part. We must therefore beware of projecting onto the ancient Greeks our own contemporary system for organizing the modes of behavior involving

---

[70] For an extensive discussion about the Castoriadian terms "creation" and *eidos* in history, see also chapter 2 above, pp. 13–14.

[71] Vernant 1988:50. Vernant's work is all the more remarkable, when one considers that his article was published nearly forty-five years ago, when the trend in classical scholarship (with a few notable exceptions) was toward a pervasive humanism resonating with an old-fashioned and out-of-date German Idealism, obliterating, as it were, all the differentiations and subtleties in concepts with which we are now familiar through new theories in philosophy, political and social sciences, gender studies, feminist thought, and poetics.

the will, the structures of our own processes of decision and our own models of the commitment of the self in the action.[72]

We have to realize, therefore, that the "conceptual system involved in our representation of what is willed"[73] differs significantly from that of the ancient Greeks.

I shall leave aside for the moment the problematic use of the notion of will in classical texts (but will return to it shortly), in order to examine one crucial deviation from modern concepts, notably that we seek "sequences of actions purely human,"[74] devoid of divine involvement in any process of decision making; the lack of the "purely human" in the ancient tradition leads us to seeing decisions as emanating from a "bound will," or (as in Homer) of a "double motivation." When the decision proves catastrophic, as with Patroclus,[75] the poet inserts into the process the factor of a mental blindness (*atê*) that produces confusion.[76] This confusion of mind, quite often considered of divine provenance, entails an error or "crime" that destroys the mortal, who, under the influence of *atê*, cannot see clearly and so is unable to predict the consequences of action. In the workings of *atê*, the ignorance (the *agnoia*) is embedded in the crime; ignorance becomes intrinsic to the crime. In this sense the mortal is not the author in the full sense of the term,[77] and the crime becomes objective.[78]

This is the Homeric concept of crime, in contrast to the later Aristotelian formulation where "men are responsible for this ignorance," and therefore emerge as subjects bearing full responsibility for the crime.[79] In this sense, between Homer and Aristotle, noting the significant intermediate stage of the

---

[72] Vernant 1988:50–51.

[73] Vernant 1988:54.

[74] Ibid. This is one of the categories that constitute the modern concept of the will, according to Vernant; the others are: 1) individual as agent; 2) subjective responsibility taking the place of the objective crime: and 3) the degree of the interconnection between the intentions of the human agent and the deeds brought to accomplishment. All of these will be tackled in the course of the present chapter.

[75] Discussed extensively above, at 5.2, pp. 130–132.

[76] Karakantza 2014:122–123, 132–134.

[77] Vernant 1988:63.

[78] Vernant 1988:68.

[79] καὶ γὰρ ἐπ᾽ αὐτῷ τῷ ἀγνοεῖν κολάζουσιν, ἐὰν αἴτιος εἶναι δοκῇ τῆς ἀγνοίας (*Nicomachean Ethics* 1113b 30–31); ὅσα δι᾽ ἀμέλειαν ἀγνοεῖν δοκοῦσιν, ὡς ἐπ᾽ αὐτοῖς ὃν τὸ μὴ ἀγνοεῖν (1114a1–2); also 1114a7–8; εἰ δὲ μὴ ἀγνῶν τις πράττει ἐξ ὧν ἔσται ἄδικος, ἑκὼν ἄδικος ἂν εἴη (1114a12–13). Man as the origin of his actions (1113b15–20): τὸ δὲ λέγειν ὡς οὐδεὶς ἑκὼν / πονηρὸς οὐδ᾽ ἄκων μακάριος ἔοικε τὸ μὲν ψευδεῖ τὸ δ᾽ ἀλη- / θεῖ· μακάριος μὲν γὰρ οὐδεὶς ἄκων, ἡ δὲ μοχθηρία ἑκού- / σιον. ἢ τοῖς γε νῦν εἰρημένοις ἀμφισβητητέον, καὶ τὸν / ἄνθρωπον οὐ φατέον ἀρχὴν εἶναι οὐδὲ γεννητὴν τῶν πράξεων / ὥσπερ καὶ τέκνων ("The saying 'No one is voluntarily wicked, nor involuntarily blessed', seems partly false, and partly true. For no one is involuntarily blessed, but wickedness is voluntary; otherwise, we shall have to disagree with what we have just said, and

fifth century BCE with the inception of law courts and dramatic performances, we move from an objective crime to the emergence of subjectivity and responsibility of humans as moral agents.[80] Vernant sees the individual in fifth-century Athens as a political subject, notably as "subject to the law,"[81] as stated earlier, instantiating (as it were) a stage of this process of transition.

Of course, counter-arguments exist regarding the workings of *atê*, which downplay the involvement of a god as an agent in the Homeric or dramatic action: the divine involvement does not detract from a hero's responsibility for his own action. *Atê* manifests itself only when the mortal works toward it. Even in cases of forceful studies of *atê*, such as the death of Patroclus in the *Iliad* or Aeschylus' *The Persians*, the "mortal works towards it": Patroclus pursues his own *kleos* oblivious to the warnings of Achilles, and Xerxes relentlessly incites his own arrogance and irreverence. This tangible intervention of the divine needs a well-established mortal foundation in order to materialize.[82] Yet *atê* lays the grounds for considering the double motivation in Homer, as well as the "bound will" of the tragic hero, with variable attribution of responsibility between the divine and the human.

5.3.1 The Notion of the Will

However, one major aspect of human dependence or independence, in relation to the divine, needs clarification before constructing a persuasive argument regarding the notion of the will. Vernant rightly argues that between "the idea of ignorance that causes the misdeed" (*agnoia* due to religious forces) and "the ignorance that excuses it" (the *akousion* of the action in the judicial terminology of the fifth century BCE), the category of the will is nowhere implied,[83] and, additionally, that in Aristotle "the idea of a free power of decision remains alien to his thought."[84]

---

deny that a human being is a first principle or the begetter of his actions as he is of his children," trans. Crisp).

[80] Vernant 1988:69.

[81] Vernant 1988:82.

[82] Karakantza 2013: "The provenance of *atê* could be divine, as in books 9 and 19 [of the *Iliad*], or primarily human, as is in the case of Patroclus. It seems that *atê* is directed by Zeus at mortals that have made themselves vulnerable to a certain error" (133); see also Yamagata 1991:9, 12 and 1994:57–60.

[83] Vernant 1988:65.

[84] Vernant 1988:59. See also Frede 2011:2–4, 157; Dihle 1982:45; Kahn 1988:234–259; Kenny 1979 passim. As for the precariousness in the notion of the will, Kahn begins his contribution in Dillon and Long 1979, titled "Discovering the Will: From Aristotle to Augustine," as follows: "It is clear that there is a problem about the will in ancient philosophy, but it is not so clear just what the problem is. At one time it seemed that there was a general agreement that the notion of the will

Along with Vernant, who raises questions arising from the notions of will (and the related notions of agency, intention, volition, and the like), we should note that the notion of the will is highly problematic (let alone the notion of a free will) when used before the Stoics, and consequently its use should be redefined in the context of Greek tragedy. When we, like Vernant, turn to Aristotle for enlightenment,[85] we realize, with the guidance of Michael Frede,[86] that the philosopher did not have a notion of the will, for he lacked the appropriate notion of choice in the way that a modern person would understand it. Not all of our actions are due to a mental event (a choice or decision to act); there is the case of "the choice without will"[87] when acting against reason (or on a non-rational desire). This is attributed to a failure of "training, practice, exercise, discipline, and reflection"—in short, to a lack of education or upbringing that "accounts for *akratic* action (ἀκρασία)."[88] Closer to what we understand as will are the Aristotelian notions of "willing or wanting something" (βούλεσθαι / βούλησις) and the notion of "choice" (προαιρεῖσθαι / προαίρεσις).[89] This latter is a "special form of willing" for two reasons. First, because "choosing" depends

---

was lacking in Greek philosophy." He then suggests that we need to consider what our concept of the will is, for we need to clarify this "before we start looking for traces of the will in antiquity, or looking for the gaps that show that this concept is lacking" (234–235). This is to acknowledge the long tradition of the investigation into the divergences or congruities of the notion since antiquity.

85   Vernant 1988:56–58.

86   Frede's book was published posthumously in 2011 (edited by A. A. Long) as *A Free Will: Origins of the Notion in the Ancient Thought.*

87   Frede 2011:19–30; "not everything voluntary is an object of choice" and *Nicomachean Ethics* 1112a15.

88   *Nicomachean Ethics* 1141b21–1146b5 and 1145a2–1154b32; *Eudemian Ethics* 1223a37–1223b31 and 1246b13 (ἀκρασία); Frede 2011:24.

89   προαίρεσις (rational choice, or disposition to choose), βούλησις / βούλευσις (wish) and their interaction are explored in *Nicomachean Ethics* 1111b5–1112a17 and 1112a20–1113a15, respectively. See, in particular, the two following illustrative passages; first, *Nicomachean Ethics* 1111b26–30: ἔτι δ' ἡ μὲν βούλησις τοῦ τέλους ἐστὶ μᾶλλον, ἡ δὲ προαίρεσις τῶν πρὸς τὸ τέλος, οἷον ὑγιαίνειν βουλόμεθα, προαιρούμεθα δὲ δι' ὧν ὑγιανοῦμεν, καὶ εὐδαιμονεῖν βουλόμεθα μὲν καὶ φαμέν, προαιρούμεθα δὲ λέγειν οὐχ ἁρμόζει· ὅλως γὰρ ἔοικεν ἡ προαίρεσις περὶ τὰ ἐφ' ἡμῖν εἶναι ("again, wish is more to do with the end, rational choice with what is conducive to the end; for example, we wish to be healthy, but we rationally choose things that will make us healthy; and we wish to be happy, and say that we do, but to claim that we rationally choose to be so does not sound right. For in general rational choice seems to be concerned with things that are in our power," trans. Crisp). And second, βούλησις as deliberation (στοχασμός), *Nicomachean Ethics* 1112b11–16: βουλευόμεθα δ' οὐ περὶ τῶν τελῶν ἀλλὰ περὶ τῶν πρὸς τὰ τέλη. οὔτε γὰρ ἰατρὸς βουλεύεται εἰ ὑγιάσει, οὔτε ῥήτωρ εἰ πείσει, οὔτε πολιτικὸς εἰ εὐνομίαν ποιήσει, οὐδὲ τῶν λοιπῶν οὐδεὶς περὶ τοῦ τέλους· ἀλλὰ θέμενοι τὸ τέλος τὸ πῶς καὶ διὰ τίνων ἔσται σκοποῦσι ("We deliberate not about the ends, but about things that are conducive to ends. For a doctor does not deliberate about whether to cure, nor an orator about whether to persuade, nor a politician whether to produce good order; nor does anyone else deliberate about his end. Rather they establish an end and then go on to think about how and by what means it is to be achieved,"

strictly on whether it is up to us (ἐφ' ἡμῖν) to do something or make something happen;[90] but the "capacity to do things" does not necessarily coincide with "willing to do things."[91] Second, because choices can be explained "in terms of the attachment of reason to the good"[92] and *not* (again necessarily) in terms of the will. Failure in the development of an individual human nature (due to immature development of character) results in failure to attain the good, something related, not to the will, but rather to the conditions of one's life (often beyond the control of the individual). Moreover, "just as there is no notion of a will in Aristotle, there is also no notion of freedom";[93] this makes the reference to a free will in classical texts even more problematic. In the Aristotelian view, there are regularities in this world that dictate a course of action. The celestial cosmos is "governed by a strict regularity,"[94] while human affairs, although presenting a certain latitude for free action, are again somehow circumscribed "because of imperfect realizations of human nature";[95] only the virtuous person can make the appropriate choices.

We need to advance several centuries, to Stoicism (notably, to Epictetus, in the first and second centuries CE), before we have, for the first time, a notion of will "as an ability of the mind or of reason to make choices and decisions,"[96] which comes about as a "natural development" of the unitary idea of the Stoics that the soul *is* a reason, and therefore what we are *is* essentially rational.[97] The Aristotelian *proairesis* is taken up by Epictetus, this time to denote "the ability to make choices, of which willings are just products";[98] and this is "indeed," according to Frede, "the first time that we have any notion of a will."[99]

Not only in Greek tragedy, but in our own times as well, the notion of free will is precarious. John Hyman, a contemporary philosopher, questions the notion of the will altogether (in antiquity, as well as in modernity and postmodernity), following a long line of nineteenth- and twentieth-century

---

trans. Crisp). See also: *Eudemian Ethics* 1226a20–b30, 1227a5–18, 1226b2–20; *Nicomachean Ethics* 1113a10–11 and 1139a22–b5.

90   *Nicomachean Ethics* 1111b30, 1112a17, 1112a30, 1113b17–19; Frede 2011:27; Kahn 1988:240.

91   Not all voluntary actions result from *proairesis*: *Nicomachean Ethics* 1112a14–15, 1135b8–11; *Eudemian Ethics* 1223b38–1224a7 and 1226b34–36. Not every action with *proairesis* need follow actual deliberation: *Nicomachean Ethics* 1117a17–22.

92   *Nicomachean Ethics* 1112a15–1113a14 and 1113b3–4; *Eudemian Ethics* 1226a7–13; *Eudemian Ethics* 1226b9–20; Frede 2011:27, 157; Cooper 1975, chapter 1 passim.

93   Frede 2011:27.

94   *Metaphysics* 12.7–9. Frede 2011:28; Frede and Charles 2000 ad loc.

95   Frede 2011:30.

96   Frede 2011:48.

97   Frede 2011:32–33.

98   Frede 2011:46.

99   Ibid.

philosophers who have also criticized this idea. He advocates that in place of the "will" we should explore instead the "four dimensions of human agency" (physical, ethical, psychological, and intellectual).[100] The differentiation of action into these four dimensions is preferable to using such notions as volition or intention, which are thought to be the cause of the human act.[101] Of course, Hyman writes, it is "widely regarded as axiomatic" that the "will [is] the source of all voluntary or intentional action."[102] However, under closer scrutiny the notion of will collapses into the four aforementioned dimensions of human agency, which, although partially overlapping, represent distinctive areas of that agency:[103] action emanates from the physical dimension; choice, from the ethical; desire and intention from the psychological; and reason and knowledge from the intellectual.

I append this formulation of the "fragmentation of the will" without any intention of entering into the contemporary debate about the existence of the notion (which is beyond the scope of this book), but to highlight the precariousness of the use of the term and its ensuing misunderstandings. It is also helpful because we realize that it is rather the notions of the self and of human agency that we should touch on if we want to understand the individual in tragedy. Despite the brilliance of Vernant's analysis in "Intimations of the Will in Greek Tragedy,"[104] the use of the notion of the will complicates rather than facilitates our understanding of human action in tragedy. In the following pages, I shall be concerned with the notion of the self and the subjective responsibility connected with the action of the autonomous individual, thus extending my analysis in chapter 3. Exploring the boundaries of the action of a human agent will help us understand where, I argue, the focus of the Sophoclean treatment of the Oedipus story is placed.

5.3.2 Subjective Responsibility and individualism

When considering subjective responsibility as the result of judicial reforms,[105] and the related notions of the self and the subject, we touch on another aspect

---

[100] Hyman 2015:4.

[101] Hyman 2015:1–2.

[102] Hyman 2015:1.

[103] Hyman 2015: "In the physical dimension the concepts of agent, power, and causation are attached; in the ethical dimension the concepts of voluntariness and choice; in the psychological dimension the concepts of desire, aim, and intention; in the intellectual dimension the concepts of reason, knowledge, and belief" (4).

[104] Leonard 2015:9.

[105] I would like to refer here to the interesting idea of the "self as a unitary entity," which antedates Vernant's "self as the political subject" by a century, dating back to the sixth century BCE in

of Vernant's approach that is open to criticism. Vernant refers to the "difficult, multiple, and incomplete self," and the "weakness of action" in Greek tragedy; in this formulation, the self again emerges as somehow fragmented, despite the "subjectivity" for which he advocated earlier in his essay. Of course, this emphasis on fragmentation resonates very well with the "antihumanistic ring" Miriam Leonard detects, which is in alignment with the structuralist movement and its questioning of the "primacy of the subject,"[106] and which is also corroborated by the Foucauldian notion of men's "discontinuous history."[107] So in this sense the incompleteness of the self in Greek tragedy, as postulated by Vernant, reflects a "critique of the structuralist and post structuralist about the political subject,"[108] rather than an inherent incongruity in the conceptualization of the notion of the self in fifth-century Athens. Vernant gives us more insight into "the humanism in structuralism than [he] does about legislation in fifth-century Athens."[109]

I corroborate Leonard's critique by returning to some of the points I raised earlier in the book[110] that will help us reconsider Vernant's "difficult, multiple, and incomplete self" in tragedy, and the "incomplete transition" to newer forms of thought, which are not yet fully materialized.

As I advocated earlier, at the end of the sixth century BCE there was a new social signification attached to the abstractions of "Athens" and "Athenians," which pointed to the will of the Athenians to become an empowered body politic that could collectively effect change in the public realm. The Athenians wished to have an independent polis not adherent to Sparta; they also refused to think of themselves (to *imagine* themselves, in Castoriadian terminology) as clients to local aristocrats, nor did they tolerate tyranny. The political *praxis* during the turbulent years between 510 BCE (the abolition of tyranny) and 508 BCE (the Athenian Revolution and the ensuing Cleisthenian reforms) marks the autonomy of a collectivity in the process of developing strong ties between its members and, undoubtedly, creating a new civic identity. This civic identity, which marks the interconnection and interdependence between the individual

---

Ionia, and connected to widespread monetization and subsequent emergence of the unitary and unchanging *Being* (the first principle) of the physical philosophy, as argued by Richard Seaford in *Money and the Early Greek Mind* (2004) and, later, in his paper "Monetisation and the Genesis of the Western Subject" (2012); as well as in several other publications: "Tragedy, Ritual, and Money" (2004), "Money and the Confusion of Generations in Sophocles' *Oedipus Tyrannus*" (2007), and "Money and Tragedy" (2008). In a sense, the "economic subject" of Seaford is posited against Vernant's individual "subject to the law."

[106] Leonard 2005b:133.

[107] Leonard 2005b:135.

[108] Ibid.

[109] Leonard 2015:9.

[110] See chapters 2 and 3 above.

subjectivity and the collective character of the Athenians, has been examined in chapter 3. I will only remind the reader here that a marked trait of the self in the polis is the accountability of the individuals to their community. The self in this sense is so strongly political that it becomes much broader than Vernant's political subject, who is principally subject to the law.

With this new concept of "Athens" and "Athenians" in mind, we can understand better how the new political system was conceived and developed so as to produce the radical, direct, participatory, and deliberative democracy of classical Athens as we know it. Fragmenting and reassembling the body politic, Cleisthenes lays the foundation for a system that sees the common traits binding the citizens together behind the multiformity and multiplicity of region, social class, wealth, education, political beliefs, and aspirations. Each new Cleisthenian tribe is living proof of the new ideology of working together and of being together in making polities—in various rituals, festivals, and dances for the city, as well as in battle and in collective burial. The Athenians spent most of their adult lives as members of their political tribe, as political beings. To my mind, this new powerful civic self is strongly represented in Attic tragedy, where the deliberations of those on stage, whether protagonists or the members of the chorus, refer to the wide range of issues associated with this very identity, as I argued earlier in this book. I cannot see anything fragmentary or incomplete in Greek tragedy;[111] on the contrary, fierce debates, strong opinions, and immovable attitudes are the material out of which tragedy is made.

5.3.3 Divine and Human Action: A New Creation

Vernant contended, however, that in tragedy the transition between the older forms of moral action and the self and the new innovations are not clearly demarcated[112] because of an incomplete process. I think that, despite Vernant's strong structuralist methodology, this idea resonates with an older trend of historicism that sees evolution as a mainly linear progression—the old will be gradually replaced by the new in a continuous line of successive forms and structures. This view of cultural history is no longer adequate, which constitutes the second parameter of the critique that I bring to the discussion. At any given moment in a human society, structures (intellectual, ethical, emotional, behavioral, and so on) exist as a synthesis of various strata, where the old and new exist synchronically in varying proportions and relations. When we come to classical Athens and the tragic genre, we can understand the co-existence of the

---

[111] See also Valakas 2009:191.
[112] Vernant 1988:79.

divine and the human, not as an incomplete transition, but as a new "creation" in the sense that Castoriadis defines it; not as a new discovery of something that was there before, undiscovered, but as a process of "constituting the new,"[113] which is an "active constitution," during which the Athenians re-conceptualize their "social imaginary significations."[114] In the words of Castoriadis:

> The Athenians did not find democracy amidst the other wild flowers growing on the Pnyx, nor did the Parisian workers unearth the Commune when they dug up the boulevards. Nor did either of them 'discover' these institutions in the heaven of ideas, after inspecting all the forms of government, existing there from all eternity, placed in their well-ordered showcases. They invented something, which, to be sure, proved to be viable in particular circumstances, but which also, once it existed, changed these circumstances essentially—and which, moreover, 25 centuries or 100 years later, continues to be 'present' in history.[115]

For Castoriadis, society "institutes itself in instituting the world of significations that is its own, in correlation to which, alone, a world can and does exist for it";[116] in other words, "society brings into being a world of significations and itself exists in reference to such a world."[117] Of course, this has to be understood in the context of the process of the "self-institution" of Athenian society, where an institution, which is a socially sanctioned symbolic network, comprises both a functional and an imaginary component.[118] Since Greek tragedy in particular is one of the main domains of the imaginary, where the re-conceptualization of social significations are formed and explored, we would expect to find there this active creation that comprises the notion of self, the individual, and the agent in the socio-historical context of fifth-century Athens. Human agency presupposes autonomy, and refers to "the relationship between the individual and society, and to the individuals' self-constitution within their specific social context in order to become subjects of action capable of transforming their reality."[119] This creation, of course, acknowledges the "pre-political" (in Castoriadis's sense) existence of the gods and their oracles, and the constraints they impose on mortal lives. The "pre-political" is never fully eradicated, and under certain

---

[113] Castoriadis 1997a:132–133.
[114] Castoriadis 1997a:341.
[115] 1997a:133.
[116] Castoriadis 1997a:359.
[117] Ibid.
[118] Castoriadis 1997a:132.
[119] Tovar-Restrepo 2012:70.

circumstances will resurface again, when classical political thought weakens in the face of other structures, where the active citizen is replaced by an individual subject to a Hellenistic king or Roman emperor. However, in Greek tragedy, when we are still *en plein* classical thought, viable forms of the individual, in correlation with the collective, are tried out so as to ensure the continuation of the unobstructed life of the polis. To this end, the social significations should be re-imagined or thought of and consequently sustained or modified;[120] "whatever has been imagined strong enough," argues Castoriadis, "to shape behavior, speech, or objects can, in principle, be re-imagined (represented) by somebody else."[121]

5.3.4 Rounding up the Argument

Consequently, I consider as fallacious (and an easy way out) any idea that the existence of the gods and their oracles dominate, dictate, and predetermine the thoughts and actions of the characters in a dramatic play; an idea prevalent among laymen and scholars alike. When it comes to Greek literature, nowhere do we find fiercer debates between the dramatic personae employing rational argumentation with a clearer view of the world and their position within it than in Greek tragedy. The comportment of the persons shows a clear evaluation of their position and the possibilities open to them, calculation of how to achieve aims, the making of choices, and the plans and strategies that constitute the essential components of agency and self.[122] If in this strategic planning crucial fragments of information are missing, as with Oedipus, this does not vitiate these actions of the essential parameters of human agency. Most of us (human beings in the twenty-first century CE with a well-established notion of the self) have found ourselves in similar situations where our evaluation of our lives—and our choice-making—has led to mis-planning because of deficient data.

Returning to the actions of Oedipus in Sophocles' play, all the parameters comprising human agency in action can be discerned: having a notion of the self (albeit with erroneous data), evaluating his life according to this notion, making

---

[120] I have argued elsewhere at length about the "correcting mechanism" of Attic tragedy in relation to the contemporary institutions of society, for tragedy addresses and affects their imaginary component. These institutions are the focal point of a society, such as the Athenian, that manifests itself as a *societas instituans*, and not a *societas instituta* (an *instituting* and not an *instituted* society; Castoriadis 1997a:369–373). The body of citizens create, deliberate, and constantly modify these very institutions by using several mechanisms, paramount among which is Attic tragedy; the end-point of this activity is the well-being of the citizens within their *polis* (Karakantza 2011a:22–25).

[121] 1997b:270.

[122] Taylor 1985:102–104, 106.

calculations, and making decisions so as to plot the course of his life. However, these actions, no matter how important, are not, on their own, enough to make him a moral agent. Oedipus needs to recognize some aspirations that fall into the category of evaluating one's life as worth living: a morally sound measuring up to "human feelings like pride, shame, guilt, sense of worth, love,"[123] and their like.[124] Moreover, the different possibilities, and the choices between them, are evaluated, with the clear intention on Oedipus' part to live at last a life worth living, eschewing even the remote possibility of killing his father and marrying his mother. In the way that Sophocles handles the story of Oedipus, I can see no fatalistic or deterministic or divinely bound action, but I can see a vital agent, a subject with a strong notion of himself when evaluating, calculating, deciding, planning, and measuring up his actions against highly moral standards. In this sense, the action of self-blinding—which is, admittedly, a choice with a will— encapsulates all his previous actions.

We can also understand fate in *Oedipus Tyrannus* (that is, the circumscribed limits of the hero's actions) as "the enabling circumstance that allows tragic events to take place."[125] In this sense, the oracle/divine action *is* what Peradotto calls "the narrative itself." In our play Oedipus acts and responds to the partic- ular circumstances as a human agent and a strong evaluator, with high moral standards. Dodds, as early as 1966, refuted the common assumption of divinely bound action in *Oedipus Tyrannus* by stating that "everything that [Oedipus] does on the stage from first to last he does as a free agent."[126] In my opinion, this emerges with crystal clarity in the play; Sophocles' topic is the transcendent ability of mortals to rise in stature above all external constraints.

To ease the minds of modern readers regarding these constraints (be they the gods, necessity, or fate), we should bear in mind that it is in our own society that we no longer conjoin religious faith with belief in prophecy; but this was not the case in the ancient world, whether pagan or Christian.[127] So, the crucial question in *Oedipus Tyrannus* must be formulated thus: whether Oedipus acts in a manner "true to himself"[128]—that is, true to his character as portrayed

---

[123] Taylor 1985:100.

[124] Taylor 1985:106. In *Oedipus Tyrannus* what is meticulously studied are all the actions that comply with the "performance" criterion.

[125] Rehm 2003, especially chapter 3, pp. 65–86.

[126] In the renowned paper "On Misunderstanding the *Oedipus Rex*" (1966:42).

[127] This is a well-known idea, beautifully formulated already by Doods in *Pagan and Christian in an Age of Anxiety* (1965:47).

[128] Sorabji 2006: "the idea of being true to yourself" found in the late Stoics has Presocratic anteced- ents in Democritus' exhortation "not to undertake activities beyond <one's> own capacity and nature" and even in Socrates' refusal to evade his execution as not being right for him, since he never left Athens before, except on military service (167). This falls within the wider issue of the idea of the individual persona that implies also an ethical dimension (157).

throughout the play. Are his actions and decisions in accordance with what we have come to know as Oedipus? Do they point to the individuality of Oedipus and relate to his ethical dimension? Rush Rehm argues regarding Orestes, where similar issues of coercion and agency are raised regarding the killing of his mother in the *Oresteia*, that "no one but Orestes must commit this crime, which is another way of saying that murdering his mother Clytemnestra and her lover Aegisthus, for killing his father Agamemnon, is part and parcel of what it means to *be* Orestes."[1]

From that perspective, the notion of identity for which I have argued throughout the present chapter emerges: what is to *be* Oedipus? Oedipus' actions, from first to last, are implicit in his character. Or, to quote again Cameron's words regarding his self-blinding, that is the crucial proof of Oedipus' subjectivity and agency; this act "is made to represent and somehow contain all the other acts which have gone before it."[2] Oedipus' choices, as we have seen, are explained in terms of the attachment to the good, for he earnestly strove to attain a life free from parricide and incest. Contrary to the theories that see in him a tyrannical disposition,[3] he is a good king, commanding approval and respect from the people of Thebes; and this reflects the line of conduct that he has pursued throughout his life, despite the lamentable outcome of the series of revelations that have constructed the new narrative of his life.

I conclude this excursus into the pressing and contentious issue of human agency and the subjective individuality that is embedded in the tragic situation in *Oedipus Tyrannus* (as is in most Greek tragedies) by stating that Oedipus is nowhere powerless in the hands of his gods, despite the renowned constraints to his life. In *Oedipus Tyrannus* the struggle of the individual in articulating his reasoning while rationally debating his position in this world, and notably in the quest for his identity, emerges with great clarity. Sophocles' Oedipus is not bound by a family curse as in Aeschylus. He commits crimes in ignorance (*agnoia*), for which he alone is responsible to the extent that he does not understand the signs of his identity (which are intentionally blurred). In a contemporary court of law he would have been absolved. He uses all his intellectual

---

[1] Rehm 2003:66; see also "in another culture, we might expect such a tragic vision to produce a sense of *powerlessness* before the multiple forces that lie beyond human control. But not in fifth-century Athens" (2003:67, my emphasis).

[2] Cameron 1968:105.

[3] Explored in chapter 4.7 above, pp. 84–99.

powers to understand and act according to a set of values that constitute a life worth living. He is a strong evaluator and a moral agent because what he does, he does with courage, intelligence, and determination. He confronts all the constraints of his life with the utmost fortitude. If at the end he falls, he does so with his immense dignity intact.

APPENDIX 1

Cornelius Castoriadis

S OME INTERESTING BIOGRAPHICAL points: Cornelius Castoriadis was born in 1922 in Constantinople (Istanbul) and died in Paris in 1997. When he was only a few months old, his family fled to Athens to escape the tragic consequences for the Greek population in Turkey following the collapse of the Greek front in the Greco-Turkish War (1919–1922). He was awarded his first degree in Economics, Political Science, and Law by the University of Athens in 1942. While still in high school, he joined the Athenian Communist Youth, and in 1941 the Communist Party of Greece, only to leave one year later to become an active Trotskyite. In the turbulent and repressive years of the German occupation of Greece and the internecine Civil War that followed shortly after, Castoriadis was persecuted by both the Germans and the Communist Party because of his radical left beliefs. In 1945, together with a substantial number of other Greek intellectuals and artists of the time, he boarded the New Zealand ocean liner "Mataroa" to escape persecution; he then settled in Paris. His escape was made possible by a generous scholarship from the French Institute of Athens with the personal intervention of its Director, Octave Merlier.

From his long career as a philosopher and political activist, I will single out two major involvements. First, the famous political group and its eponymous journal, *Socialisme ou Barbarie* (*Socialism or Barbarism*), which he co-founded with Claude Lefort and lasted from 1948–1966. In the years prior to the radical movement of May 1968, the journal, under the direction of Castoriadis, is believed to have played a pivotal role in influencing intellectuals and activists of the time. Second is the publication in 1975 of his seminal book *L'Institution Imaginaire de la Société* (*The Imaginary Institution of Society*), where the author presents his theory of the self-instituting society, social imaginary significations, and social change as a radical creation developed over years. The philosopher's interest in ancient Athenian democracy had always been vigorous, but gained further momentum when he became Director of Studies at the celebrated École des Hautes Études en Sciences Sociales (EHESS), from 1979 to 1997. Three volumes of his seminars on ancient Greece from that period have been published posthumously, with topics ranging from Homer and Heraclitus, to Attic tragedy and Thucydides. As ancient Athens was an essentially autonomous society, it became Castoriadis's cardinal theoretical paradigm for alternative and viable political organizations appropriate to his contemporary world.

APPENDIX 2

Cleisthenes

A CLASSIC BOOK ON THE CLEISTHENIC reforms remains *Clisthène l' Athénien. Essai sur la représentation de l' espace et du temps dans la pensée politique grecque de la fin du VIe siècle à la mort de Platon* by Pierre Lévêque and Pierre Vidal-Naquet, published in 1964. In 1969, another extensive study on Cleisthenes was published by Clarendon Press: *Nomos and the Beginnings of the Athenian Democracy*, by the German-American classical scholar Martin Ostwald. Ostwald then pursued his themes in a subsequent book: *From Popular Sovereignty to the Sovereignty of the Law* (1986).

This interest in Cleisthenes, however, as one of the "founding fathers" of Athenian democracy was not always the case. Mogens Herman Hansen's contribution to the volume *Ritual, Finance, Politics: Athenian Democratic Accounts Presented to David Lewis* (1994) has the telling title "The 2500th Anniversary of Cleisthenes' Reforms and the Tradition of Athenian Democracy" (25–37). In this contribution, he writes: "both in our sources for Athenian democracy and in the tradition about Athenian democracy Cleisthenes is a subordinate character, and it is only in this century that he has become the focus of attention in studies of Athenian democracy" (25). For centuries, Cleisthenes was overshadowed by Solon and Pericles. Only after the publication of Aristotle's *The Constitution of Athens* in 1891 did attention shift to Cleisthenes, for the philosopher gives us "the longest and most detailed account of Cleisthenes' work" in chapters 20–22 (26). Hansen further remarks:

> ... even today it is disputed whether Cleisthenes deserves to be credited with the introduction of democracy in Athens. Following the fourth-century tradition some modern historians will have the birth of Athenian democracy pushed back to Solon. Others believe that the essential elements of popular rule did not emerge until after Ephialtes' reforms. For my own part, I recommend that we trust Herodotus when he tells us that it was Cleisthenes who gave power to the people (27).

Relevant to the entire discussion are, of course, the individual contributions to the *Origins of Democracy in Ancient Greece*, edited by Raaflaub, Ober, and Wallace (2007).

APPENDIX 3

The Heroic Self

I WILL BEGIN BY CONSIDERING THE heroic self, with the Iliadic Achilles as my case in point. What are the salient characteristics of Achilles' individual distinctiveness and uniqueness in terms of psychological states, his physical presence, or bodily states? We are told of his beauty (which is, however, a quality of all Iliadic heroes),[1] his training as an exceptional warrior, and his capabilities as a *rhêtor* in the army's assembly (again, characteristics shared by many heroes in the Iliad). The Achilles of our *Iliad* is mostly famous for his anger, which erupts at the opening of the *Iliad* and results in his withdrawal from battle for most of the narrative time of the poem. He only rejoins the fray in Book 19. Achilles' anger constitutes a re-reading of the Trojan War by Homer; our Achilles (the image of him borne in our communal consciousness) is the Homeric Achilles.[2]

However, this intense emotion, instead of being an introspective reflection of the inner soul of the hero, is expanded by the poet to its collective dimension. From the very first moment of this eruption of anger, we are told about the consequences for others of this bout of emotional turmoil and ensuing withdrawal from the fighting. Homer describes the bleak consequences of Achilles' anger for the Achaeans and the Trojans, for the dead and the living, for the gods and the mortals, even in the celebrated proem of the epic. These dire repercussions are aggravated by Achilles asking his mother to extract the promise from Zeus to favor the Trojans until "many will die" and his comrades in arms come beseeching his assistance. In doing so, he flouts the system of values of the heroic society of which he is so prominent a member and traduces every possibility of remaining an exemplar to his peers. In the Embassy of Book 9, he is criticized heavily by his fellow-warriors and friends, who expound upon the appalling damage his self-obsession has wrought on the Achaeans. The ideal of

---

[1] The exception of ugly Thersites proves the case of the highly attractive appearance of the Iliadic heroes, for he belongs to an inferior social class. He has an appalling physical appearance and he fails in public speech, both areas of excellence of the aristocratic warriors.

[2] West 2011:44–46, 81.

behavior in the heroic community is epitomized not by Achilles but by Hector, who dismisses his beloved wife's advice to stay within the city walls and organize the defense of Troy from within, to preserve his life. His reply is cast in the following celebrated lines (*Iliad* 6.441-446):[3]

ἦ καὶ ἐμοὶ τάδε πάντα μέλει γύναι· ἀλλὰ μάλ' αἰνῶς
αἰδέομαι Τρῶας καὶ Τρῳάδας ἑλκεσιπέπλους,
αἴ κε κακὸς ὣς νόσφιν ἀλυσκάζω πολέμοιο·
οὐδέ με θυμὸς ἄνωγεν, ἐπεὶ μάθον ἔμμεναι ἐσθλὸς
αἰεὶ καὶ πρώτοισι μετὰ Τρώεσσι μάχεσθαι
ἀρνύμενος πατρός τε μέγα κλέος ἠδ' ἐμὸν αὐτοῦ.

Yes, Andromache, I worry about all this myself,
But my shame before the Trojans and their wives,
With their long robes trailing, would be too terrible
If I hung back from battle like a coward.
And my heart won't let me. I have learned to be
One of the best, to fight in Troy's first ranks,
Defending my father's honor and my own.

Hector, above all, cannot disdain battle and stand shamed before his fellow citizens, as he has been raised from birth to fight in the vanguard of the Trojan line as the foremost defender of the city. This formulation of duty overriding self-interest has often been conceptualized in terms of cooperative vs. competitive values. Arthur W. H. Adkins in his classic book *Merit and Responsibility* of 1960 formulated this distinction and conflict of values. However, we need to make some amendments before embarking on the specific arguments about the particularity and accountability of the Homeric heroes—that is to say, before balancing the unique characteristics of a person with his public persona.

Cooperative and Competitive Values; Questioning the Dichotomy

In Adkins' view, the competitive values (promoting recognition of the individual through personal achievement) override the cooperative (or "quiet") values ideally promoting cooperation at a communal level. Competitive values defeat co-operative ones because the latter attract less admiration from society.[4] In

---

[3] Trans. Lombardo.

[4] Adkins 1960:55; see also p. 36: "In comparison with the competitive excellences, the quieter co-operative excellences must take an inferior position; for it is not evident at this time that the

Adkins' interpretive framework, not only are intentions irrelevant,[5] but martial prowess alone is paramount.[6] Following this reasoning then, Homeric heroes are impelled to pursue their personal *timê* and *kleos* at the expense of others' *timê* and *kleos*, and this would be considered as a normal, and normative, *ethos*. In this respect Achilles, whose pursuit of his *timê* is the most egotistic and obsessive, could be seen as the prototypical hero, the measure of all others.[7]

In fact, however, Achilles' behavior is not the norm in the *Iliad*, nor does it comply with the commonly accepted ethics of his fellow warriors,[8] as many incidents in the *poem* bear witness. He puts his heroic *timê* above the communal wellbeing of the Achaeans, and consequently spurns the battlefield. He does not act as is expected of him, which is evidenced by the strong disapproval of his friends of the Embassy (Book 9). Moreover, when he actually rejoins the fray, he violates all conceivable aspects of the heroic code in a cumulative frenzy of killing (Book 21) and finally treats Hector's body in blatant defiance of both human and divine laws (Books 22–24).[9] Achilles *violates* the ethics of the Iliadic warrior, as upheld by heroes such as Ajax, Diomedes, Odysseus, Menelaus, Hector, and Aeneas; *ethics* he himself embodied before the outburst of his *mênis*.

---

security of the group depends to any large extent upon these excellences." This idea is repeated again on p 46: "as soon as a crisis forces the essential framework of values into view, the competitive values are so much more powerful than the cooperative that the situation is not treated in terms of the quiet values at all; and as it is precisely with such crises that the concept of moral responsibility is concerned, it is evident that such terms as *aidôs* and *aeikes*, however useful to society in general, cannot affect the development of the concept of moral responsibility, for they are ineffective at the crucial moment." In this framework of interpretation, the author claims that even when Agamemnon admits his wrongdoing against Achilles in Book 19 there is no moral responsibility for his actions (52); the only flaw of Agamemnon is that he "falls short in success of war" (51), which for Adkins requires only competitive values.

5   Adkins 1960:35–36, 49.

6   Adkins 1960:51–52.

7   Achilles as the archetypal warrior for his "self-awareness and for his wrath," but he also oscillates between excellence and bestiality (best and beast): King 1987:228; he serves as a paradigm of a war hero for later literature (King 1987 passim). Many further studies have noted the peculiarity of his character and position in the *Iliad*; as the "best of the Achaeans" (Nagy 1999:26–41); as having an evolving character shifting from anger to pity (Schein 1984:89–167); withdrawing from suffering and receding to the politics of pity (Hammer 2002:207–229); representing an internal ambiguity of the heroic code consisting of values of cooperation and erosion (Zanker 1994:42); Muellner (1996) studies his *mênis* not in qualitative terms but as a driving theme of the *Iliad* (starting at book 1) and follows its teleology, which dissolves into *philotês* (Book 24).

8   Lloyd-Jones 1983:17.

9   This behavior is dictated by what I call "the second round of Achilles' anger" (Books 19–24). I do not use the term *mênis*, since this is the technical term to describe the anger addressed against Agamemnon, which is officially denounced in Book 19 (μήνιδος ἀπόρρησις). It should be noted, however, that various verbal forms deriving form *mênis* are used by the poet to describe Achilles' maniacal killing of the Trojans and the maltreatment of Hector's body (observe the use of words ἐμμανής, μεμαώς).

In her last meeting with Hector, Andromache describes how Achilles treated her father, whom he had killed, with honor by giving him an appropriate heroic burial and accepting the ransoms offered for her mother, setting her free. In addition, Achilles used to fight in the front rank to achieve both success for the Achaeans *and* his personal *kleos* (Book 1).

The combining of personal gain and collective cause while observing the warriors' code of honor is the mode of fighting proper to an Iliadic hero, as Cairns illustrates in his book *Aidos* (1993). He offers a better insight into the Homeric ethics than the earlier dichotomy of Adkins: "to be concerned with one's own honor is to envisage oneself as one among others, also bearers of honor; thus to limit one's own claim to honor is to accept one's status vis-à-vis others, to inhibit self-assertion is to recognize how this conduct would impinge upon the honor of others ... ."[10] In this sense, "[the code of honor] integrates self-regarding and other-regarding, competitive and co-operative standards into a remarkably unified whole."[11] This last idea is similarly put forward by Hammer: "Homeric society constructs the notion of action in such a way that the excellences to which Adkins points are tied to an issue of community maintenance. ... although excellence *appears* to create a competitive individualism, it is an excellence carefully tied to the internal gradations of status and obligation *within the community*."[12] This is exactly what the *Iliad* conveys to its audience. I subscribe to the view that the code of honor observes individual and collective interests and that the overvaluation of personal interests at the expense of the common wellbeing is rejected squarely in the Homeric society.

---

[10] Cairns 1993:13.
[11] Cairns 1993:14.
[12] Hammer 2002:79.

Bibliography

Adkins, A. W. H. 1960. *Merit and Responsibility: A Study in Greek Values.* Oxford.

———. 1972. *Moral Values and Political Behaviour in Ancient Greece.* London.

Ahrensdorf, P. J. 2009. *Greek Tragedy and Political Philosophy: Rationalism and Religion in Sophocles' Theban Plays.* Cambridge.

Alexiou, M. 1974. *Ritual Lament in Greek Tradition.* Cambridge.

Athanasiou, A. 2006. *Φεμινιστική Θεωρία και Πολιτισμική Κριτική.* Athens.

Bain, D. 1979. "A Misunderstood Scene in Sophocles' *Oidipous* (*O.T.* 300–462)." *Greece and Rome* 26:132–145.

Bakogianni, A. 2011. *Electra Ancient and Modern: Aspects of the Reception of the Tragic Heroine.* Bulletin of the Institute of Classical Studies, Supplement 113. London.

———. 2013. *Dialogues with the Past: Classical Reception Theory and Practice.* 2 Vols. Bulletin of the Institute of Classical Studies, Supplement 126.1-2. London.

Banwell, S. and M. Fiddler. 2018. "Gendered Viewing Strategies: A Critique of Holocaust-related Films that Eroticize, Monsterize, and Fetishize the Female Body." *Holocaust Studies* 24:150–171.

Bassi, K. and J. P. Euben, eds. 2010. *When Worlds Elide: Classics, Politics, Culture.* Lanham, Md.

Battezzato, L. 2005. "Lyric." In Gregory 2005:149–166.

Beattie, T. 1999. *God's Mother, Eve's Advocate: A Marian Narrative of Women's Salvation.* Bristol.

Beer, J. 2004. *Sophocles and the Tragedy of Athenian Democracy.* Westport, CT.

Beier, T., ed. 2007. *Generationskonflikte auf der Bühne.* Tübingen.

Belfiore, E. S. 2000. *Murder among Friends: Violation of Philia in Greek Tragedy.* Oxford.

Bloom, H., ed. 2007. *Homer's* The Iliad. New York.

Blundell, M. W. 1989. *Helping Friends and Harming Enemies: A Study in Sophocles and Greek Ethics.* Cambridge.

Bollack, J. 1990. *L' Oedipe Roi de Sophocle. Le texte et ses Interprétations.* 4 vols. Villeneuve.

Brodribb, S. 1992. *Nothing Mat(T)ers: A Feminist Critique of Postmodernism.* North Melbourne, Vic, Australia.

Bryant, J. M. 1996. *Moral Codes and Social Structure in Ancient Greece: A Sociology of Greek Ethics from Homer to the Epicureans and Stoics*. Albany.

Budelmann, F. 2000. *The Language of Sophocles: Communality, Communication and Involvement*. Cambridge.

———. 2006. "The Mediated Ending of Sophocles' Oedipus Tyrannus." *Materiali e Discussioni per l' Analisi dei Testi Classici* 57:43–61.

Burkert, W. 1985. *Greek Religion. Archaic and Classical*. Trans. J. Raffan. Oxford. Originally published as *Griechische Religion der archaischen und klassischen Epoche. 1977*. Stuttgart.

Burian, P. 2009. "Inconclusive Conclusion: The Ending(s) of Oedipus Tyrannus." In Goldhill and Hall 2009:99–118.

Butler, J. 1986. "Variations on Sex and Gender: Beauvoir, Wittig, and Foucault." *Praxis International* 5:505–516.

———. 1988. "Performative Acts and Gender Constitution: An Essay in Phenomenology and Feminist Theory." *Theatre Journal* 40:519–531.

———. 1993. *Bodies that Matter. On the Discursive Limits of Sex*. NY.

———. 2000. *Antigone's Claim. Kinship Between Life and Death*. NY.

Cairns, D. L. 1993. *Aidos: The Psychology and Ethics of Honour and Shame in Ancient Greek Literature*. Oxford.

———. 2013. "Divine and Human Action in the Oedipus Tyrannus." In Cairns 2013, 119–172.

———, ed. 2013. *Tragedy and Archaic Greek Thought*. Swansea.

Calame, C. 1996. "Vision, Blindness, and Mask." In Silk 1996:17–39.

Cameron, A. 1968. *The Identity of Oedipus the King: Five Essays on Oedipus Tyrannus*. NY.

Carter, D. M. 2006. "At Home, Round Here, Out There: The City and Tragic Space." In Rosen and Sluiter 2006:139–172.

———. 2007. *The Politics of Greek Tragedy*. Exeter.

———, ed. 2011. *Why Athens? A Reappraisal of Tragic Politics*. Oxford.

Castoriadis, C. 1983. "Greek Polis and the Creation of Democracy." *Graduate Faculty Philosophy Journal* 9.79–115.

———. 1995. *Χώροι του ανθρώπου*. Trans. Z. Σαρίκας. Athens. Originally published as *Domaines de l' homme*. 1986. Paris.

———. 1997a. *The Imaginary Institution of Society*. Trans. K. Blamey. Cambridge. Originally published as *L' Institution Imaginaire de la Société*. 1972. Paris.

———. 1997b. *Castoriadis Reader*. Ed. and Trans. D. A. Curtis. Cambridge, MA.

———. 2001. "Αισχύλεια Ανθρωπογονία και Σοφόκλεια Αυτοδημιουργία του Ανθρώπου." In *Ανθρωπολογία, Πολιτική, Φιλοσοφία. Πέντε διαλέξεις στη Βόρειο Ελλάδα*, 11–36. Athens.

———. 2007. *Η ελληνική Ιδιαιτερότητα. Από τον Όμηρο στον Ηράκλειτο. Σεμινάρια 1982-1983.* Ed. E. Escobar, M. Condicas, and P. Vernay. Ed. Z. Καστοριάδη (for the Greek edition). Trans. Ξ. Γιαταγάνας. Athens. Originally published as *Ce qui fait la Grèce. D' Homère à Héraclite. Séminaires 1982-1983. La création humaine II.* 2005. Paris.

———. 2008. *Η Ελληνική Ιδιαιτερότητα. Η Πόλις και οι Νόμοι. Σεμινάρια 1983-1984.* Ed. E. Escobar, M. Condicas, and P. Vernay. Trans. Z. Καστοριάδη. Athens. Originally published as *Ce qui fait la Grèce, Vol. 2: La Cité et les lois. Séminaires 1983-1984. La création humaine III.* 2008. Paris.

Cavanagh, S. L. 2017. "Antigone's Legacy: A Feminist Psychoanalytic of an Other Sexual Difference." *Studies in the Maternal* 9:1–33.

Christ, M. R. 2006. *The Bad Citizen in Classical Athens.* Cambridge.

Cooper, J. M. 1975. *Reason and Human Good in Aristotle.* Cambridge, MA.

Crisp, R. 2014. *Aristotle. Nicomachaean Ethics.* Cambridge.

Culler, J. 1981. *The Pursuit of Signs: Semiotics, Literature, Deconstruction.* Ithaca, NY.

Cusland, J. C. R., and J. Hume, eds. 2009. *The Play of Texts and Fragments: Essays in Honor of Martin Cropp.* Mnemosyne Supplement 314. Leiden.

Dain, A. and P. Mazon. 1967–1972. *Sophocles.* 3 vols. Paris.

Davidson, J. F. 1985. "Sophoclean Dramaturgy and the Ajax Burial Debates." *Ramus* 14:16–29.

Davies, M. 1991. *Sophocles' Trachiniae.* Oxford.

Dawe, R. D. 2006 [1982]. *Sophocles. Oedipus Rex.* Cambridge Greek and Latin Classics. 2nd ed. Cambridge.

Delcourt, M. 1938. *Stérilités Mysterieuses et Naissances Maléfiques dans l' Antiquité Classique.* Liège.

———. 1944. *Oedipe; ou la Légende du Conquérant.* Paris.

———. 1957. *Héphaistos; ou la Légende du Magicien.* Paris.

Devereux, G. 1973. "The Self-blinding of Oidipous in Sophocles: *Oidipous Tyrannos.*" *The Journal of Hellenic Studies* 93:36–49.

de Jong, I. J. F., and A. Rijksbaron, eds. 2006. *Sophocles and the Greek Language: Aspects of Diction, Syntax and Pragmatics.* Mnemosyne Supplement 269. Leiden.

de Polignac, F. 1995. *Cults, Territory, and the Origins of the Greek City State.* Trans. J. Lloyd. Chicago. Originally published as *La Naissance de la Cité Grecque: Cultes, Espace, et Société VIIIe-VIIe siècles avant J.- C.* 1984. Paris.

de Sélincourt, A. (revised with an Introduction and notes by A. R. Burn). 1972. *Herodotus. The Histories.* London.

de Ste. Croix, G. 2004. *Athenian Democratic Origins: and Other Essays.* Ed. D. Harvey and R. Parker. Oxford.

Dieteren, F., and E. Kloek, eds. 1990. *Writing Women into History.* Amsterdam.

Dihle, A. 1982. *The Theory of the Will in Classical Antiquity.* Berkeley.

Dillon, J. M. and A. A. Long, eds. *The Question of Eclecticism: Studies in Later Greek Philosophy.* Berkeley.

Dodds, E. R. 1959. *The Greeks and the Irrational.* Sather Classical Lectures 25. Berkeley.

———. 1965. *Pagan and Christian in an Age of Anxiety: Some Aspects of Religious Experience from Marcus Aurelius to Constantine.* Cambridge.

———. 1966. "On Misunderstanding the *Oedipus Rex.*" *Greece & Rome* 13:37–49.

Dover, K. J. 1974. *Greek Popular Morality in the Time of Plato and Aristotle.* Oxford.

Duffy, W. 2010. "Aias and the Gods." In Myrsiades 2010:149–169.

Easterling, P. 1982. *Sophocles. Trachiniae.* Cambridge Greek and Latin Classics. Cambridge.

Edmunds, L. 1985. *Oedipus: The Ancient Legend and Its Later Analogues.* Baltimore.

———. 1996. *Theatrical Space and Historical Place in Sophocles' Oedipus at Colonus.* Lanham, Md.

———. 2000, "The Teiresias Scene in Sophocles' *OT,*" *Syllecta Classica* 11:34–73.

Edmunds, L. and A. Dundes, eds. 1983. *Oedipus: A Folklore Casebook.* New York.

Ehrenberg, V. 1973. *From Solon to Socrates: Greek History and Civilization during the Sixth and Fifth Centuries B.C.* London.

Elster, J., and H. Landemre, eds. 2012. *Collective Wisdom: Principles and Mechanism.* Cambridge.

Euben, J. P. 1986. *Greek Tragedy and Political Theory.* Berkeley.

———. 1990. "Identity and the *Oedipus Tyrannos.*" In *The Tragedy of Political Theory: The Road Not Taken,* 96–111. Princeton NJ.

———. 1992. "How to Study Ancient Moral and Political Philosophy." *Polis* 11: 3–27.

Finglass, P. J. 2007. *Sophocles: Electra.* Cambridge Classical Texts and Commentaries 44. Cambridge.

———. 2011. *Sophocles: Ajax.* Cambridge Classical Texts and Commentaries 48. Cambridge.

———. 2018. *Sophocles: Oedipus the King.* Cambridge Classical Texts and Commentaries 57. Cambridge.

Farnell, L. R. 1921. *Greek Hero Cults and the Idea of Immortality.* Oxford.

Fisher, N. R. E. 1992. *Hybris: A Study in the Values of Honour and Shame in Ancient Greece.* Warmister.

Foley, H. P. 1993. "The Politics of Tragic Lamentation." In Sommerstein, Halliwell, Henderson, and Zimmermann 1993:101–143.

———. 2003. "Choral Identity." *Classical Philology* 98:1–30.

Foucault, M. 1974, *The Order of Things: An Archaeology of the Human Sciences.* London. Originally published as *Les Mots et les Choses.* 1966. Paris.

———. 1977. *Discipline and Punish: The Birth of the Prison.* Trans. A. Sheridan. London. Originally published as *Surveiller et Punir. Naissance de la Prison.* 1975. Paris.

———, ed. 1980. *Herculine Barbin, Being the Recently Discovered Memoirs of a Nineteenth Century Hermaphrodite.* Trans. R. McDougall. New York. Introduction by Foucault only for the English edition. Originally published as *Herculine Barbin, dite Alexina B.* 1978. Paris.

———. 1988–1990. *The History of Sexuality.* 3 vols. Trans. R. Hurley. New York. Originally published as *Histoire de la Sexualité.* 1976–1984. Paris.

———. 2000–2002. "Truth and Juridical Forms." In *Essential Works of Foucault 1954-1984*, vol. 3: *Power* (ed. J. D. Faubion). Trans. R. Hurley and Others, 1–89. London.

Frazer, J. G. 1921. *Apollodorus: The Library.* 2 vols. Loeb Classical Library. Cambridge, MA.

Frede, M. 2011. *A Free Will: Origins of the Notion in Ancient Thought.* Ed. A. A. Long. Sather Classical Lectures 68. Berkeley.

Frede, M. and D. Charles, eds. 2000. *Aristotle's Metaphysics Lambda. Symposium Aristotelicum.* Oxford.

Freud, S. 1977. *Three Essays on the Theory of Sexuality and Other Works.* Ed. and Trans. A. Richards. The Penguin Freud Library, vol. 7. London. Orig. pub. as *Drei Abhandlungen zur Sexualtheorie.* 1905. Leipzig-Vienna.

———. 1988. *Case Histories II.* Ed. and Trans. A. Richards. The Penguin Freud Library, vol. 9. London.

Gallop, J. 1982. *The Daughter's Seduction: Feminism and Psychoanalysis.* Ithaca, NY.

Gardiner, C. P. 1987. *The Sophoclean Chorus: A Study of Character and Function.* Iowa City, IA.

Garvie, A. F. 1998. *Sophocles* Ajax. Warminster.

Gildenhard, I., and M. Revermann, eds. 2010. *Beyond the Fifth Century: Interactions with Greek Tragedy from 400 BCE to Middle Ages.* Berlin-New York.

Gill, C. 1996 *Personality in Greek Epic, Tragedy, and Philosophy: The Self in Dialogue.* Oxford.

———. 2006a. *The Structured Self in Hellenistic and Roman Thought.* New York.

———. 2006b. "Achilles' Swelling Heart." In Bloom 2007:95–108.

Giosi, M. J. 1996. *Μύθος και Λόγος στον Σοφοκλή.* Athens.

Girard, R. 1972. *La Violence et le Sacré.* Paris.

Goff, B., ed. 1995. *History, Tragedy, and Theory.* Austin.

———. 2004. *Citizen Bacchae: Women's Ritual Practice in Ancient Greece.* Berkeley.

Goffman, E. 1968. *Stigma: Notes on the Management of Spoiled Identity.* London.

———. 1986. *Reading Greek Tragedy.* Cambridge.

Goldhill, S. 2009. "The Audience on Stage: Rhetoric, Emotion, and Judgment in Sophoclean Theatre." In Goldhill and Hall 2009:27–47.

———. 2012. *Sophocles and the Language of Tragedy.* Oxford.

Goldhill, S. and E. Hall, eds. 2009. *Sophocles and the Greek Tragic Tradition.* Cambridge.

Goodhart, S. 1978. "Ληστὰς Ἔφασκε: Oedipus and Laius' Many Murderers." *Diacritics* 8:55–71.

Gould, J. 2001. *Myth, Ritual, Memory, and Exchange. Essays in Greek Literature and Culture.* Oxford.

Gould, T. 1965a. "The Innocence of Oedipus. The Philosophers on Oedipus the King." *Arion* 4.3:363–386.

———. 1965b. "The Innocence of Oedipus. The Philosophers on Oedipus the King II." *Arion* 4.4:582–611.

———. 1966. "The Innocence of Oedipus. The Philosophers on Oedipus the King III." *Arion* 5.4:478–525.

Goux, J.-J. 1993. *Oedipus, Philosopher.* Trans. C. Porter. Stanford. Originally published as *Oedipe Philosophe.* 1990. Paris.

Gregory, J. ed. 2005. *A Companion to Greek Tragedy.* Oxford.

Griffith, M. 1999. *Sophocles' Antigone.* Cambridge Greek and Latin Classics. Cambridge.

Hall, E. 2010. *Greek Tragedy: Suffering Under the Sun.* Oxford.

———. 2012. "The Necessity and Limits of Deliberation in Sophocles' Theban Plays." In Ormand 2012:301–315.

Hame, K. 2008. "Female Control of Funeral Rites in Greek Tragedy: Klytaimestra, Medea, and Antigone." *Classical Philology* 103:1–15.

Hammer, D. 2002. *The Iliad as Politics. The Performance of Political Thought.* Norman, OK.

Hansen, M. H., ed. 1993. *The Ancient Greek City State: Acts of the Copenhagen Polis Centre.* Vol. 1. Copenhagen.

———. 1994. "The 2500th Anniversary of Cleisthenes Reforms and the Tradition of Athenian Democracy." In Osborne and Hornblower 1994:25–37.

———. 2006. *Polis: An Introduction to the Ancient City-State.* Oxford.

———, ed. 2007. *The Return of the Polis: The Use and Meanings of the Word Polis in Archaic and Classical Sources.* Papers from the Copenhagen Polis Centre 8. Historia 198. Stuttgart.

Harris, E. M. 2006. *Democracy and the Rule of Law in Classical Athens: Essays on Law, Society, and Politics.* Cambridge.

Harris, W. V., ed. 2008. *The Monetary Systems of the Greeks and Romans.* Oxford.

Heath, M. 1987. *The Poetics of Greek Tragedy.* Stanford.

Hegel, G. W. F. 1892–1896. *Lectures on the History of Philosophy*. 3 vols. Trans. E. S. Haldane and F. H. Simson, London.

Herman, G. 2006. *Morality and Behaviour in Democratic Athens: A Social History*. Cambridge.

Hesk, J. 2003. *Sophocles* Ajax. London.

Hewitson, G. 1999. *Interrogating the Masculinity of Rational Economic Man*. Cheltenham, UK.

Hook, D. 2006a. "Psychoanalysis, Sexual Difference, and the Castration Problematic." In Shefer, Boonzaier, Kinguwa 2006:49–59.

———. 2006b. "Lacan, the Meaning of the Phallus, and the Sexed Subject." In Shefer, Boonzaier, Kinguwa 2006:60–84.

Honig, B. 2013. *Antigone Interrupted*. Cambridge.

Hyman, J. 2015. *Action, Knowledge, and Will*. Oxford.

Irigaray, L. 1985. *Speculum of the Other Woman*. Trans. G. G. Gill. Ithaca, NY. Originally published as *Speculum de l' Autre Femme*. 1974. Paris.

———. 1993. *Je, Tu, Nous: Toward a Culture of Difference*. Trans. A. Martin. New York. Originally published as *Je, Tu, Nous: Pour une Culture de la Différence*. 1990. Paris.

———. 1994. *Thinking the Difference: For a Peaceful Revolution*. Trans. K. Montin. London. Originally published as *Le Temps de la Différence: Pour une Revolution Pacifique*. 1989.

Jebb, R. C. 1887. *Sophocles. Part I*: The Oedipus Tyrannus. 2nd ed. Cambridge.

———. 1892. *Sophocles. Part V*: The Trachiniae. Cambridge.

———. 1896. *Sophocles. Part VII*: The Ajax. Cambridge.

Jouanna, J. 2018. *Sophocles. A Study of His Theater in Its Political and Social Context*. Trans. S. Rendall. Princeton. Originally published as *Sophocle*. 2008. Paris.

Kahn, C. H. 1988. "Discovering Will: From Aristotle to Augustine." In Dillon and Long 1988:235–259.

Kamerbeek, J. C. 1953. *The Plays of Sophocles. Part I*: The Ajax. Leiden.

———. 1963. *The Plays of Sophocles. Part IV*: The Oedipus Tyrannus. Leiden.

———. 1965. "Prophecy and Tragedy," *Mnemosyne* 18:29–40.

Karakantza, E. D. 2004. *Αρχαίοι Ελληνικοί Μύθοι. Ο Θεωρητικός Λόγος του 20ού Αιώνα για τη Φύση και την Ερμηνεία τους*. Athens.

———. 2011a. "Polis Anatomy: Reflecting on Polis Structures in Sophoclean Tragedy." *Classics Ireland* 18:21–55.

———. 2011b. "In Quest of the Father in the Narratives of Origin and Movement in Oedipus Tyrannus." *Mètis* 9:149–164.

———. 2011c. "To Befriend or Not to Befriend? A Note on Lines 678–683 of the Deception Speech in Ajax." *Logeion* 1:41–47.

———. 2013. "Throwing out the Menos with the Bath Water. The Sophoclean Text vs Peter Stein's Electra (2007)." In Bakogianni 2013:61–78.

———. 2014. "Who is Liable for Blame? Patroclus' Death in Book 16 of the *Iliad*." In *Crime and Punishment in Homeric and Archaic Epic*. Ed. M. Χριστόπουλος and M. Παΐζη. Proceedings of the 12th International Symposium on the *Odyssey* (Ithaca, 3–7 September, 2013), 121–140. Ithaca.

———. 2017. "Dying Becomes Her: Posthumanism in Sophocles' *Antigone* in the Light of Lásló Nemes' *Son of Saul*." *Logeion* 7: 21–41.

———. Forthcoming (a). "Antigone Goes to School. G. Kakoudaki's Production of the Sophoclean Play (2014) for Teenage Audiences."

———. Forthcoming (b). "Beauty and the Beast: An Interpretation of Sophocles' *Trachiniae*."

Kearns, E. 1989. *The Heroes of Attica*. Bulletin of the Institute of Classical Studies. Supplement 57. London.

Kenny, A. 1979. *Aristotle's Theory of the Will*. New Haven.

King, K. C. 1987. *Achilles: Paradigms of the War Hero from Homer to the Middle Ages*. Berkeley.

Kirkwood, G. M. 1958. *A Study in Sophoclean Drama*. Ithaca.

Kitto H. D. F. 1994. *Sophocles. Antigone. Oedipus the King. Electra*. Ed. with an Introduction and notes by E. Hall. Oxford.

Knox, B. M. W. 1957. *Oedipus at Thebes*. New Haven.

———. 1964. *The Heroic Temper: Studies in Sophoclean Tragedy*. Berkeley.

Konstan, D. 1997. *Friendship in the Classical World*. Cambridge.

———. 2010. "Are Fellow Citizens Friends? Aristotle versus Cicero on Philia, Amicitia, and Social Solidarity." In Rosen and Sluiter 2010:233–248.

Kosticova, A. 2013. "Postmodernism: A Feminist Critique." *Metaphilosophy* 44:24–28.

Kovacs, D. 2002. *Euripides. Helen. Phoenician Women. Orestes*. Loeb Classical Library 11. Cambridge, MA.

———. 2009a. "Do We Have the End of *Oedipus Tyrannus*?" *The Journal of Hellenic Studies* 129:53–70.

———. 2009b. "The Role of Apollo in *OT*." In Cusland and Hume 2009:357–368.

Kresic, S., ed. 1981. *Contemporary Literary Hermeneutics and Interpretation of Classical Texts*. Ottawa.

Kristeva, J., J.-C. Milner, and N. Ruwet, eds. 1975. *Langue, Discours, Société. Pour Émile Benveniste*. Paris.

Krostenko, B. A. 2001. *Cicero, Catullus and the Language of Social Performance*. Chicago.

Lacan, J. 1978. *The Four Fundamental Concepts of Psychoanalysis.* Ed. J.-A. Miller. Trans. A. Sheridan. New York. Originally published as *Quatre Concepts Fondamentaux de la Psychanalyse.* 1973. Paris.

———. 1990. *Television.* Trans. D. Hollier, R. Krauss, A. Michelson. New York. Originally published as *Télévision.* Paris. 1974.

———. 2001. *Écrits. A Selection.* Trans. A. Sheridan. London and New York. Originally published as *Écrits.* 1966. Paris.

Lardinois, A. 2006. "The Polysemy of Gnomic Expressions and Ajax's Deception Speech." In de Jong and Rijksbaron 2006:213–223.

Latacz, J. 1996. *Homer: His Art and his World.* Trans. J. P. Holoka. Ann Arbor, MI. Originally published as *Homer. Der erste Dichter des Abendlandes.* 1989. Munich.

Lattimore, S. 1975. "Oedipus and Teiresias." *California Studies in Classical Antiquity* 8.105–111.

Leeb, C. 2017. *Power and Feminist Agency in Capitalism: Toward a New Theory of the Political Subject.* New York.

Leonard, M. 2005a. *Athens in Paris: Ancient Greece and the Political in Post-War French Thought.* New York.

———. 2005b. "Tragic Will and the Subject of Politics." *Phoenix* 59:133–142.

———. 2006. "Lacan, Irigaray, and Beyond: Antigones and the Politics of Psychoanalysis." In Zajko and Leonard 2008:121–140.

———. 2015. *Tragic Modernities.* Cambridge, MA.

Levêque, P., and P. Vidal-Naquet. 1996. *Cleisthenes the Athenian; An Essay on the Representation of Space and Time in Greek Political Thought from the End of the Sixth Century to the Death of Plato.* Trans. D. A. Curtis. Atlantic Highlands, NJ. Originally publishd as *Clisthène l' Athénien. Essai sur la représentation de l' espace et du temps dans la pensée politique grecque de la fin du Vie siècle à la mort de Platon.* 1964. Paris.

Lévi-Strauss, C. 1963. *Structural Anthropology.* Trans. C. Jacobson and B. G. Schoepf. New York. Originally published as *Anthropologie Structurale.* 1958. Paris.

———. 1969. *The Elementary Structures of Kinship.* Trans. J. H. Bell, J. R. von Sturmer, and R. Needham. Boston. Originally published as *Les Structures Élémentaires de la Parenté.* 1949. Paris.

———. 1973. *Anthropologie Structurale II.* Paris.

———. 1975. "Mythe et Oubli." In Kristeva, Milner, and Ruwet 1975:294–300.

Lewis, D. M. 1963. "Cleisthenes and Attica." *Historia* 12:22–40.

Liapis, V. 2012. *"Oedipus Tyrannus."* In Ormand 2012:84–97.

Lloyd-Jones, H. 1983. *The Justice of Zeus.* 2nd ed. Sather Classical Lectures 41. Berkeley.

————, ed. and trans. 1994a. *Sophocles: Ajax, Electra, Oedipus Tyrannus*. Loeb Classical Library 20. Reprint with corrections 1997. Cambridge, MA.

————, ed. and trans. 1994b. *Sophocles: Antigone, The Women of Trachis, Philoctetes, Oedipus at Colonus*. Loeb Classical Library 21. Reprint with corrections 1998. Cambridge, MA.

Lloyd-Jones, H. and N. G. Wilson.1990. *Sophoclis Fabulae*. Oxford.

Lombardo, S. 1997. *Homer. Iliad*. Introduction by S. Murnaghan. Indianapolis.

Loraux, N. 1993. *L' invention d' Athènes: Histoire de l' oraison funèbre dans la cité classique*. Paris.

Lorraine, T. E. 1990. *Gender, Identity, and the Production of Meaning*. Boulder, CO.

Lovatt, H. 2013. *The Epic Gaze: Vision, Gender and Narrative in Ancient Epic*. Cambridge.

MacCary, W. T. 1982. *Childlike Achilles: Ontogeny and Phylogeny in the* Iliad. New York.

MacDowell, D. M. 1986. *The Law in Classical Athens*. Ithaca.

MacIntyre, A. 2007. *After Virtue. A Study in Moral Theory*. 3rd ed. London-New York.

Makrinioti, D., ed. 2004. Τα όρια του σώματος. Trans. K. Athanasiou et al. Athens.

Meir, C. 1997. *Η Πολιτική Τέχνη της Αρχαίας Ελληνικής Τραγωδίας*. Trans. Φ. Μανακίδου. Athens. Original publication as *Die politische Kunst der griechischen Tragödie*. 1988. Munich.

Mikalson, J. D. 2005. *Ancient Greek Religion*. Oxford.

Muellner, L. 1996. *The Anger of Achilles: Mênis in Greek Epic*. Ithaca, NY.

Mulvey, L. 1975. "Visual Pleasure and Narrative Cinema." *Screen* 16:6–18.

Murnaghan, S. 2011. "Choroi Achoroi: The Athenian Politics of Tragic Choral Identity." In Carter 2011:46–268.

————. 2012. "Sophocles' Choruses." In Ormand 2012:220–235.

Murray, A. T., rev. W. F. Wyatt. 1999. *Homer. Iliad*. 2 vols. Loeb Classical Library 170 and 171. 2nd ed. Cambridge, MA.

Myrsiades, K. 2010. *Approaches to Homer's* Iliad *and* Odyssey. New York.

Nagy, G. 1999. *The Best of the Achaeans: Concepts of the Hero in Archaic Greek Poetry*. Baltimore.

Newton, R. M. 1991. "Oedipus' Wife and Mother." *Classical Journal* 87:35–45.

North, H. 1966. *Sophrosyne: Self-Knowledge and Self-Restraint in Greek Literature*. Ithaca, NY.

Ober, J. 1989. *Mass and Elite in Democratic Athens: Rhetoric, Ideology and the Power of the People*. Princeton.

————. 1993. "The Polis as a Society: Aristotle, John Rawls, and the Athenian Social Contract." In Hansen 1993:129–160.

———. 1996. "The Athenian Revolution of 508/7 B.C: Violence, Authority, and the Origins of Democracy." In *The Athenian Revolution: Essays on Ancient Greek Democracy and Political Theory*, 32–52. Princeton.

———. 2002. "Social Science History, Cultural History, and the Amnesty of 403." *Transactions of the American Philological Association* 132:127–137.

———. 2005. *Athenian Legacies: Essays on the Politics of Going on Together.* Princeton.

———. 2007. "I Besieged that Man. Democracy's Revolutionary Start." In Raaflaub, Ober, and Wallace 2007:83–104.

———. 2008a. *Democracy and Knowledge: Innovation and Learning in Classical Athens.* Princeton.

———. 2008b. "The Original Meaning of 'Democracy': Capacity to Do Things, not Majority Rule." *Constellations* 15:3–9. Princeton/Stanford Working Papers in Classics.

———. 2012. "Epistemic Democracy in Classical Athens; Sophistication, Diversity, and Innovation." In Elster and Landemre 2012:118–147.

Opstelten, J. C. 1952. *Sophocles and the Greek Pessimism.* Amsterdam.

Ormand, K., ed. 2012. *A Companion to Sophocles.* Chichester, West Sussex.

Osborne R., and S. Hornblower, eds. 1994. *Ritual, Finance, Politics: Athenian Democratic Accounts Presented to David Lewis.* Oxford.

Osborne, R. 2009. *Greece in the Making 1220-479 BC.* 2nd ed. London-New York.

Ostwald, M. 1969. *Nomos and the Beginnings of the Athenian Democracy.* Oxford.

———. 1982. *Autonomia: Its Genesis and Early History.* Chico, CA.

———. 1986. *From Popular Sovereignty to the Sovereignty of the Law: Law, Society, and Politics in Fifth Century Athens.* Berkeley.

———. 1988. "The Reform of the Athenian State by Cleisthenes." In *The Cambridge Ancient History*, 303–346. Cambridge.

Parker, R. 1996. *Athenian Religion: A History.* Oxford.

Patterson, C. B. 2006. "The Place and Practice of Burial in Sophocles' Athens." *Helios* Supplement 33, 9–48.

Pearson, A. C. 1924. *Sophoclis Fabulae.* Oxford Classical Texts. Reprint with corrections 1928. Oxford.

Pelling, C. 1997. *Greek Tragedy and the Historian.* Oxford.

———. 2000. *Literary Texts and the Greek Historian.* London.

Peradotto, J. 1992. "Disauthorizing Prophecy: The Ideological Mapping of *Oedipus Tyrannus.*" *Transactions of the American Philological Association* 122:1–15.

Poe, J. P. 1987. *Genre and Meaning in Sophocles'* Ajax. Frankfurt am Main.

Pozzi D. C., and J. M. Wickersham, eds. 1991. *Myth and the Polis.* Ithaca, NY.

Pucci, P. 1988. "Reading the Riddles of Oedipus Rex." In *Language and the Tragic Hero: Essays on Greek Tragedy in Honor of Gordon Kirkwood*, ed. P. Pucci. 131–154. Atlanta.

———. 1991. "The Endless end of the *Oedipus Rex*." *Ramus* 20:3–15.

———. 1992. *Oedipus and the Fabrication of the Father: Oedipus Tyrannus in Modern Criticism and Philosophy*. Baltimore.

———. 1994. "Gods' Intervention and Epiphany in Sophocles." *American Journal of Philology* 115:15–46.

Raaflaub, K. A., J. Ober, and R. W. Wallace. 2007. *Origins of Democracy in Ancient Greece*. Berkeley.

Rehm, R. 2003. *Radical Theatre: Greek Tragedy and the Modern World*. London.

Reinhardt, K. 1979. *Sophocles*. Trans. H. Harvey, and D. Harvey. NY. Originally published as *Sophokles.*, *1947*. Frankfurt am Main.

Remes, P., and J. Sihvola, eds. 2008. *Ancient Philosophy of the Self*. Berlin and Heidelberg.

Renger, A.-B. 2013. *Oedipus and the Sphinx: The Threshold Myth from Sophocles through Freud to Cocteau*. Trans. D. A. Smart and D. Rice, with J. T. Hamilton. Chicago.

Revermann, M. 2010. "Situating the Gaze of the Recipient(s): Theatre-Related Vase Paintings and their Context of Reception." In Gildenhard, and Revermann 2010:69–97.

Roberts, D. H., F. M. Dunn, and D. Fowler, eds. 1997. *Classical Closure: Reading the End in Greek and Latin Literature*. Princeton.

Rinon, Y. 2008. *Homer and the Dual Model of the Tragic*. Ann Arbor, MI.

Rosen, R. M., and I. Sluiter, eds. 2006. *City, Countryside, and the Spatial Organization of Value in Classical Antiquity*. Mnemosyne Supplement 279. Leiden.

———, eds. 2010. *Valuing Others in Classical Antiquity*. Mnemosyne Supplement 323. Leiden.

Rowe, C., 1995. *Plato: Statesman*. Warmister.

Rowe, C., and S. Broadie. 2002. *Aristotle Nicomachean Ethics*. Oxford.

Salzman-Mitchell, P. 2005. *A Web of Fantasies: Gaze, Image, and Gender in Ovid's Metamorphoses*. Columbus.

Schein, S. L. 1984. *The Mortal Hero: An Introduction to Homer's* Iliad. Berkeley.

Seaford, R. 1985. "The Destruction of Limits in Sophokles' Elektra." *Classical Quarterly* 35.2: 315–328.

———. 2004a. *Money and the Early Greek Mind: Homer, Philosophy, Tragedy*. Cambridge.

———. 2004b. "Tragedy, Ritual, and Money." In Yatromanolakis and Roilos 2004:71–93.

———. 2007. "Money and the Confusion of Generations in Sophocles' *Oedipus Tyrannus*." In Beier 2007:23–28.

———. 2008. "Money and Tragedy." In Harris 2008:49–65.

———. 2012a. *Cosmology and the Polis: The Social Construction of Space and Time in the Tragedies of Aeschylus*. Cambridge.

———. 2012b. "Monetisation and the Genesis of the Western Subject." Historical Materialism 20:1–25.

Segal, C. 1981a. "The Music of the Sphinx: The Problem of Language in *Oedipus Tyrannus.*" In Kresic 1981, 151–163.

———. 1981b. *Tragedy and Civilization: An Interpretation of Sophocles.* Cambridge, MA.

———. 1986. *Interpreting Greek Tragedy: Myth, Poetry, Text.* Ithaca-London.

———. 2001. Oedipus Tyrannus: *Tragic Heroism and the Limits of Knowledge.* 2nd ed. New York.

Shefer, T., F. Boonzaier, and P. Kinguwa, eds. 2006. *The Gender of Psychology.* Cape Town.

Sicherl, M. 1977. "The Tragic Issue in Sopphocles' *Ajax.*" *Yale Classical Studies* 25:67–98.

Silk, M. S., ed. 1996. *Tragedy and the Tragic: Greek Theatre and Beyond.* Oxford.

Söderbäck, F., ed. 2010. *Feminist Readings of Antigone.* Albany, NY.

Sommerstein, A. H., S. Halliwell, J. Henderson, and B. Zimmermann, eds. 1993. *Tragedy, Comedy and the Polis: Papers from the Greek Drama Conference (Nottingham, 18–20 July 1990).* Bari.

———. 2011. "Sophocles and the Guilt of Oedipus." *Cuadernos de Filología Clásica. Estudios Griegos e Indoeuropeos* 21:103–117.

Sorabji, R. 2006. *Self: Ancient and Modern Insights about Individuality, Life, and Death.* Oxford.

Sourvinou-Inwood, C. 1989. "Assumptions and the Creation of Meaning: Reading Sophocles' *Antigone.*" *The Journal of Hellenic Studies* 109:134–148.

———. 1990. "Sophocles' *Antigone* as a Bad Woman." In Dieteren and Kloek 1990:11–40.

———. 1987–1988. "Sophocles' *Antigone:* 904–920. A Reading." *Annali dell'Instituto Universitario Orientale di Napoli (A.I.O.N.)* 9–10, 19–35.

Stanford, W. B. 1963. *Sophocles* Ajax. London.

Strauss Clay, J. 2011. *Homer's Trojan Theater: Space, Vision, and Memory in the Iliad.* New York-Cambridge.

Taxidou, O. 2004. "Oedipus/Anti-Oedipus: The Philosopher, the Actor, and the Patient." In *Tragedy, Modernity and Mourning,* 42–69. Edinburg.

Taylor, C. 1985. *Human Agency and Language.* Philosophical Papers I. Cambridge.

———. 1989. *Sources of the Self: The Making of the Modern Identity.* Cambridge.

———. 2004. *Modern Social Imaginaries.* Durham-London.

Taylor, C. C. W. 2006. *Nicomachaean Ethics, Books II–IV.* Trans. and Commentary. Oxford.

Tovar-Restrepo, M. 2012. *Castoriadis, Foucault and Autonomy: New Approaches to Subjectivity, Society, and Social Change.* London.

Tredennick, H. 1969–1975. *Aristotle. The Metaphysics.* 2 vols. Loeb Classical Library. Cambridge, MA.

Tridimas, G. 2011. "Cleisthenes' Choice: The Emergence of Direct Democracy in Ancient Athens." *The Journal of Economic Asymmetries* 8:39–59.

Valakas, K. 2009. "Theoretical Views of Athenian Tragedy in the Fifth c. BC." In Goldhill and Hall 2009:179–207.

Vernant, J.-P. 1988a. "The Lame Tyrant. From Oedipus to Periander." In Vernant and Vidal-Naquet 1988:207–236.

———. 1988b. "Ambiguity and Reversal: On the Enigmatic Structure of Oedipus Rex." In Vernant and Vidal-Naquet 1988:113–140.

———. 1988c. "The Intimations of the Will in Greek Tragedy." In Vernant and Vidal-Naquet 1988:49–84.

Vernant, J.-P., and P. Vidal-Naquet. 1988. *Myth and Tragedy in Ancient Greece.* Trans. J. Lloyd. New York. Originally published as *Mythe et tragédie en Grèce ancienne,* 2 vols. 1972 and 1986. Paris.

Vidal-Naquet, P. 1986. *The Black Hunter. Forms of Thought and Forms of Society in the Greek World.* Trans. A. Szegedy-Maszak. Baltimore. Originally published as *Le Chasseur Noir. Formes de Pensée et Formes de Société dans le Monde Grec.* 1981. Paris.

Vidal-Naquet, P. 2003. *Ο Θρυμματισμένος Καθρέφτης. Αθηναϊκή Τραγωδία και Πολιτική.* Trans. X. Μεράντζας. Athens. Originally published as *Le Mirroir brisé. Tragédie athénienne et politique.* 2001. Paris.

Warner, R. 1972. *Thucydides: History of the Peloponnesian War.* Introduction and notes by M. I. Finley. London.

Whitman, C. H. 1951. *Sophocles: A Study in Heroic Humanism.* Cambridge, MA.

Whitehead, D. 1986. *The Demes of Attica. 508/7–CA. 250 B.C. A Political and Social Study.* Princeton.

West, M. L. 2011. *The Making of the Iliad.* Oxford.

Williams, B. 2008. *Shame and Necessity.* With a new foreword by A. A. Long. Berkeley-Los Angeles.

Winnington-Ingram, R. P. 1980. *Sophocles: An Interpretation.* Cambridge.

Wyke, M., ed. 1998. *Parchments of Gender: Deciphering the Bodies of Antiquity.* Oxford.

Yamagata, N. 1991. "Phoenix's Speech—Is Achilles Punished?" *Classical Quarterly* 41:1–15.

———. 1994. *Homeric Morality.* Mnemosyne Supplement 131. Leiden.

Yatromanolakis D., and P. Roilos, eds. 2004. *Greek Ritual Poetics.* Hellenic Studies Series 3. Cambridge, MA.

Zajko, V., and M. Leonard, eds. 2008. *Laughing with Medusa: Classical Myth and Feminist Thought.* Oxford.

Zanker, G. 1994. *The Heart of Achilles: Characterization and Personal Ethics in the* Iliad. Ann Arbor, MI.

Index Locorum

General Index

abstract notions/abstractions: of Athens/Athenians, 16, 18, 23, 141
accountability: to the society of peers, 27–30
Achilles, 26–28, 58, 129–132, 137, 153–156
Adeimantus, 24
Adkins, Arthur W. H.: *Merit and Responsibility*, 154–156
Aeschylus, 54n45, 117n2, 146; The Persians, 137
agathon/agathos bios, 30
Agamemnon, 35–36, 130, 146, 155n4, 155n9
agency, human: 140, 143
agent, human: 45n19, 122, 125, 129, 133–134, 136n74, 140, 145
agnoia, 136–137, 146
Ajax, 32–33, 78, 109, 114n233, 118, 155
akratic action (ἀκρασία), 138
Andromache, 77n115, 154, 156
Antigone, 6, 75–77
Assembly, 5, 12n12, 16n27, 22, 29, 153
Athens, 4, 15, 18–19, 21, 23–24, 25–26, 29, 86–87, 90–92, 99; *Athens in Paris*, 85n136, 93n173; classical, 13, 29–31, 98; contemporary, 149–150; democracy in, 12–13, 19, 151; democratic, 4, 12, 98 (*see also* Cleisthenic reforms); fifth-century, 134, 137, 141, 143, 146n129; Oedipus in, 84n134

apolides, 4
apolis, 4, 6. *See also under* Sophocles: *hypsipolis–apolis*
Apollo, 42, 54–56, 60, 65, 67, 69, 100–103, 118n4, 125–130, 132
Aristogeiton, 86, 87n143
atê, 136–137
Athenian Revolution, 13, 15–17, 23, 26, 141
autonomos/autonomy, 4, 13, 29; individuals/city-state, 26

Bacchiads, 86
Bain, David, 66
Black Hunter, 11
body politic, 4–5, 13, 15–17, 21, 23, 24, 141–142; collective (*dêmos*), 12–13; democratic, 97; legislative, 29. *See also* gendered body
Boulê, 15, 17
Burkert, Walter, 50
Butler, Judith, 6, 73, 74; *Antigone's Claim*, 75–76; *Bodies that Matter*, 78

Cadmus, 47n22, 48, 49
Cairns, Douglas, 127–131; *Aidos*, 156
Caldwell, Richard, 58
Cameron, Alister, 63, 113, 118, 146
Carson, Anne: *Antigonick*, 118
Castoriadis, Cornelius, 5 13–14, 20, 23n54, 149–150; *The Imaginary Institution of Society*, 5n2, 14, 149;